What I Learned from My Dog

Chicken Soup for the Soul: What I Learned from My Dog
101 Stories about Our Best Friends
Amy Newmark

Published by Chicken Soup for the Soul, LLC www.chickensoup.com

The publisher gratefully acknowledges the many individuals who granted Chicken Soup for the Soul permission to reprint the cited material.

Front cover courtesy of iStockphoto.com (©Iuliia Zavalishina)
Back cover and interior image created by Daniel Zaccari using man courtesy of iStockphoto.com (©GlobalStock) and dog partly generated using Adobe Firefly from the prompt "profile of dog with green field background"

Photo of Amy Newmark courtesy of Susan Morrow at SwickPix

Cover and Interior by Daniel Zaccari

Publisher's Cataloging-in-Publication Data

Names: Newmark, Amy, editor.
Title: Chicken soup for the soul : what I learned from my dog , 101 stories about our best friends / Amy Newmark.
Description: Cos Cob, CT: Chicken Soup for the Soul, LLC, 2025.
Identifiers: LCCN: 2025930455 | ISBN: 978-1-61159-119-4 (paperback) | 978-1-61159-354-9 (ebook)
Subjects: LCSH Dogs--Anecdotes. | Dogs--Literary collections. | Dog owners--Anecdotes. | Human-animal relationships--Anecdotes. | Self-help. | BISAC PETS / Dogs General | PETS / Essays & Narratives | SELF-HELP / Motivational & Inspirational
Classification: LCC SF426.2 .C458 2025 | DDC 636.7--dc23

Library of Congress Control Number: 2025930455

PRINTED IN THE UNITED STATES OF AMERICA
on acid∞free paper

30 29 28 27 26 25 01 02 03 04 05

What I Learned from My Dog

101 Stories about Our Best Friends

Amy Newmark

Chicken Soup for the Soul, LLC
Cos Cob, CT

Changing the world one story at a time®

www.chickensoup.com

Table of Contents

❶

~My Very Good, Very Bad Dog~

1. The Slim Jim Caper, *Jody Lebel* 1
2. The Eviction, *Mark Rickerby* 5
3. The Dog Who Could Open Doors, *Lorraine Rose* 8
4. Flunking Obedience Class, *Irene Maran* 12
5. When 5% Isn't Enough, *Winter D. Prosapio* 14
6. A Dog with Friends, *Becky Alexander* 16
7. Forbidden Fruit, *Chip Kirkpatrick* 19
8. The Simple Things, *Marianne Reese* 22

❷

~Always an Adventure~

9. The Doggy Door, *Kim Engelmann* 27
10. My Dog Got Stuck Up a Tree, *Ali Hall* 31
11. Harley the Huntress, *Anne Calvert* 34
12. Bruno Needs Viagra, *Louise Butler* 37
13. Sunday Surprise, *Laura Vertin* 40
14. Maxine's Mail, *Debra White* 43
15. Cody and the Bone, *Laura McKenzie* 45
16. Mackie's Game, *Constance Rutherford* 47
17. Tommy and the Cottonmouth, *Marilyn J. Wolf* 49

3

~That Heroic Dog~

18. Senior Class, *Dave Bachmann* 53
19. Faithful Flicka, *Marie T. Palecek* 57
20. Mama Knows Best, *David Weiskircher* 61
21. Dog, *Sue Sussman* 64
22. Night Watch, *Deidra Parham* 67
23. My Canine Nanny, *Billie Holladay Skelley* 69
24. A Neighborhood Hero, *Ree Pashley* 72
25. An Angel in a Fur Coat, *Robyn Gerland* 74

4

~Changed by the Dog~

26. Priorities, *Lois Tuffin* 77
27. Him and Me, *Anna I. Smith* 80
28. Eating Rocks, *Amanda Ann Gregory* 83
29. Old Dog, New Tricks, *Kristin Evans* 87
30. Great Expectations, *Sandra Martin* 90
31. Their Best Day Ever, *Alex Flowers* 93
32. I Owed It All to Lilly, *Laurie Dell'Accio* 96
33. Single Dog-Parenting, *Sally Meadows* 100
34. Unexpected Lessons, *Aimee C. Trafton* 103
35. Unleashing Confidence, *Anne Taylor* 105

5

~Meant to Be~

36. Double Rescue, *Maiya Katherine* 109
37. The Eclipse Dog, *Jeffree Wyn Itrich* 112
38. A Sweet Ray of Hope, *Debbie LaChusa* 116
39. Rebel Heart, *Jessi Waugh* 120

40. Message from an Angel, *Amy Soscia* 122
41. The Power of Canine Connection, *Jill L. Ferguson* 127
42. The Rescue, *Judy Kellersberger* 130
43. The Interview, *Nemma Wollenfang* 134
44. Pawprints on My Heart, *Lindsay Detwiler* 137
45. The Boomerang Dog, *Jillian Van Hefty* 140

6

~A Dog's Purpose~

46. Iggy, *Kathryn Haueisen* 144
47. Otis, *Judy Kelly* 147
48. Charlie's Playground, *Genesis F.* 150
49. Magic Potion, *Amy McHugh* 152
50. Mother Merlin, *Linda Mihatov* 156
51. The Great Dog Cure, *Miranda Phelps* 158
52. The Seventh Juror, *Joyce Newman Scott* 162
53. Collie, *Laura McKenzie* 166
54. The Brothers, *Cheri Bunch* 169

7

~A Natural Therapist~

55. Anything But Ordinary, *Jane M. Biehl* 173
56. Dog with a Loving Heart, *Robin Stearns Lee* 176
57. From Protected to Protector, *Nancy K.S. Hochman* 180
58. The Dog We Needed, *Catherine Kenwell* 183
59. Strider's Sixth Sense, *Dawn O'Herron* 185
60. A Bond, *Kathleen Gemmell* 187
61. About a Dog Named Sam, *Nanette Norgate* 190
62. A "Tail" from the Other Side, *Paula Marie Usrey* 193
63. A Dog Called Delta, *Elton A. Dean* 196
64. He Brought Back My Dad's Smile, *Katrin Babb* 199

8

~Special Bonds~

65. A Light in the Darkness, *Camille Hartnett* 203
66. Echoes of Love, *Kim Garback Diaz* 206
67. My Temporary Tommy, *Melanie Chartoff* 209
68. The Wonder Dog, *Annmarie Sitar* 213
69. To Love Again, *Rose Panieri* 216
70. The Most Special Visits, *Woody Woodburn* 220
71. Imaginary Dogs, *Ellie Sanchez* 223
72. Cardinal Blessings, *Margie Pasero* 225
73. Sunny and Emie, *James B. Zambelli* 228
74. Murphy and Jerry, *Dr. Dale Atkins* 231

9

~Learning to Love the Dog~

75. Don't Pick Me, I'll Pick You, *Misty Rae* 235
76. DadsRules4TheDog.doc, *Karl Haffner* 238
77. The Gentle Giant, *Doug Sletten* 241
78. Never Judge a Pug by His Breed, *Anita Gait* 243
79. Strength Through Weakness, *Ellen L. Fannon* 247
80. Whiskers and Tears, *Kristi Cocchiarella FitzGerald* 250
81. Matchmaker, Matchmaker, *Melissa R. Friedman* 253
82. Delighted to Meet You, *Sheri Block Glantz* 257
83. A Change of Heart, *Elizabeth S.* 260
84. Stepping Up, *Kathy Valentino* 263

10

~What a Clever Dog~

85. Going with the Flow, *Lisa Timpf* 268
86. My Little Tap Dancer, *Mary Z. Whitney* 270
87. This Dog Kept Her Hair Appointment, *Carolyn Campbell* ... 272

88. What My Dog Taught Me About Trust, *Amy Catlin Wozniak* 274
89. The Day I Learned to See Dogs Differently, *Angela Kennedy* 277
90. Charlie Hero, *Marla H. Thurman* 280
91. I'll Hide, You Seek! *Emily C. Marszalek* 284
92. A Winner After All, *Sarah Stuart* 287
93. My Dog Can Talk, *Alli Straus* 291

11

~Who Rescued Whom?~

94. Along Came a Spider, *Corrie Lopez* 296
95. Sunny Delight, *Carol W. Huff* 299
96. Anxious Alice, *Carina Middleton* 303
97. Running Partners, *Bianca Sanchez* 306
98. I've Been Waiting for You, *Laurel L. Shannon* 310
99. A Golden Gift, *Mary Beth Magee* 313
100. Amazing Gracie, *Marla Anne Bernard* 317
101. Magical Maggie, *Veronica Saldate* 320

Meet Our Contributors 323
Meet Amy Newmark 337
Thank You 339

My Very Good, Very Bad Dog

The Slim Jim Caper

Dogs are great. Bad dogs, if you can really call them that, are perhaps the greatest of them all.
~John Grogan

This time, the store owner called the police. Randy had shoplifted from his establishment before, but I had always been able to fix it — usually by paying double the price of the purloined item. Peering through the faceted glass of my front door, I could see Mr. Pachenko pacing the brick-edged sidewalk, his face pale with anger, while two police officers stood at my front door.

Mr. Pachenko owned the corner food mart in our mostly residential neighborhood of gentrified townhouses. Most of them had window boxes filled with flowers. There was a quiet park nearby. Crime was rare.

For a moment, I foolishly thought about pressing myself against the wall and pretending I hadn't heard the loud knocking. But I knew I had been seen coming down the hallway toward the front door.

The pounding came a second time, heavier and more demanding.

"You stay in the living room," I told Randy. "I'll go talk to them." He had gone back to sitting on the couch, but his eyes were huge.

I opened the door.

"Ms. Lebel?" It was the taller of the two cops, the younger one. His uniform was as crisp as his voice. His name badge said Carter.

I knew this situation was not good. The sickening image of Randy in the back of their patrol car, face pressed against the window as they drove away, made my knees weak.

"Yes, Officer, I'm Jody Lebel."

"Ma'am, we have a complaint that…"

Mr. Pachenko couldn't hold it in a moment longer. He burst up the porch stairs, his portly body pushing between the officers.

"I tol' you I wasna gonna put up with this," he said, poking his finger at me. "This last time."

The older officer gently maneuvered the shopkeeper back down the steps. "Sir," he admonished, "let us handle this."

Mr. Pachenko held his ground on the first stair. "Yes, yes. Do job. Yes. Is good." He shook a fist in the air aimed at no one in particular. "Is two times already this week. He need to be punished."

"Mr. Pachenko," I pleaded, "it's only a few Slim Jims. Let me pay for them."

"That is not issue," he retorted. His accent became thicker as his irritation rose. "He have no respect, no manners. He come in store, look me straight in eye, grab bunch of Slim Jims, and before I get around counter, he is running down street."

I looked ashamedly at the officers. "He just loves those things," I said lamely.

"Is that all he takes?" said the older cop.

"That's it."

I looked down at Mr. Pachenko. "Why don't you put them behind the counter where he can't reach them?"

"Oh, now you tell me how to run store?"

Officer Carter pulled out his notepad and started to write. "All right, how many times has this happened?"

"It's been going on for a while, I know," I said. "Believe me, I've talked to him. It's like he can't control himself."

"Pah," Mr. Pachenko spat out. He squared his shoulders, and his eyes grew large and dark as he delivered his final blow. "He will control self when locked up. This I want."

"Okay," said the older cop, "let me get this straight. Randy comes into your store and steals Slim Jims right in front of you. Is that it?"

"Yes, Officer," the store owner said, his respect for law enforcement apparent in his tone.

"It's not much of a crime," I started to say.

The officer interrupted me. "It's shoplifting, a misdemeanor, ma'am." He gave me a hard look meant to put me in my place. It worked.

"Why don't you just keep a box of Slim Jims in the house?" This came from the older cop, a seasoned man who, judging by his demeanor, probably considered the paperwork he would have to do more distasteful than the crime.

"They don't sit well with his stomach. He's up all night, and that means I'm up all night."

"Mr. Pachenko, why don't you go back to your store? We'll get this handled," said the older officer.

Mr. Pachenko hesitated.

"Go on now," Officer Carter said firmly. "We'll see to this."

Mr. Pachenko stomped away. "I want this stopped," he threw back gruffly over this shoulder. "No more. You hear me? No more."

"What if I speak to him?" the older cop said kindly.

"Yes, yes," I said. "That's a great idea."

Officer Carter began tapping his pen on his notepad, barely concealing his annoyance. I ignored him and appealed directly to the cop with the heart.

"Maybe the uniform will scare him." I tried to put on a little smile, but it might have come across as a grimace. "Come in," I said, pulling the door open.

Randy and I had been together since high school. I adored him. I couldn't picture my life without him. Even for a day.

"He's in there," I said, gesturing to the far end of the hallway. "In the living room."

As we approached, three pair of feet working the creaks out of the old, wooden floor, Randy could be seen on the couch holding a Slim Jim. No shame at all.

The officers stopped abruptly on the threshold. "This is Randy Lebel?"

"Yes."

Both men turned abruptly and strode purposefully down the hall and straight out the front door. I heard it slam behind them. In that moment, I realized that my fists had been clenched.

"You just dodged a huge bullet, dude," I said, plopping down on the couch next to him. Randy's big, brown eyes locked on mine.

"Don't even try to get out of this with that look," I scolded. "You're still in big trouble."

But I couldn't stay mad for long. Soon, I was scratching him behind his ears, his favorite place. Randy bent his head down to that Slim Jim between his front paws and chewed off the plastic wrapper. Enraptured by the spicy treat, he began to drool.

—Jody Lebel—

The Eviction

Dogs act exactly the way we would act
if we had no shame.
~Cynthia Heimel

Charlie was a dream pet at home, but when we took him outside, he became a furry tornado, barking at other dogs and pulling on the leash until my shoulder nearly came out of its socket. We didn't walk him; he dragged us. He once pulled my wife into the street and almost got her run over by a car.

I tried everything to break him of these bad habits, but nothing ever worked. He never bit anyone—he wouldn't hurt a fly—but when people saw a German Shepherd mix running toward them and their dogs while barking excitedly, the mere horror alone was sufficient to make Charlie—and me by association—very unpopular.

I was gardening one day when I heard what sounded like a little girl screaming in the front yard. I looked around and realized that Charlie was no longer in his usual spot next to me.

Terrified that he had frightened a child, I ran toward the front and saw our mailman standing there as stiff as a board with Charlie sniffing his feet. There was no child in sight.

"Is this..." the mailman squeaked.

He coughed, and then his voice returned to its usual Sam Elliott bass.

"Uh, is this your dog?"

I apologized profusely and called Charlie into the yard. The mailman grunted and walked away. I didn't take it personally. He was grumpy on his best days. I did feel bad, however, because the age-old rivalry between mail carriers and dogs is legendary. I yelled, "He really is friendly!"

If only everyone else could have seen Charlie as I did — as a super-affectionate, expert-level cuddler and all-around lovebug. But everyone outside the house only saw his wild side.

It's probably my fault for not training him correctly. Truth be told, I kind of admired his free spirit. I feel the same about dogs as I do about gardens. A perfectly manicured garden doesn't have as much charm as one with a little wildness left in it — an untamed corner where the vines intermingle and bees, butterflies, and hummingbirds reign supreme, beyond the human need to control everything. Dogs are mostly wolves, after all, and should be allowed a bit of ferality.

Charlie's masterpiece of misbehavior occurred one day when I decided to take him to an event called Nuts for Mutts that was being held at a local junior college. I figured he would fit right in. His long Collie fur and German Shepherd body were often perplexing to people with purebred dogs. His coat contained every color of the canine spectrum — black, brown, blond, red, and white — and there was no discernible pattern to it, as if the genes never quite agreed on what kind of dog he was. His fur stuck up in random tufts and his tail was so bushy that I often joked he was a giant squirrel.

After entering the gate at Nuts for Mutts, I immediately regretted the decision to take him. His meltdowns were bad enough when we passed another dog on the sidewalk in our neighborhood, but seeing hundreds of dogs of every variety seemed to unleash (no pun intended) a kind of thermonuclear explosion in his brain. Charlie was so excited that he seemed to levitate as he pulled, barked, and tried to squirm out of his collar. I tried to calm him down, but he wouldn't even look at me.

After an hour or so, an official approached me. I thought he was going to talk about how cute and high-spirited Charlie was. Nope. He said, "I'm sorry, but your dog is too disruptive. People are complaining. I'm going to have to ask you to leave." I couldn't exactly argue with him. My wife and children stayed as Charlie and I walked sadly back to our car.

Talk about your uncomfortable rides home. Even after Charlie had come to his senses, he still couldn't look at me.

"I hope you're happy," I said. "Kicked out of Nuts for Mutts. Whoever heard of such a thing?"

He looked down as if somewhere in his doggy mind he knew it was his fault that, out of hundreds of dogs, he was the only one who was evicted from the premises. They definitely weren't nuts for this particular mutt.

I suppose I should have been angry, but looking at him so disappointed gave me the same feeling I got after one of my daughters lost a big softball game. I tousled his fur and told him that instead of going straight home, we would go to our favorite dog park, where standards weren't quite so high, and he could run around with dogs he knew and bark as much as his heart desired.

The dog park certainly did the trick. He completely forgot about the humiliation of being escorted out of a mutt show. But as I watched him frolic, I felt resentment growing in me. I'd heard of dog snobs before, but mutt snobs? I had a mind to write a darn good letter, but I never did. Instead, just as I found ways to seek out "my people," I found my dog's pack: the untrained, infrequently washed, rough-and-tumble, Heinz 57 mutts. They were the renegades who didn't just walk on the wild side but lived there permanently.

It has been ten years since Charlie passed, but I still think of him every day. He was such a good dog that I'm sure he got an immediate pass into heaven. I just hope he doesn't get kicked out.

— Mark Rickerby —

The Dog Who Could Open Doors

A door is what a dog is perpetually on the wrong side of.
~Ogden Nash

He was a blend of Golden Retriever and Irish Setter, with a reddish-gold coat, long and slightly wavy, and a pure white face. His large paws, sporting tufts of fur, resembled webbed feet. His back legs were bowed like an ancient grandpa's, bent and wobbly.

My sister Ann jammed on her brakes to avoid hitting him as he stood in the bend of our narrow country road. She got out of the car and approached him as he wagged his tail, his eyes forlorn and grateful. His collar, empty of tags, pinched too tightly around the matted fur of his neck.

He jumped into Ann's back seat. She arrived at our farmhouse with a fanfare of horn honking to summon me and my husband Tony to come and greet her bedraggled passenger. She had rescued many cats and dogs, so we weren't surprised when she appeared with another needy animal.

He seemed malnourished and was covered with fleas. Tony and I had space in our home — and hearts willing and open for a dog in need. We volunteered to keep him overnight, but he couldn't be kept in the house. Before Ann left that evening, we settled him into our outdoor kennel with a blanket, food, and water. He seemed more content than we were; we hated leaving him outdoors, even in the August warmth. So, we had a restless night and walked up the hill to the kennel with a flashlight at 1:00 AM and again at 4:00 to check on him.

The next day, I drove him to Animal Control to see if anyone had left a notice. I felt relief, in a way, that no one had; I wanted to give this lovely fellow the home he deserved. I glimpsed my passenger from the rearview mirror as he sat on the back seat. His ears were badly infected, and the hair drooped down from them, sooty as charcoal, long matts resembling dreadlocks. That's when I named him Marley, after the great Jamaican performer, Bob Marley.

"This is probably the worst ear infection I've ever seen," our vet said. He indicated that Marley looked to be about fourteen and would never have normal hearing again. "Old for a big dog, and he probably hasn't been abused given his friendliness. But he sure has been badly neglected."

On Marley's first night inside, he slept in the kitchen on a comfy dog bed near the louvered doors that hooked shut. But when we awoke in the morning, we discovered Marley curled up on the sofa!

The two doors between the kitchen and the living room were always latched overnight. And yet each morning that first week, the doors would be open. Tony and I blamed each other for forgetting to secure them.

And then one day the mystery was solved: We spied Marley jiggling the louvered doors with his nose and paws to release the hooks and then tap the latch with his chin.

Soon after, we discovered that Marley's talent at opening doors was life-threatening due to the plowing and other machine work we did on our eight acres. Our black Labs, free to roam, were trained to avoid the electric fence. We assumed Marley was too old (and hearing-impaired) to learn. So, he had to be confined to the house, with the screen door secured tightly to keep him in the kitchen.

But he figured out how to escape over and over again. He always returned though.

One fateful afternoon, he escaped through the door, and this time he didn't come back. By evening, it was pouring rain. Tony and I searched the woods and the riverbank. We inched our way down winding country roads, our flashlights beaming through the dusk, but we couldn't catch a glimpse of him. And he wouldn't have heard us anyway if we'd shouted his name.

We feared that he had either perished in the river or followed some hikers up the Appalachian Trail, which runs past our house. By nightfall, I was distraught.

The next morning, we approached hikers on the Appalachian Trail. Miraculously, by afternoon, one young hiker said he had just seen a dog that fit Marley's description down by the river.

After a heavy rain, the Housatonic River is a powerful torrent. We feared Marley would be swept away. We dashed down the trail and across the road to the spot the hiker had mentioned. We eased down a rocky ledge to the riverbank, and there stood Marley on a wide, flat rock, surrounded by the rushing water.

Without hesitating, Tony forged in, slipping on the slimy algae coating the rocks, the bottom half of his jeans ballooning in the current. All the while, Marley stood on the rock, placidly wagging his tail, waiting for yet another rescue.

At last, Tony made it to Marley, hoisted him in his arms, and pushed his way back through the surge, almost toppling under the dog's weight. He struggled up the muddy embankment, with Marley's furry legs wrapped around him.

The next day, I called Invisible Fence. I had thought that old Marley could never learn but he took to his training quite well. He needed a little extra time and patience to catch on, but within a month, he'd given up wandering off. He was free to roam the property now.

Eventually, his bowed back legs began to weaken. He struggled to get up, and he became incontinent. We knew his time had arrived.

As I held him on my lap, I whispered into his hairy ear, "You've meant so much to us, Marley." My husband's gentle hands stroked Marley's soft belly as the vet helped him drift away.

Marley, the dog who could open doors, certainly opened our hearts. And as he wandered one last time toward divine territory, we trusted that the louvered doors to heaven were already unhooked for him. In fact, those doors might as well have been wide open because Marley would have unhooked them anyway!

— Lorraine Rose —

Flunking Obedience Class

Accept the challenges so that you can feel the exhilaration of victory.
~George S. Patton

My daughter Vicki had high expectations when she enrolled Cody in dog obedience class. "He's going to be a star like Lassie or Rin Tin Tin," she said.

"He's got to pass the six-week course before he barks out his valedictorian speech," I shot back.

Cody was nine months old, a playful German Shepherd growing by leaps and bounds. He exhibited a fierce curiosity about everything with which he came in contact. Even a brisk walk on a leash couldn't settle him down. Either he tugged on it or chewed it to pieces.

A time-out cage took up a quarter of my daughter's family room. This was Cody's quiet place where he could relax and chew a bone. But when he finished, he was off and running again, frightening the small children in the neighborhood and knocking the mail from the mailman's hands.

The first night of obedience school was successful. Cody sniffed and interacted with several dogs while Vicki met their owners. When not distracted by other canines, Cody perked up his ears and seemed to be listening and following instructions. My daughter insisted he was a good student although he was a bit high-strung and bursting with puppy energy.

The weeks passed quickly, and graduation night arrived. Vicki's husband, in-laws and I were invited to this special event. I made a poster that said, "Way to Go, Cody!" It showed two dog paws high-fiving each other. My handbag held a graduation gift: a rawhide bone wrapped in fancy paper.

Vicki walked Cody out into the mix of dogs lined up on the gymnasium floor. The instructor called out commands. The dogs responded. When they were asked to "lie down" and "stay," all of them obeyed — except Cody. He thought it would be more fun to bite another dog's ear. When the command was given to "sit," Cody jumped up and searched for a treat. My daughter's face turned bright red. A command was given for the dogs to "sit and stay" while the owners were instructed to walk away. Probably overwhelmed by these confusing orders, our puppy stretched out on the floor and fell into a deep sleep.

At the end of the evening when the certificates were handed out, Cody had failed with "flying colors." My daughter was invited to attend "summer school" with Cody at a reduced rate.

We couldn't get angry at a puppy so full of life, so we celebrated anyway. Trying to console my daughter, I reminded her that she never made the honor roll in high school but had still become successful. Sometimes, it takes a little longer for some of us to reach our goals.

Instead of summer school, Cody was sent to an out-of-state obedience school run by a retired Navy SEAL. When he returned two weeks later, Cody had been transformed. Hooyah!

— Irene Maran —

When 5% Isn't Enough

Humor is merely tragedy standing
on its head with its pants torn.
~Irvin S. Cobb

It was bound to happen. There was no reason to think that we would be spared. After all, we lived in an area with evidence of these encounters, and it didn't take a statistician to recognize that we were overdue.

Things started out innocently enough. I opened the door to the backyard so Rosie, our Great Pyrenees mix, could run around one last time that evening. Since it was right around the Fourth of July, Archer, our Terrier mix, declined to go out. (He is not a fan of fireworks.)

I will forever be grateful for Archer's reluctance that fateful night.

Rosie leapt off the deck as she always does, determined to chase off all the imaginary critters in the far corner of the yard. Then, she stopped in mid-run.

"Oh, no," I said. I actually said something else, but it was not suitable for polite company. At the exact moment when I saw her spin on her heels and head for the deck, an unmistakable whiff of something not good filtered up into my nose from below the deck.

"Rosie! No!" I shouted, desperate to get her away from under the deck where I knew darn well that a critter—a very specific kind of critter—was hanging out.

But it was too late. She was already under the deck. I called her, hoping that I could stop her in mid-stride. Then, the whiff turned into a hurricane.

I shouted a whole lot of things not suitable for polite company. Rosie ran up to me with a toxic cloud surrounding her. I pulled her inside the house, hoping the skunk would dash off.

Rosie immediately ran to her bed and started rubbing her face all over it.

My husband Adam then shouted things also not suitable for polite company. Rosie blinked her eyes, which were weeping thanks to the full shot of skunk defense she got right in the face. We took her back outside and began washing her over and over and over and over. It was mostly ineffective, which we realized when we went inside.

"She has to live outside," Adam announced.

"She is not living outside," I said, rubbing more shampoo on her. "She'll just get sprayed again."

"She can't come inside," he said.

"She has to come inside," I said. "She'll just get sprayed again."

"She has to sleep in her crate," he said.

Since she usually sleeps under my side of the bed like a giant meerkat, I agreed.

If you've ever tried to sleep with a 72-pound, wet, skunked dog in a giant dog crate next to your bed, you know it was a very, very long night.

After about a week and despite numerous washings, Rosie had about five percent of her skunk smell remaining. Let me tell you, five percent is about 4.99 percent too much skunk smell.

These days, the skunk has moved on to a more dog-free area, but just in case, I go out beforehand as an advance scent scout every night. Better safe than smelly.

— Winter D. Prosapio —

A Dog with Friends

Dogs got personality. Personality goes a long way.
~Quentin Tarantino

Sam positioned himself twenty feet from the hurdle and performed his warm-up exercise — bouncing from front paws to back paws to front paws to back paws. He stopped to focus for a moment on the four-foot structure and then rocketed forward, stretching his Beagle body. He easily sailed over the white wood fence. Having escaped the confines of his yard, he trotted across the driveway to join me on my walk along Mountain Home Road.

That's how it went every day.

Sam was not my dog, just my committed companion while walking through the countryside. We would stroll to the end of his rural road, make a U-turn, and walk back past his house. Instead of ending there, however, he'd continue with me as I turned left on Ghost Hill Road and walked down the hill to my house. After a brief goodbye, he always moseyed home.

On one blue-sky October day, Sam saw a blond German Shepherd along our walking route and gave her a sociable bark. The German Shepherd's ears perked up. Sam barked again as if to say, "It's a beautiful day! Won't you join us?" The dog ran to us and fell in step beside Sam. Now, it was a Beagle, a German Shepherd, and me.

A bit farther along the route, Sam spotted a black-and-white Border Collie relaxing on a front porch. Sam barked, and I speculated what he said in dog language: "Hey friend. You look bored. Want to walk with us?" The Border Collie stared at first but soon accepted Sam's offer. Now, it was a Beagle, a German Shepherd, a Border Collie, and me.

Just before making our left to start down Ghost Hill, a medium-sized gray dog of unknown lineage raised her head as our entourage neared and let out a bark of delight. Sam was clearly delighted as well and barked back a long response. I imagined it went something like this: "We are on an incredible adventure! Would you like to come along?" Without hesitation, the gray dog bounded across her yard to us. Now, it was a Beagle, a German Shepherd, a Border Collie, a gray dog of unknown lineage, and me.

Once we were on Ghost Hill Road, a little Yorkshire Terrier yipped wildly and spun in circles. Sam, of course, barked his invitation to join our motley group, and the brown Terrier fell in behind us. Now, it was five dogs and me. So much for a peaceful walk on a fresh fall day.

Then, I heard car engines. One car was coming down Ghost Hill in one lane, and another was coming up Ghost Hill in the other lane.

"Sam, get off the road!" I yelled. Usually, he heeded my warnings, but this time there was too much barking and yipping and chaos. "Sam, car!" I yelled again. Dogs were scattered all across the road. I stepped off the road into the grass and literally covered my eyes.

Both cars rolled to a stop. As one driver got out of his car, I exclaimed helplessly, "Not one of these dogs is mine!"

"No, but that one right there is mine." The man pointed at Sam. "I have a fenced yard. I have no idea how he keeps getting out."

Uh-oh. Sam was in trouble. I didn't rat him out, though. How could I? He was such a free spirit. No fence could contain him. He had roads yet to walk, adventures yet to experience, friends yet to make.

The man picked up Sam and set him in the passenger seat. As they pulled away, I couldn't help but smile because I knew Sam would be joining me on my walk the following day.

Watching Sam make new pals taught me a lot about friendship. Dogs — and people — are attracted to a welcoming spirit. Sam asked everybody to be his friend, whether blond and tall or brown and small. He made the first move too, gave the first bark. His happy example inspired me to invite new relationships into my life. Now, my days have extra joy and even a touch of carefree chaos. Clearly, Sam was right. The walk is lots more fun when shared with others.

— Becky Alexander —

Forbidden Fruit

Never trust a dog to watch your food.
~Author Unknown

I was born with a green thumb, a skill I inherited from my mother, who could jam a toothpick in the ground and it would grow. I have grown many types of vegetation: fruits, vegetables, orchids, and exotics. Sadly, my wife Grace has no such skills. She can merely walk past a healthy green plant and it will soon turn brown, wither and die.

I have planted many citrus trees on our property, and each year we harvest bushels of delicious citrus. But apples are Grace's favorite fruit and she often said she wished I could grow apples for her. We live in northeast Florida though, and it's not apple-growing country. Apples need 500–1,000 hours of bone-chilling cold to set the blossoms, and we don't have that much cold. But I did learn about a variety developed in Israel called Anna that requires less cold and can tolerate heat.

I ordered three and planted them in our yard. Every February, they would be covered with blossoms. Then they would drop them.

But there was one year when one tree held on to one blossom. And Grace watched that flower like a hawk. When a small, green ball began to form, she became the tree's guardian and protector.

She drew up a schedule for watering and fertilizing. If a bird or squirrel looked like they were heading to the tree, she would chase them away. Any weed that came up within five feet of the tree was ripped from the earth and tossed on the compost pile.

And Barney was not allowed to pee on the tree.

Barney was our big, yellow Labrador Retriever. There was never a sweeter dog. He loved everybody, and everybody loved him. Many of our neighbors did not know our names, but everybody knew Barney. People often parked their cars and walked to our fence just to pat his head. There was an elementary school nearby, and each day we heard a chorus of young voices sing out, "BARNEY! BARNEY! I LOVE YOU, BARNEY!"

Barney was also a bona fide eating machine! We only knew of two foods he wouldn't eat: strawberries and pistachio pudding. Anything and EVERYTHING else could, would and did go down his maw. Large rib bones, corn cobs, potato skins. Even kale.

And it didn't have to be edible! I kept finding bits of aluminum foil in my backyard. I was mystified until I saw my elderly neighbor leaning over the back fence, handing a large package well wrapped in foil to our pooch. I confronted her and learned that this eighty-year-old, dedicated vegetarian went to the grocery store each week to buy her veggies, fruits, nuts and berries—and the biggest pot roast she could find, which she lovingly prepared for my dog. She said she was afraid that, if dirt got on the meat, it might make Barney ill. I assured her that a bit of dirt wouldn't hurt him, but I was concerned about the copious amounts of foil he was ingesting.

It got worse! I had a greenhouse filled with my vast collection of cacti and succulents. One of my prize specimens was a large pot of small barrel cacti. They were the size of baseballs, and each sported dozens of needles. I noticed some were missing and wondered why anybody would steal them one at a time! Then, I saw Barney lying under a tree, carefully chewing on something. I pried his jaws open and reached in his mouth to investigate. I let out a yelp and pulled out a thoroughly chewed cactus, still covered with needles, many of which were deeply imbedded into my hand. I still don't understand how he could chew on them!

Back to the apple...

Grace inspected the fruit every day, making sure that no worm or insect attacked that single apple. And she was checking its growth and ripeness. Finally, the day arrived when she determined it was time to "harvest the crop." Most people would simply grasp the apple, give it a twist and a tug, and be done.

But not my wife!

Grace believes there are certain events in life that require a certain decorum or bit of panache. And the success of this apple was one. She returned to the house, reviewed her vast collection of woven baskets, and selected the perfect one. She folded a linen napkin and placed it in the bottom. She daintily pulled on her gardening gloves and collected her shears.

She returned to the tree, but it was empty! She frantically searched the ground, but the apple wasn't there. She had only been gone for two minutes.

Then, she realized Barney was not at her side. He was always with us whenever we were outside. She saw him at the far end of the yard, and his back was to her—a sure sign he was doing something he shouldn't be doing. And she knew where her apple was!

I was watching from the kitchen, and I saw my wife drop the basket and shears and pull off her gloves. Then, she put her head down and charged across the yard. My wife, who is not at all athletic, became an Olympian that day. Legs churning, arms pumping, she tackled that dog with a ferocity that would make any NFL linebacker proud. She straddled Barney, pulled his jaws open, and stuck her hand into his mouth. Seconds later, she stood and, in triumph, held aloft a slightly chewed and spit-covered apple!

She marched into the house, went to the kitchen sink, and proceeded to scrub the fruit. Then, she cut it in half, and like the original Eve in the Garden of Eden, she offered me half. Unlike Adam, I refused.

"No," I told her. "You earned this apple. It's all yours!"

Then, with equal amounts of amusement and squeamishness, I watched her eat it. When she finished, all that remained was the stem.

I smiled at her. She smiled at me. And I didn't kiss her for three days!

—Chip Kirkpatrick—

The Simple Things

Dogs love to go for rides. A dog will happily
get into any vehicle going anywhere.
~Dave Barry

Whenever our daughter Melanie would arrive to pick up her girls, our Golden Retriever, Gixxer, would greet her at the door and whine with excitement. He would prance by her side, never taking his gaze off her. He wanted more than her attention.

"I can't today, Gixxer. I'm in a hurry," Melanie said while patting the top of his head. "Girls, let's go!" she yelled down the stairwell.

I sympathized with Gixxer as he sat patiently in front of Melanie, giving her his best impression of sad puppy eyes. "I'm sorry, little guy. She doesn't have time for you today."

"Mom! Way to make me feel bad." Melanie scratched Gixxer behind his ears. She made the mistake of cupping her hands around his ears, tilting his head to look into his soulful, brown eyes. She couldn't refuse him now. "Ugh. Fine! Let's go." She waved for Gixxer to follow. "Make sure the girls are ready by the time we get back!"

Gixxer bolted past her in a race to the front door. He bounced up and down on his front paws, his tail wagging like a helicopter rotor. Once Melanie opened the door and waved him on, he darted through the threshold, bounded off the porch, and planted himself next to her car door, wiggling with excitement. She opened the passenger door, allowing him to sit in the front seat. As she started the car, she lowered the window for him.

A few minutes later, my granddaughters and I watched them pull up to the curb. We giggled at Gixxer's cuteness as he appeared to be smiling, panting with his tongue hanging out of his mouth. A quick drive around the block and he was happy.

Melanie opened the door for Gixxer, and he quickly exited. "Goodbye, Dudicle." (That was her nickname for him.) She couldn't help but smile.

After our granddaughters gave Gixxer kisses on either side of his head, saying their goodbyes, he padded to my side and sat as we watched them drive away.

The next day when Melanie arrived to pick up the girls, Gixxer met her at the front door, whining with excitement like usual. She walked past him, brushing her hand across his head. "I don't have time today. I'm serious this time. I'm already late."

I watched as Gixxer pranced next to Melanie. His gaze focused on her eyes, begging for attention. She refused to look at him.

"Poor Dudicle, Melanie never has time for you anymore," I said, using the most sympathetic voice I could muster.

Melanie grimaced, turned on her heel, and said between gritted teeth, "Fine! Let's go! But the girls better be outside and waiting when we get back." She feigned anger, but I knew it wouldn't last.

We were all outside ready to greet Gixxer as they returned from their short drive around the block. He jumped out of the car, tail wagging, tongue flapping, happy to see us. Melanie's annoyance abated.

A few months later, Melanie and her family came to show us their new SUV. Her husband Corey informed me that dogs weren't allowed in their new car. They wanted to keep it looking nice, free of dog fur.

Good luck with that, I thought.

When it was time for them to leave, we all went outside to say our goodbyes. My granddaughter opened the back door of their SUV and Gixxer promptly jumped in, sitting right in the middle of the seat. Corey had been distracted by talking to my husband Gene and didn't notice that Gixxer had gotten in the car until he opened his door.

"What's Gixxer doing in the car?" Corey looked pointedly at Melanie as she started the ignition. "I thought dogs weren't allowed in this car."

"The rules don't apply to Gixxer. Get in. We're taking him around the block," she said.

"But..." Corey stopped himself short, shaking his head. He must have figured it was a losing battle when it came to Gixxer. It reminded me of the time when Gixxer spent the night at their house. Corey slept on the couch while Gixxer slept on the bed with Melanie.

After they dropped off Gixxer and we watched them drive away, Gene said, "Boy, does he have them trained. You won't catch me caving in like that."

I rolled my eyes, knowing that Gixxer had my husband wrapped around his furry paws. A few days later, Gixxer proved it to be true.

I sat on the porch, watching Gene work on his truck. Finished, he slammed down the hood and pushed the doors closed that had been open. He sat next to me, letting out an exhaustive sigh. "That was no fun," he said, wiping sweat from his forehead.

"Um, why'd you leave Gixxer in the truck?" I tilted my head toward the truck.

Gene glanced at the truck, squinting his eyes as he peered at the tinted windows. "He's not in the truck."

"Yes, he is. He's in the back seat."

"When did he get in the truck?" Gene ambled to the truck and opened the back door. "Gixxer! What are you doing in there? Come on, get out." He waved his hand for Gixxer to exit. Gixxer moved to the other side, lowering his head, avoiding Gene's gaze. "Come on, get out." Gixxer sat defiantly, turning his head to avoid eye contact.

"He's not going to get out until you take him for a ride around the block," I called out.

"I'm not doing it! If he thinks he can sucker me into taking him for a ride, he has another think coming!" He glared at Gixxer. "Come on, get out!" He thrust his arm to signal Gixxer to exit. Gixxer didn't move, still avoiding eye contact. Gene slammed the door and went around to the other door. Gixxer moved to the opposite side. "Gixxer, out! Now!" Gixxer ignored him, turning his head toward the window.

Gene huffed and crossed his arms as he sat hard next to me. "I'm not doing it. He can sit in there all day for all I care."

I dangled the truck keys in front of my husband. He snatched them out of my hand, mumbling under his breath as he stomped to the truck, turned the ignition, lowered the back window, and drove around the block. Once home, he opened the door, and Gixxer jumped out, running to me with his tail wagging.

Although Gixxer is no longer with us, his enduring spirit lives within our hearts. He made us smile every day and he was a constant reminder that it's the simple things in life that bring joy.

— Marianne Reese —

Always an Adventure

The Doggy Door

In order to really enjoy a dog, one doesn't merely try to train him to be semi-human. The point of it is to open oneself to the possibility of becoming partly a dog.
~Edward Hoagland

I had just finished installing a doggy door in the back of the house, and I couldn't wait to show Linda. Linda is my rescue dog who is about the size of a small elephant. She is gangly and brown with spikey fur and a bulbous nose. She loves everyone and everything—mostly. However, she had a bad habit that may have been why I found her in the pound. Linda was notorious for sitting at the door and whining to go out, even if you had just let her out and back in five minutes before. She had the knack of knowing right when you had settled into the comfort of your armchair. That's when she whined. She wanted you to get up, open the door, and let her out. She did this five times an hour.

There was more. Sometimes, after you got up from the comfort of your chair to open the door, she wouldn't go out. She'd look at you, eyes smiling, and dash away back into the house. It was a game that she made up all by herself, for people to play when they were extremely tired at night. Linda won every time. If you didn't get up, she increased the volume of her plaintive whine. If you still resisted, her whine turned into a primitive, wolf-type howl. No matter how much you didn't want to, you did eventually respond.

So, the doggy door installation was actually for the bipeds in the family who liked to sit in comfortable chairs after seven at night. It was for those who liked to watch movies all the way through without interruption or finish a conversation without going to the door.

I brought Linda into the back room and showed the doggy door to her proudly that day, talking in high-pitched tones as one would talk to a toddler. I wanted her to be excited. I wanted her to be thrilled at the prospect of autonomy and choice represented by the hinged plastic panel that would easily give way to a small shove and set her free to roam the fenced-in yard.

"Look, Linda! Wow! You have your own door! It's great to have your own door!"

Linda took one look at the door and froze. I reached down and swung the plastic panel back and forth, back and forth, with great enthusiasm.

"See! Look, Linda! You can go in… You can go out! You can go in… You can go out! All by yourself!"

I swung the door at least nine times. Linda still hadn't moved except to flatten her tiny ears back against her massive skull. Then, she put her head down slightly, looking up at me from the top of her eyeballs. Her eyes glistened and she hunched her shoulders up around her neck, still frozen in place, as if she were reliving some past trauma. Had she had a near-death experience before I rescued her from the pound? A doggy door perhaps opening up as she journeyed toward the light?

I opened and closed the doggy door once more. She'd had enough. She put her tail between her legs and flew down the hall, sliding on the hardwood floor into the main bedroom. I found her hiding under the bed, panting.

I had to go to work so I left her there. That night, on my return, Linda was standing on the other side of the sliding glass door, greeting me. She was wagging her tail, with her whole body following suit. When I entered the house, she squealed joyously, and for all I could observe, she seemed to have recovered completely from the morning's trial. She even had her favorite Santa Claus stuffy, which was not a stuffy, in her mouth. I say this because "SC," as we called this limp, bedraggled dog toy, has no stuffing at all. With entrepreneurial skill, Linda had removed both of SC's eyes and pulled out all the stuffing through the tiny eyeholes with her teeth. So, I thought ruefully, if she could pull stuffing through tiny Santa Claus eyeholes to create this limp, red rag of a toy, why couldn't she pull herself through an XTRA LARGE doggy door to go outside?

I wanted to sit in a comfortable chair that night and not be bothered. I took Linda by the collar and showed her the doggy door again. "Look, Linda! This is great! Yeah! It's great!"

Her ears flattened against her head. She began to struggle to get away. So, I let her go, and I went outside with her favorite treat: a peanut-butter pretzel. She never could get enough of those. I opened the doggy door from outside, peering into the house, with treat in hand.

"C'mon, girl! C'mon! It's nice out here! We can do this! Yes, we can!"

All my efforts to coax her were met with silence. I popped the peanut-butter pretzel into my mouth and sighed.

When I went back inside, I found Linda curled up in the cat's crate. Yes, we have a cat, too. Her name is Harriet. Harriet is completely anti-social, which is why I don't talk about her.

Linda was sitting on Harriet's little pink bed inside the crate, covering the bed entirely except for a piece of the blanket that stuck out on one side by her rear end with the words embroidered "I'm a Brat." I couldn't have agreed more. How Linda had jammed herself into that tiny space and curled her long, bony legs up around herself, I will never know. She stayed there all night while Harriet sat on the area rug staring Linda down.

I gave up on the doggy door. Linda was back to her game the next evening, continuing to whine and disrupt bipeds in comfortable chairs after seven at night. The days of winter wore on toward spring, and the motionless doggy door hung in the back room, shunned and silent.

Finally, one day when I came back from work and opened the gate into the yard, I noticed something was different. It took me a moment, but then I realized that no dog was staring at me and wriggling joyously from inside the sliding glass door. Grabbing the mail, I looked around furtively but there was no sign of Linda. I was becoming concerned, but then she appeared, bounding around the side of the house with SC in her mouth. She was absolutely beside herself with joy. She greeted me by banging her tail on a nearby tree trunk, keeping the beat, while shoving her face into my hands.

"Linda! How did you get outside, girl?"

Had she used the doggy door? I scarcely dared to think it might be true. Another biped had probably come home early and let her out. Still, miracles can happen. I went inside and walked to the back of the house where the trauma-inducing plastic panel hung. I had not realized yet that Linda, uncharacteristically, was not following me. Then, it happened. Like a torpedo launched at a target, Linda came crashing through the doggy door from outside, running toward me at full tilt. She shoved her enormous nose into my stomach, still holding SC carefully in her mouth.

"You did it, Linda!" I exclaimed. "You used your door! Good girl, Linda! Good girl!"

Linda flung herself at me again in absolute delight, wriggling and wagging. What had caused the shift in her canine brain from "scary doggy door" to "user- friendly doggy door"? I didn't really care, but I was about to find out.

Seconds later, in the midst of Linda's celebration, as I crouched down and stroked her massive head, praising her effusively for de-traumatizing herself, another dog came bounding into the house — through the now very "user-friendly" doggy door. It was a dog I had never seen before: a kind of stocky Bulldog, with muddy paws, sporting strings of drool at the sides of his mouth. They flew up in the air as he bounded toward me.

That is how we acquired Lincoln. He had no ID tags, and though we posted an ad, no one claimed him. Later, we found the hole he had dug underneath the fence to get to Linda. Despite all his weaknesses and incessant slobber, the fact that Lincoln had taught Linda to use the doggy door obligated us, of course, to provide him with a home. Not only that, but after seven when the bipeds were in their comfortable chairs, Lincoln and Linda preferred each other's company to ours, racing in and out of the doggy door.

— Kim Engelmann —

My Dog Got Stuck Up a Tree

Every survival kit should include a sense of humor.
~Author Unknown

The high-pitched barking stopped me in my tracks. Jasper and I exchanged glances and instinctively knew that Zac was up to no good. We turned in the direction of the yelps. Zac sounded more like a seal than a dog. We knew what that meant. Either he'd found prey or he was in trouble.

Zac had come to me all skin and bones at just over a year old. Rejected from five households, he was withdrawn and morose. I guess he expected to be abandoned again. It took a month before he wagged his stumpy tail, but over time he learned to put his trust in me. Now, he wiggles his whole body with joy.

Life with Zac is unpredictable. He is goofy, wild, and determined. He has given me more gray hairs than any other life stressor.

Princess Jasper and I ran toward Zac's barking, jumping over rocks and tree roots and scratchy plants. When we finally reached ground zero for the barking we didn't see him. Until I looked up.

I didn't know whether to laugh or cry. Zac was up a tree and balancing precariously on a branch, face-to-face with a giant, hissing-and-spitting ginger cat.

The tree had grown at an angle, giving Zac a ramp to run up. But then he had jumped off the trunk and onto adjoining branches.

The branch that Zac wobbled on hung over a 20-meter drop onto a rocky shoreline. There was no room for him to turn around, and I doubted he could shimmy backwards to the tree trunk, which he couldn't even see behind him. At best he was facing broken bones.

I needed help, and I needed it fast.

I had no signal to make a call, so I bolted a mile to the nearest house. I stashed Jasper back in the car as I passed it.

"Excuse me, but my dog's stuck up a tree. Any chance I can borrow your phone?"

Dogs don't climb trees! They must have thought I was bonkers. You know what they say: If it looks like a duck and quacks like a duck, it must be a duck. I looked bonkers and sounded like it. I'm not even sure who I planned to call.

The occupants of the house looked understandably suspicious and confused. But they opened the door wider and motioned for me to enter. I bent down to undo the laces of my hiking boots. I had to be polite even though every second counted.

Then, I heard them say, "What, you mean *that* dog?"

Had I forgotten to close the door of the car? Had Jasper managed to get out? I turned around, ready to scold Jasper and order her back to the car when I saw Zac galloping toward me. His oversized tongue lolloped out the side of his enormous grin. He was in one piece, all four legs functioning as normal, and miraculously with no open wounds.

The combination of adrenaline and relief swiped my legs from under me, and I wilted to the ground. Zac stumbled onto my lap, all 32 kg of him, and licked my face. I wanted to be angry with him, but he wouldn't have understood. I embraced him, knowing we had been granted bonus time together. Tears of gratitude streamed down my cheeks as he raised his muzzle to the sky and sang his familiar song of happiness.

"Ow, ow, ow, ow, ow!"

How he got down from that tree, I will never know. But I do know that Zac helped me build faith that there is always an escape route. Although it feels like my poor heart can't take many more of his antics, Zac has helped me believe that even when we imagine the worst, everything will be okay in the end.

—Ali Hall—

Harley the Huntress

Humor is emotional chaos remembered in tranquility.
~James Thurber

I was a single mom for several years, sharing custody with my former husband. When I was house hunting, a must-have was a fenced yard. I found the perfect house for my family with a nice yard, in a quiet neighborhood on a loop, where most of the houses backed up to woods. Many mornings, I would sit out back listening to the birds and watching the squirrels run up and down the trees. Occasionally, I saw an armadillo gathering leaves and sticks. A few times, I watched possums in the tree while I sat on my living room sofa. There was plenty of wildlife to enjoy.

At the time, I also had a problem: I collected dogs. I didn't think of it as a problem, but when I brought in the fourth one, people in my life became concerned. I was put on dog probation. I was also on book probation, but that's a story for another time.

So, there we were: four dogs, two children, and me. Our pups were wonderful companions and greatly loved, but we stayed busy trying to keep them from escaping under the fence. One in particular — Harley — was determined to get out and see the world. And she did, way too often for my liking. Besides being Houdini, Harley is our huntress. She is not a big girl, maybe forty-five pounds. Our guess is she is a Feist mix. Her coat is black and smooth, and her body thin and muscular.

She mostly brings me moles. Moles in the hallway, moles under the bed, and one glorious time, a mole *in* my bed. She's good at what she does. We thought about starting a reality show: "Harley, Mole Huntress."

One fine day it was not a mole. I could deal with moles. But I was not prepared for this. While sipping coffee and looking out my kitchen window into the backyard, I saw my sweet Harley with a little extra pep in her step. The girl looked proud of herself. I squinted and tried to figure out what was in her mouth. It didn't take me long once I realized that sticks don't bend in the middle and hang down to the ground.

I hollered for my daughter Abigail and then went to the garage for a shovel. I'm not sure of my logic on that, but that is what I did. Shovel in hand, I announced, "Harley has a snake!"

It went downhill from there. Harley was not giving up her prize. We chased her around the backyard, pleading with her to drop the slithery serpent. As we closed in on her, she finally dropped it. I told Abigail to pick up Harley and hold onto her. When she had a good hold on our squirming, undeterred pup, I scooped up the snake on my spade—you know, the kind of shovel that is not meant to carry long snakes any distance at all—and then walked toward the house. There was no real plan other than for my daughter to hold Harley while I picked up the snake. If I was thinking at all, I would have gone to the wooded area and put the snake over the fence. At this point, I felt sure the dog had already killed it.

I was carrying the snake on the spade. There was much more snake hanging off each side of the spade than there was on it. Adrenaline had been coursing through my veins, but now I was sure we had the situation under control.

Then, Harley wriggled free from Abigail's arms and came right for me and the snake. I was doing my best to hold the spade and the dangling snake as high in the air as possible while screaming for my daughter to grab Harley. She darted and jumped higher than I'd ever seen. There was no doubt in my mind that she is part Feist, part kangaroo. I was still balancing the snake on the spade and trying to keep it from Harley. I swung the snake around, Harley jumped at it,

Abigail reached for the dog, and SMACK! In my attempt to keep the snake away from Harley, I turned and smacked Abigail in the face with the snake. I froze.

"You hit me with the snake!" Abigail cried. "You hit me with the snake, and I heard it hiss!"

She had Harley, I had the snake, and we stared at each other for what felt like minutes and then started laughing. We went back to the house, and I laid the snake across the back patio to decide what to do with it. It did not slither away. It did not move.

Abigail came out of the house after securing Harley. We stared at the snake. When we looked later it was gone. We could only hope.

—Anne Calvert—

Bruno Needs Viagra

You are wise to remember that a well-developed sense of humor is the pole that adds a balance to your steps as you walk the tightrope of life.
~William Arthur Ward

Bruno was a Shih Tzu, one of those cute, cuddly lapdogs that trot around the ring in dog shows with a fetching little bow holding long, silky hair out of their eyes. But Bruno didn't have a bow, and he never trotted. He was selfish, undisciplined, loud, and crude. He charged at full speed in and around the furniture, leaving a trail of urine in his wake.

The only good thing about Bruno was that he was not mine. The dog had been given to my niece by a suitor who was trying to stay in her good graces. It didn't help. The guy was phased out, but the dog remained.

I was not the only person in the family who disliked Bruno. My brother-in-law disliked the suitor, disliked the dog, and definitely disliked the pee pads that decorated my sister's beautiful home to accommodate Bruno's stubborn refusal to be house-trained. In fact, I never once heard my brother-in-law refer to the dog as anything but "the little bastard."

We stopped seeing Bruno when my husband and I retired two states away in the lower Rio Grande Valley of Texas, just twenty miles from the U.S./Mexico border. In fact, we forgot all about him.

Like many retirees, if our insurance did not offer us a good deal on prescriptions, we would walk across the International Bridge to

Nuevo Progreso, Tamaulipas, Mexico. There, we would find a score of pharmacies, American-educated pharmacists, and name-brand medicines, most of them made in Europe and sold to us for a fraction of the cost that the same meds would cost in the United States.

Tom and I are a healthy pair, but we did go to one particular shop for Tom's cholesterol medicine. The pharmacist, a University of Texas grad, had that gift that some people have for always putting a name with a face. Even seeing us only three or four times a year, Arturo always greeted us by name and with that gracious warmth that characterizes the people of Mexico.

One March morning, we got a call from my sister. She kept the usual pleasantries to a minimum and dove into the purpose of her call.

"Louise, you live near the border, right?"

"Sure do. A thirty-minute drive if the traffic isn't bad."

"And you can get medicine there, even without a prescription?"

"Yes, is there a problem?"

"Well," she paused, "yes." Longer pause. "Is it true that you can get Viagra there, really cheap?"

My jaw fell open.

"You can get it by the gross for next to nothing, and you don't need a prescription. But I don't think you are supposed to use it without talking to a doctor first."

"Oh, it's not for anyone here," my sister explained. "It's for Bruno."

Bruno! I didn't even know the little pest was still alive. And the thought of him needing a boost in his love life was even more remote. As it turned out, love had nothing to do with it.

"Bruno is having heart problems. He has passed out several times, and the vet said he needs Viagra."

For those who might be wondering why increasing a Shih Tzu's sex performance might help a dog with a bad heart, let me explain. Viagra is simply the brand name for sildenafil, a drug that has been used for decades to increase blood flow by dilating blood vessels. It was used for circulatory problems long before it was used for problems with ED.

The vet had given my sister a script for Viagra and told her to have it filled at the pharmacy. It would be ground down, put in a solution, and given to Bruno a few drops each day. No problem at all, until Sis's husband found out how much it was going to cost to keep "the little bastard" alive. No, no, no, they were not going to spend that kind of money on that dog.

At that point, our proximity to the border became Plan B. I would get Viagra in Mexico at a more reasonable price, mail it to Colorado, save Bruno's life drop by drop and day by day, and be reimbursed for my trouble. Plans, of course, are one thing, execution another.

Recognizing the need for haste, Tom and I took the trip across the Bridge the next day. We got to the pharmacy, and Arturo greeted us with his usual warm handshake, wanting to know how he could help us.

I jumped right in, asking for Viagra. Without skipping a beat, Arturo's attention went straight to my husband. He started explaining that Tom would not even need to take a whole pill; just cutting it in half would be more than enough.

"Oh, no," I interrupted, leaping to my husband's defense. "It isn't for him. It is for my sister's dog."

Arturo looked at me with a mixture of surprise, sympathy and barely contained amusement. "Of course," he said.

Tom, on the other hand, gave me one of those looks that says, "We'll talk later."

But we didn't. At least not right away.

We met friends for lunch at a popular restaurant, shopped a little, and then headed back across the border, at which point all purchases are checked and any appropriate taxes are paid. As we approached the U.S. checkpoint, Tom turned to me and said, "If they ask about the Viagra, don't tell them it's for your sister's dog. No one believes that."

I started to point out that I was only telling the truth, but then I stopped. Tom was right. Nobody's dog eats their homework, and nobody needs Viagra for their dog.

Bruno had enough Viagra for the final year of his life. The story lives on in our family, although Tom never finds it as funny as I do. I think the sympathy on Arturo's face haunts him.

— Louise Butler —

Sunday Surprise

One of the most enduring friendships
in history — dogs and their people,
people and their dogs.
~Terry Kay

We had just accepted the fact that Simi was expecting her first litter of puppies. At only fifteen months old, she wasn't much more than a puppy herself, but we could no longer ignore the physical signs.

Although Simi was quite young, the father-to-be was not. At eleven years old, Zeus was a senior dog. Yet here they were, about to be parents for the first time. While the expansion of our fur family was unplanned, our human family was still excited about the news, especially our children.

Simi had a favorite yellow squeaky toy that she was rarely seen without. It was common to see her running in the yard with it in her mouth as she played. As we arrived home from church one Sunday morning, we saw her in the front yard with her favorite yellow toy halfway out of her mouth. The fact that she didn't run to greet us was odd. She remained by the pine trees, standing and watching us as we unloaded from the car.

After we had eaten lunch and cleaned the kitchen, I glanced out the window to see Simi lying in the yard near the pine trees. After a moment, she stood up with her yellow toy still in her mouth, turned around and lay right back down. I called my husband over to the window to look, and he confirmed my suspicion that the time had come for the puppies. We called for the kids and headed outside to prepare her an area where she could be comfortable. She remained in the same spot by the pine trees but wagged her tail as we approached to check on her.

Sure enough, we could see the contractions of her belly and noted a difference in her breathing. We led her to her garage birthing suite as we made bets on how many puppies she would have. She was petite for a Great Dane and didn't appear to be much larger than her normal size, so we were expecting two or three puppies.

Zeus joined us in the garage. By this time, Simi was lying in front of me. I realized that she was using her beloved yellow chew toy to help manage her pain as she labored. With every contraction, she'd pick the toy back up until the contraction ended when she would put it back down. After about half an hour, the first puppy arrived to our squeals of excitement. After Simi cleaned the puppy, she lay back down and grabbed her toy as she prepared for the next round of contractions.

Five hours and five more puppies later, we were still in the garage. Simi was quite tired and seemed to appreciate the support from Zeus and her humans. With each new puppy, she would clean it up, sigh loudly and pick up her yellow chew toy. By now, her head was resting in my lap as I rubbed her gently and spoke softly to her as she continued laboring. The guesses and excitement had shifted to naming the puppies and wondering how many more were in there.

Five hours and six more puppies later, my husband and I called it a night with the final count at fourteen puppies. Zeus, Simi, and the puppies remained in the birthing suite with food, water, and the trusted yellow chew toy nearby. Simi was exhausted.

We were in shock, wondering how we would care for fourteen Great Dane puppies. Regardless of the daunting task that lay before us, we went to bed thankful that all the puppies and Simi seemed healthy.

I was awakened the next morning by my husband's gentle shake. "You aren't going to believe this. There are fifteen," he said. We went from two Great Danes to seventeen in less than twelve hours. Seventeen dogs living in our garage. Wow.

Although one of the puppies didn't survive, the first few weeks went smoothly, given the circumstances. I was able to come home at lunch most days to check on the new family. Simi established a system of cleaning, nursing, and caring for the puppies. It was beautiful to see how easily she and Zeus adjusted to being parents. When the kids got home from school, they would cuddle and care for the pups, who were beginning to grow and become more active.

The following few weeks proved to be much more challenging as the puppies grew. We live in rural Georgia with owls, hawks, and other puppy predators nearby. We needed to move the puppies out of the garage while still protecting them. We created a puppy complex with a covered sleeping area and open play area, with controlled access. The puppies had almost doubled in size and were quite active and noisy. My mom would help check on them during the day and helped us with supervision when we let them outside of the complex for free play. Keeping up with fourteen energetic puppies was no easy feat!

Fortunately, we were able to find homes for the puppies with relative ease as they were old enough to be weaned just before Christmas. We kept one of the boys, Thor, who brought us much joy.

Zeus died about four months after the puppies were born. Thor lived until he was six and died peacefully at home with Simi by his side. Simi remains highly active and energetic, even at ten years old. We had her spayed as soon as she recovered from the delivery, so that was her one and only litter.

Simi now has an adopted Bassett Hound brother, Copper. Recognizing that she is reaching the high end of her life span, we cherish our time with her. We often look back at photos of all those puppies and fondly remember that Sunday surprise.

— Laura Vertin —

Maxine's Mail

If we couldn't laugh, we would all go insane.
~Jimmy Buffett

I have absolutely no idea how my dog Maxine's name ended up on a mass-marketing list, but sometime in the spring of 1991, shortly before I moved away from Cambridge, Massachusetts, a few offers trickled in. Physicians Mutual Insurance Company of Omaha offered Maxine a Hospital Plus Protection Plan. It didn't say if it applied to animal hospitals.

The Award Claim Center from Redlands, California, mailed an urgent notice confirming that my dog would receive a cash prize. It said, "You are CONFIRMED." The Craftmatic Adjustable Beds company of Trevose, Pennsylvania, said she was eligible to receive their free catalog simply by calling their toll-free number.

International Correspondence Schools sent her information about training for a better job, one that paid more money. Then, the Ford Motor Company offered Maxine a guide to car and truck buying.

The U.S. Olympic Committee cordially invited her to make Olympic history. A sweepstakes notified Maxine that she won a contest. Wow, Maxine, what a lucky dog. To receive her award, she had to send $12.75.

Not long after I arrived in Boulder, Colorado, dozens of new offers for Maxine flooded my mailbox. Some days, Maxine had more mail than I did. Lots of companies wanted Maxine as a customer. The Encyclopedia Britannica wanted to sell her a complete set. Magazine subscriptions started arriving. The American Running and Fitness

Association wanted to send a free gift. That made sense since we jogged every day. Maybe they could send her a canine heart monitor. I worried sometimes that I overworked her.

But the clincher came when dunning notices arrived, threatening to sue Maxine. The Security Control Service from Newport, Delaware, said they were retained to collect Maxine's unpaid balance from a magazine subscription she allegedly ordered. I called the phone number and spoke to a collection agent. He claimed that Maxine D. White ordered a subscription to a running magazine over the phone and didn't pay for it. I cracked up. Maxine White couldn't have ordered a subscription on the phone. She was a dog. He insisted she had. Go ahead and sue me, I said.

The dunning notices kept coming, so I called Julie Hayden, a television reporter whom I'd met at a shelter discussion several months earlier at the University of Colorado. She cracked up when I told her about Maxine's dilemma. Her station offered to represent Maxine in court if the collection agency came after her. Julie and a camera crew arrived at my apartment and filmed a segment about Maxine's mail. Not long afterward, the junk mail stopped coming.

All these years later, I have no idea how Maxine's name ended up on those lists.

— Debra White —

Cody and the Bone

Next to creating a life, the finest thing
a man can do is save one.
~Abraham Lincoln

Someone was pounding on our front door and yelling, "Help!" My husband Doug and I came running and quickly opened the door. Our next-door neighbor Jay had his dog Cody with him, a black Labrador Retriever who was squirming, crying, and choking. Maybe choking to death.

Our neighbor Jay and his wife Susan were "once-in-a-lifetime neighbors" who'd become dear friends over the years. They made homemade salsa and shared it with us. They came to our son's wedding. They had us over for barbecues and dinners.

Their two dogs, Lucy and Cody, were sweet. And now Cody was in trouble.

Jay was red-faced and breathing hard. "He's got a chicken bone caught in his throat, and I can't get it out! I can hold him if you can put your hand in his mouth and pull it out. He won't bite you." Doug stepped out onto our front porch and kneeled down to the dog's level. Jay pried open poor Cody's mouth. Cody cried and made high-pitched sounds of agony. He looked terrified.

Doug glanced at me, and I knew he wasn't thrilled to put his hand in the mouth of this large, panic-stricken dog. I didn't blame him, but he had no choice. Doug pushed his hand in Cody's mouth and couldn't feel anything, so he stopped to look but couldn't see anything.

Then, Doug pushed his hand farther into Cody's mouth. Way in the back he felt a piece of chicken bone wedged tightly across the roof of Cody's mouth like a chin-up bar. Doug grabbed it and pulled. Nothing. He tried again, harder. Nothing. Cody twisted his strong body to get away.

"Let's try again," Doug said. This time, Jay sat on the ground and held Cody tighter. Doug put his hand in Cody's mouth and gripped the bone. He leaned back, using his body weight, and pulled with all his might. I held my breath and prayed silently.

The bone snapped in two, and Doug quickly took the sharp pieces out of Cody's mouth. Cody, Jay and Doug collapsed on the ground and rested. Cody wiggled out of his dad's arms and went over to Doug, a few feet away. He climbed on Doug gently and kissed his face, arms and even his hands.

We could tell that Cody knew what had just happened and understood the gravity of the situation. "Wow, Doug! You've got a friend for life now!" Jay said.

We were ecstatic that Cody seemed to be okay.

The next day, Jay brought over a large bowl of fresh salsa and an invitation for a thank-you dinner. When we went to Jay and Susan's later that evening, Cody came trotting over. As soon as we sat down, Cody ran up to Doug and put his head in Doug's lap. He looked up with adoration at Doug.

Doug looked at us and said with a smile, "Yep, Cody's my friend for life!"

— Laura McKenzie —

Mackie's Game

Not all those who wander are lost.
~J.R.R. Tolkien

It had been about a month since I rescued Mackie, a six-year-old Doberman female, sweet as could be. We had established our habits, one of them a daily hike on state land along a nearby foot trail.

But on this particular day, I was delayed and distracted, and our departure time came and went. Mackie must have noted this, and when I leaned over to release her tie rope so she could come inside, she deliberately dropped her head, turned quickly away, and sprinted for the road — without me.

I wasn't a novice at chasing errant dogs, so I wasn't about to run after her on foot. Instead, I ran inside, grabbed my car keys and a leash, and sped after her.

Her first stop was a parking lot where she sniffed about and then gobbled a tidbit of something. Opening my car door, I got out and opened the rear door for her, encouraging her sweetly, "Mackie, let's go bye-bye." But as though I'd poked her with a hypodermic needle, she shot past me and back onto the road. Heart beating in my ears, I turned the car around and began following her. A car approached, I called on God for Mackie's safety, and it passed.

As this was the route we usually took to the park, Mackie was accustomed to each driveway along the way — but she hadn't been able to visit the houses. Now, she wanted to do just that. She ran right up onto a porch while my mind conjured a scene where someone opens the door, is greeted warmly by Mackie, and then grabs her collar. Well, as you can guess, that didn't happen. All I could do was watch while she sniffed about.

Eventually, she'd visited three houses, and I'd asked for God's help at each one. The last house was right next to the park entrance. I recognized this as a critical point. Once she hit the trail on the state land, I'd have to park my car and follow on foot. And then she'd likely be off the trail, into the woods, and out of sight.

Mumbling to God again, I got out, stationing myself in the middle of the driveway, hoping to grab her as she passed. Then, the sound of an approaching vehicle caused me to turn and look. It was a Jeep, which was soon beside me.

"Having car trouble?" the driver asked.

"No, dog trouble's more like it," I responded.

"Where is it?"

"She's on that porch, likely hoping for a handout."

"Oh, I can fix that. What's her name?"

"Mackie," I responded.

I watched him reach into the passenger seat, grab a McDonald's bag, and pull a half-eaten burger from its wrapper. He got out and called "Mackie!" in a smooth, enticing voice. Mackie came running, aiming her mouth at the burger in his hand. He grabbed her collar. I could have hugged my White Knight that day.

— Constance Rutherford —

Tommy and the Cottonmouth

Once you've had a wonderful dog, a life without one is a life diminished.
~Dean Koontz

When I saw that little brown face and those yellow eyes at the shelter, I knew that puppy was going to be mine. I adopted Tommy soon after my husband and I moved to Florida. He was never a cuddly pup, but he was always curious and interested in the world around him.

Before he was a year old, he had decided that his job in life was to be our protector. He took his job very seriously. My fat, round puppy grew into ninety pounds of solid muscle with long, strong legs, a wide head, and a powerful chest.

At home with us and with our close friends, he was funny, happy, and playful. But when strangers came to the door, he was vigilant in his duties as sheriff. Our loving, happy dog could become menacing.

I always walked him on a leash. We lived across the street from a conservation area with a mowed, grassy strip near the street. We often saw a wide variety of wild animals, from tortoises and rabbits to predators like alligators. When walking there, the wild animals would see us, and we would see them. We left them alone, and they left us alone.

Venomous cottonmouth snakes hunted in the grassy area every day. Cottonmouths were three feet long with reddish-brown, thick bodies, smaller heads, and tapered tails. When threatened, a cottonmouth will coil and open its mouth wide, showing the cottony white interior, hence the name. Tommy and I saw the snakes often enough that I could recognize their markings. They would lift their heads above the grass to see what was going on and then go back to their hunting. It was as if they thought, *Oh, it's you.* They didn't leave, and we didn't either. I had heard cottonmouths are fierce and aggressive, but these never were—at least, not to us.

One summer day, Tommy and I were enjoying a walk. He was on a long leash. He suddenly came upon an adult cottonmouth that was dark brown with very dark markings. It wasn't one of our regulars. Before I could get him away, the dog and snake were face-to-face. I froze. I didn't want to scare the snake by making Tommy move quickly. It might bite him, and he might not survive. I kept thinking, *No sudden moves, no sudden moves.* At least the snake wasn't coiled. Very, very slowly, I put more slack in the leash so my dog could move quickly if needed.

I was terrified. All I could do was stand quietly and watch as they slowly stretched out and sniffed each other. The snake was touching Tommy's nose with its tongue. Tommy was curiously sniffing the snake. The two of them were looking each other over.

After what seemed like an eternity, the dog and snake slowly turned away from each other. The snake put its head down and moved into the brush. Tommy looked up at me and wagged his tail. I didn't realize that I had been holding my breath the whole time. Knowing how impulsive Tommy could be, it was possible he would have snapped at the snake. I was so relieved that I started doing a silly, happy dance. I didn't care who saw me, neighbors or the cars driving past. Tommy bounced over to me with a big smile, and I gave him a huge hug.

I learned something that day. Although watching the dog and snake was very scary for me, I don't think the encounter was for either of them. Not only was there nothing I could have done, but in the end there was nothing I needed to do. The animals worked it out for themselves. Sometimes, we need to step in and make things right. Sometimes, we need to let things take a natural course. And that's okay.

— Marilyn J. Wolf —

Chapter 3

That Heroic Dog

Senior Class

Any glimpse into the life of an animal quickens our own and makes it so much larger and better in every way.
~John Muir

I'd always heard that dogs could discern things that we could not—that they had a kind of sixth sense. But after my wife and I adopted a ten-year-old Lab from a no-kill shelter (seniors adopting seniors), we became convinced that we had gotten a dog with *no* sense.

We learned that Winston liked to go on unsanctioned outings, one of which occurred after we got him home. Winston was sitting behind a screen door when a teen scooted by on his skateboard, which was, for Winston, an invitation to play. The screen door was no match for a 90-pound Labrador, and off he went.

With me running after him down a busy street in my PJs.

We also discovered that Winston had a voracious appetite, particularly for food like pizza and birthday cake, both of which he sampled from a kitchen counter we mistakenly thought was too high for him to breach.

But when Winston snagged hamburgers from a charcoal grill without singeing his paws, we began to wonder if our new dog had superpowers.

A few weeks later, we discovered he did.

It was just after midnight. My wife and I were abruptly awakened by Winston, who was frantically barking. Nothing we did seemed to calm him down.

And then the earthquake hit.

We knew immediately what was happening and stumbled to the kitchen, taking refuge under an oak table. Winston followed, wedging his considerable girth into the small space. No longer barking, he seemed satisfied that he had rescued Mom and Dad from certain disaster.

It was a 4.5 earthquake on the Richter scale, not devastating but strong enough to rattle the house and our nerves.

We now knew that we had adopted a truly unique dog. But Winston wasn't done impressing us. He had another big surprise in store.

Our neighbor was having a pool party, and we were invited. Winston was also invited as he was a well-known celebrity. The backyard was crowded with children, all known to Winston, and he moved amongst them, licking his greetings.

As children do at pool parties, they all jumped into the pool at once, mounting rafts, splashing, laughing.

Winston was not happy about it.

He began by barking. When that had no effect, he raced around the perimeter of the pool, whimpering.

My wife and I tried to intervene, but Winston continued circling the pool, clearly distraught.

And then, Winston did something we had never seen him do before. He jumped into the water.

At first, Winston bobbed and flailed, but then he became acclimated to his new setting and began dog paddling across the pool, much to the delight of the children. But Winston wasn't interested in playing. He had something else in mind and motored madly toward the deep end where one of the boys was lounging on a raft. Once there, he gripped the edge of the raft in his mouth and paddled determinedly toward the shallow end.

The children watched, astonished, as Winston grounded the raft on the steps of the pool, emerged triumphantly, and shook himself dry. The boy on the raft clambered out and moved to pet Winston. Everyone was cheering, including my wife and me.

And then, the boy from the raft dropped to the ground.

He was having a seizure. His parents, obviously experienced with this, calmly moved to his side and made him safe. It lasted but a minute, and then the boy was back, a weak smile indicating that all was well. The boy's parents thanked us, saying that what Winston had done wasn't all that unusual — at least for dogs trained to detect seizures.

Once the boy had fully recovered, Winston located a vacant chaise lounge and settled in for an afternoon snooze.

Just another day in the life of Winston: superhero dog.

In dog years, Winston was already elderly when we adopted him. But he still possessed the gumption to jump onto our bed whenever we were gone, and then hop down when we got home. The telltale sign? A dog biscuit on the bed. My wife and I always left a couple of them for Winston whenever we left. Invariably, he would leave incriminating evidence behind.

But Winston's aging hips soon made the bed an impossible peak for him to scale. And that's when we discovered another amazing thing about our aging rescue Lab.

"Remember how Winston left those treats behind on our bed?" my wife asked one day.

"Of course."

"Look what I found on the floor." She held up one of Winston's biscuits. "He wasn't leaving them by accident. He was leaving them on the bed for us. And now, because he can't get on the bed, he's leaving them *next* to the bed."

"You mean our rescue dog is leaving us treats?"

My wife didn't answer. I could see tears in her eyes.

Winston's health declined. While he remained the same old king of cuddles, he began to struggle. His around-the-block walk became a down-the-street walk. And then, one day, he stopped walking altogether.

"I called the vet," I told my wife, "and she's coming by later."

"We're probably the only people who have a vet that makes house calls," my wife suggested.

"We're the only people with a Winston."

Before the vet arrived, my wife and I went for a walk. We wanted to speak openly, and my wife was convinced that Winston could understand everything we said.

"What if it's time?" she asked.

I couldn't answer. This time, I was the tearful one.

The vet arrived, and her look of concern was disheartening. "Help me carry him to my van," she said quietly. "I'm taking him back to the clinic."

And suddenly, our Winstonless house became very quiet and empty.

The vet called much later. "He's got parvovirus. Dangerous for young dogs, usually fatal in older ones. I've started him on some medication. We'll know more in twenty-four hours." There was a long pause, and then she said, "It doesn't look good."

With nothing left but hope for tomorrow, my wife and I decided to try and get some sleep. But, a few minutes later, I found her sitting on the bed, sobbing.

"Honey, there's still a chance."

"That's not why I'm crying. Look."

"Oh."

It was one of Winston's treats. While we had been on our walk, somehow, in spite of being severely ill, he had managed to bring one of his biscuits into the bedroom for his mom and dad.

We slept little, unaccustomed to the absence of Winston's gentle snoring from his bed next to ours. In the morning, as we were having our coffee, the vet called.

Expecting the worst, I put her on speakerphone.

"When I came in this morning," she began, "Winston hadn't moved from last night. I tried to get a reaction. Food, treats, squeeze toy. Nothing. And then, as a last resort, I said, 'Winston, wanna go home and see your mom and dad?'"

At this, the vet paused as if struggling to get the words out. "He wagged his tail. I think he's going to make it."

— Dave Bachmann —

Faithful Flicka

The sheepdog is shown its possibilities, he learns what life is like for a good dog and is invited to walk in a rational world whose farthest boundaries are defined by grace.
~Donald McCaig, Nop's Hope

Spring had come early that year. With warm temperatures and snowmelt, the green hue in the upper pasture was visible from the house. Dad sent me and my older brother, Michael, to scout the area before releasing the herd to graze. He also told us to shut the gate to the lower pasture as it would still be too wet to be safe for the young calves.

"If the fence line is solid, we can turn the herd out and take a trip into the city to visit Grandma."

Grandma was three hours away. The trip was like an unexpected day off.

Michael and I were the oldest, so many of the chores landed on our shoulders. Dad taught us to inspect each fence post and the attached barbed wire carefully. We took our jobs seriously. The safety of the herd depended on us. Michael and I set off as Flicka, our tri-colored Rough Collie, led the way.

Although not as pretty as Lassie in the TV series, Flicka exceeded her Hollywood counterpart in many ways. Dad would say, "Flicka, bring 'em home." Without further instruction, Flicka would be off to round up our small herd of cattle and bring them into the barnyard.

"Poetry in motion" was how Dad described watching Flicka command respect from the herd. We never trained Flicka. She instinctively knew how to handle the herd from puppyhood. They trusted her. Even over-protective mama cows did not interfere with Flicka training their calves.

All was good in the upper pasture, so we moved the herd out in the morning. Flicka had her paws full, but she kept the herd in line. The cows were delighted to see open space again. It's amusing how a 1,200-pound cow can kick up her heels and dance across the field.

Dad paused to check the lower gate and nodded. Any job was expected to be done correctly the first time. That nod of approval meant the world to my brother and me.

"We'll be back tonight," Dad explained, "but let's leave the upper gate open. It should be warm enough for the calves to be out overnight. Sometimes, their mamas prefer the barn when the sun sets. Flicka will take care of them."

We smiled a "high-five" at each other and then raced toward the house. Flicka, as always, ran with us.

With clean clothes and sausage-stuffed pancake sandwiches, we piled into the car. Flicka watched us leave. Then, with tail high, she rejoined the herd. We knew she would listen for our return and be there to greet us. Somehow, she always knew.

As the sun peeked over the horizon, Dad muttered something about a red sky and sailor's warning, but we were too excited to pay much attention. After all, Grandma was so delighted to see us, and we were having such a great time.

By mid-afternoon, the temperature plummeted as heavy, dark clouds rolled in. Dad got quiet. Something was wrong—quiet was not one of Dad's attributes. His worry seeped into our joy like an ominous shadow. Before weather radar, farmers relied on "reading the clouds" and feelings. This feeling was not comforting.

"Sorry, Ma," Dad told Grandma. "We need to get home to check on the herd."

Grandma released no one from her care without a full belly. With a quick meal and a container of fresh-baked cookies "for the trip," we were on our way.

Spring snow is usually wet and heavy, making driving treacherous. Dad battled the snow-packed highway with near-zero visibility for over an hour. When he pulled over to put chains on the tires, a highway patrol officer informed us that they had closed the road. The spring snowstorm had morphed into a blizzard. Disheartened, we returned to Grandma's house.

Grandma's cheerful greeting dispelled some of the gloom. The warmth from the fireplace and hot chocolate comforted us while the wind howled outside. There was nothing we could do except pray.

By morning, the storm had passed. Snowplows quickly cleared the highways. Abandoned vehicles along the roadside reminded us how fortunate we were. On the way through our small Wisconsin town, Dad asked a snowplow driver if he would adjust his route to open the road to the farm.

We were filled with dread as we followed the snowplow the final mile to our home. The silence in the car was unnerving as we listened to the drone of the tires on the icy pavement.

My father's mood was alarming. With his jaw clenched and eyes riveted on the snowplow ahead, his white knuckles on the steering wheel vibrated with tension. We all felt it.

"It'll be alright." Mother's words were soft and gentle.

"Don't know about that. But we'll soon find out." His voice was flat.

For the first time, I realized that my father could not fix everything. He derived immense satisfaction from restoring things that were "beyond hope." This, however, he was powerless to fix. It was unsettling.

We found a white blanket of snow shrouding the yard and barnyard. There was no sign of life except the birds singing: no tracks, movement, or sounds. No herd in the barnyard. No Flicka.

Flicka's food dish on the porch was untouched. The sad reality that we had lost the herd, compounded by losing our beloved dog, felt unbearable.

Mechanically, Michael and I quickly put on our winter clothes to assist Dad in locating our herd.

An even blanket of snow covered the upper pasture. As we trudged toward it, the absence of a "moo" or bark was eerie.

"Well," Dad sighed, "at least there's no evidence of carcasses. Still, we have to find them."

The reality of his words stung my eyes. I'd dealt with death before, but never of this magnitude.

"Mooo."

Two sharp barks followed the low bellow.

"Mooo."

Dad sprinted toward the gully. Well, he sprinted as much as the deep snow allowed. My brother and I followed his trail. On top of the ravine, Dad stood in disbelief. Flicka spotted him and ran over. She was so proud of herself.

Somehow, Flicka had moved the entire herd into the gully and out of the wind. We could see her tracks circle the gorge as she had worked tirelessly to keep them in a tight bunch. Their body heat under the insulating blanket of snow enabled the calves to stay warm. Miraculously, we had not lost a single cow or calf.

Dad knelt in the snow with his face buried in Flicka's fur. His shoulders shuddered as he hugged her. Finally, Dad stood up, wiped the tears from his eyes, and gazed at the herd.

"Come on, girl, let's bring 'em home."

— Marie T. Palecek —

Mama Knows Best

You can't buy love, but you can rescue it.
~Author Unknown

It's probably not every day you see a guardian angel running along a four-lane road in pursuit of two overly rambunctious dogs. But that's what happened.

It all started a few weeks earlier when I stopped at a pet store to get birdseed. Tagging along was Maddie, my red-coated Border Collie.

When I got there, the store was holding an adoption event. I nearly turned and left because Maddie, though well-behaved, gets cranky around other dogs. My wife explained it was because Border Collies think they're superior dogs and don't like socializing with riffraff.

As I returned to the car, I laughed at the absurdity of what I was doing, and I stopped and said, "This is ridiculous. If I don't get the birdseed today, I'll have to return later. So, suck it up, Maddie. We're doing this for the birds. Just ignore the other dogs."

Border Collies don't miss a thing and, sure enough, when we strolled into the store, Maddie took notice of everything. She evaluated every dog we saw.

Suddenly, she skidded to a stop and focused on a crate that was slightly out of the way. She seemed frozen, so I looked closer and saw that two puppies were in the crate. They appeared to be some type of herding dog breed. What was interesting is that I'd never known Maddie to not bark at other dogs, but she wasn't barking at these two. Could it be that she recognized them as fellow herding dogs?

A person working for the pet-adoption group confirmed that the puppies were brothers who were mostly Australian Shepherds. I knew that Australian Shepherds were related to Border Collies. This woman said the puppies had been found abandoned in the woods near an old cemetery and were around twelve to sixteen weeks old.

Though their eyes locked on me, they kept stealing quick glances at Maddie. Did they know she was a herding dog? Being abandoned, I wondered what they thought of Maddie. Did they see her as a mama?

My mind started processing. I knew that herding dogs were active and powerful, but I'd had dogs like this my entire life, so I knew I could physically handle them. But what about my mental strength? I'd just lost my wife, and I was still more than a bit shaky. And what of Maddie? She'd been a massive help in caring for my sick wife. Both Maddie and I needed peaceful time for rest and reflection. How much peace would we have with two large puppies tearing through the house?

That's when I heard my wife: *If you wait for the stars to align perfectly before you do something, you'll never get around to doing anything! You love dogs, and these two will bring light to your days.*

That day, throwing common sense to the wind, I adopted both of them. As I filled out the paperwork, the person in charge said, "There's nothing that says you have to take them both, you know?"

"I lost my brother some years back, and I remember the pain of that loss. I can't split up these two. I can't put them through that."

As I loaded them in the car, the adoption person inquired if I wanted to borrow a crate to keep them confined while I drove home.

"No, thanks. She'll maintain order," I said, pointing to Maddie. Like most herding dogs, Maddie lived for order.

On the way home, the brothers were well-behaved. Being in a car seemed to amaze them more than scare them. Of course, Maddie had her eyes on them the entire time.

I named them Remy and Baux after two small towns in the south of France that Genie liked. They spent the next few weeks learning everyone's role and temperament, and I took them in the car as often as I could—and always with Maddie to further enforce that she was the boss. It didn't take them long to accept Maddie as the "mother dog." Even though they maintained their youthful spunk and spirit, they always watched Maddie to see if she approved of whatever they were up to.

A few weeks later, I swung by the UPS store to ship a large box. As I opened the rear of the SUV, I told Remy and Baux to stay in the car. Uncharacteristically, they darted past me, hopped out, and ran over to a grassy area. *No big deal,* I thought. *Maybe they just need to go to the bathroom.* That wasn't it, though. I watched in shock as they started racing down the side of the four-lane road. My heart stopped as they strayed into the road. Cars swerved to avoid them. They were too far away for me to catch them on foot, and they were ignoring my calls. I was in trouble.

That's when things got worse. After about two hundred yards, the road curved, causing me to lose sight of them. I still heard cars honking, and I was fearful I might hear a sickening thud followed by a yelp.

I had to do something, but what?

That's when I saw my answer: Maddie. She sat stoically in the front seat of the SUV, watching everything. I saw the look in her eyes. She knew! I opened the front door and looked into Maddie's eyes. As we had several times in the past, we made a mental connection. I let her out and said, "I need you to bring them back."

Maddie was off in a red flash. Miraculously, she ran along the grassy shoulder, staying out of traffic. Did she know that was safer? I lost sight of her when she came to the bend in the road, but then I heard the sweet sound of three sets of dog tags jingling.

The jingling came louder and closer, and I saw Remy and Baux running toward me. Directly behind was Maddie. She was herding them straight to me.

They immediately jumped into the open back of the SUV, and Maddie took the front seat. As I stroked her head, I said, "You're an angel, you know that?" She snorted as if to say, "No big deal."

— David Weiskircher —

Dog

The poor dog, in life the firmest friend.
The first to welcome, foremost to defend.
~Lord Byron

It's been eight years since that night in Petra—in pitch black, suffocating heat. Exhausted from three months of hard travel, my husband and I gave one last push, signing on for "Petra at Night" to see the Treasury, our last ancient ruin before heading home.

The small tour headed out, entering a long, narrow path carved between towering stone cliffs. Lines of votive candles meant to guide the way flickered powerless against the dark. I cringed at distant howling. "Wild dogs," someone said. For a half-hour, we stumbled through jagged rocks and loose stones. More howling echoed off the rocks. The cliffs closed in around us.

At last, the path opened on a sandstone temple illuminated by spotlights. We sat on rock slabs, straining to hear a flautist, her music drowned out by the howling dogs and chattering tourists.

It had been a rough travel day—up since 4:00 AM—and I'd had trouble breathing in the brutal heat. We'd expected to hear a lecture but realized the flautist was all we were getting. There were still thirty torturous minutes left in the "program." It would have been wiser to wait, to leave in the safety of the group. But we decided to head back alone.

Not quite alone.

A dog followed us into the narrow canyon. It moved wolf-like, shoulders hunched, head down. I scanned the darkness for the rest of his pack. He was alone... for now.

"If he attacks," I told my husband, "I'm attacking back."

Dog kept pace behind us.

The thing I failed to notice—the thing my lungs were now screaming—was that the path to the Treasury had been all downhill. Also, and this is true, 1.2 kilometers walking downhill equals 17,000 miles walking uphill. I slowed, sucking in air. Dog sneaked closer. I could count Dog's ribs. He was sizing us up for his next meal. I didn't take my eyes off him.

A half-hour into the climb, shouting voices pierced the darkness behind us. Dog stopped, dropping back. Seconds later, two young tourists burst out, laughing, scrambling up the rocky path. Dog lunged, barking, charging, flashing his teeth until the men raced on ahead.

"He's protecting us," said my husband.

"Seems that way," I said.

"Some animals," he said, "have a sixth sense about people who need more care than others—the sick, the elderly…"

I narrowed my eyes. "Tread lightly."

Forty minutes into the climb, my lungs threatened mutiny. I slowed, walking backward, sideways, struggling to suck in air. I drained the last of my water. Dog came closer, trotting at my side, stopping occasionally to scratch fleas.

Suddenly, two large dogs tore up the path toward us. Dog went wild, charging, biting. We pressed our backs against the canyon wall, helpless. He was a fighter, our Dog. All heart. I prayed for his safety. Held my breath until it was over. The two dogs slunk away into the night.

I wished I had water for Dog.

An hour later, we finally climbed out from the canyon walls. The land opened wide in front of us. Free at last! Just 800 feet to go… straight uphill. An unkempt man materialized from the shadows, offering an illegal taxi ride in exchange for money, a Mars bar, and our firstborn. I was tempted. Dog, an excellent judge of character, bared his teeth, making low-throated growls. The man backed away, disappearing into the dark. We kept climbing. It felt like my lungs would explode.

Minutes later, tires crunched along the rocks next us. The taxi, its lights off, inched up the hill with a passenger. Dog charged the car, running, barking, making sure it was gone from our lives.

Finally, the three of us arrived at the tour's starting point, just a half-block from our hotel. I gasped, bent forward, fists on hips, my lungs destroyed. I couldn't stand, needed a moment. After a long while, it occurred to me that I could get water and food at our hotel for Dog. I unbent.

Dog was gone.

We flew home the next day. The pulmonologist sampled a spot on my right lung. He told me what Dog knew without attending Harvard Medical School. Lung cancer. Stage four. Inoperable.

That was eight years ago... and counting. My husband had been right about Dog and his sixth sense. Dog knew. And he showed me that, when bad stuff hits, you attack it with fight and heart and you don't quit. Good Dog.

— Sue Sussman —

Night Watch

Gratitude; my cup overfloweth.
~Author Unknown

It was nearing midnight as I waited for my mother to arrive home. She was a nurse and had taken a late shift that day. Oddly, she often reminded me of how I would wait up for her to come home when I was a small child.

This night, I didn't watch alone. I had man's best friend right by my side. His name was Benji. He was just honored to be allowed inside on such a cold night. This wasn't often, so he savored every minute of it.

Eventually, we heard the quiet rumble of an engine. Of course, Benji's keen ears sent him scampering to the door before me. We stood at the door vigilantly observing as Momma collected her bags to come inside. Once inside, she put on an egg to boil while she settled in. Since my "night watch" was over, I felt relieved enough to call it a night.

I retired to my room and got in bed. Benji was still roaming around the house. He'd come into my room to settle once he finished his patrol. After all, my room was the warmest room in the house. He was free to enter and exit as he pleased because my door had a broken knob, so he could open the door with a push of his nose.

Once my head hit the pillow, I fell fast asleep. It must have been fifteen to twenty minutes later when I was awakened by Benji's wet nose moving my limp hand. He was nervously pacing by my bed. Since he stood equal height to my bed, he could easily rouse me. As soon as I opened my eyes and looked at him, he darted out the door.

I went back to sleep. I figured that he needed to be let outside before he had an accident in the house. I was going to get up—just not then.

Benji burst into my room again with the same angst as before. He put his cold, wet nose under my hand a second time. This time, I sat up, and he immediately dashed out of the room. I lay back down again. After he realized that I was not coming, Benji hurriedly returned a third time. This time, he lightly bit my hand and proceeded to pull me out of bed. That was when I smelled smoke!

I jumped to my feet and followed Benji's lead. He led me to the kitchen where a tall flame had engulfed the pot with the egg. My mother had fallen asleep with the egg boiling. I quickly grabbed the pot handle and extinguished the fire. Needless to say, I praised Benji over and over again for his vigilance.

When I finally lay down for the night, I couldn't help but think of how differently things could have been were it not for my wonder dog. Peacefully, I sank back into slumber with great confidence, knowing that Benji was on duty!

—Deidra Parham—

My Canine Nanny

No animal I know of can consistently be more
of a friend and companion than a dog.
~Stanley Leinwall

When I was in the first grade I loved school but hated walking home when the school day was over. It was a journey of several blocks, and part of this trek—around a huge, brick Army National Guard building—frightened and disturbed me. That building, along with its expansive parking lot, took up the whole corner of the block. There was no way for me to reach home except to traverse two sides of that corner and walk around it.

Nothing untoward or terrible ever happened to me there, but for some reason, this gigantic building scared me. The site frequently had multiple types of artillery, munitions, and vehicles near it, and all the activity frightened me. The soldiers performed marching exercises and fitness drills in the parking lot, and I always felt like they were watching me. When a commander would yell out orders and an entire platoon would respond in unison, I'd jump at the sounds.

The result was that I sometimes froze where I stood or walked so slowly that my mother questioned me about why it had taken me so long to get home. I came to dread the school bell because it meant I had to walk by that National Guard building and its parking lot.

The only good thing about that corner was that, once I got around it, I always ran into a friendly and very intelligent Dalmatian named

Chief. He belonged to a physician who lived on my street, and I looked forward to seeing Chief every day.

One day, early in the school year, when the National Guard corner was particularly active with moving vehicles and soldiers marching here and there, I heard a loud bang. I froze in my tracks and couldn't move. The noise hadn't disturbed anyone else, and the military activity on the corner continued like nothing had happened, but I remained glued to the spot where I first heard the bang. Nervous and frightened, my mind raced with thoughts of gunfire, bombs, and explosions. I started hyperventilating, and my legs began shaking.

Suddenly, Chief appeared at my side. He actually pushed his head under my hand and stopped when I was touching his collar. As I grabbed hold of his collar, he started walking me around the corner. This time, he didn't stop at his house but walked me all the way down the street to my house. Once there, he waited outside until I was safely inside.

Thereafter, Chief met me every day, and we walked around the corner together. It didn't matter if the parking lot was active and noisy or totally empty and quiet. Chief was there. He came when it was sunny, when it rained, and even when it snowed.

I don't know how Chief knew I needed help, but he understood somehow that I was uneasy, anxious, and scared. Everyone on our block talked about what a smart, sweet dog Chief was, and I think he sensed that I needed help.

Chief became my canine nanny who faithfully walked me home and stood guard until I was safely inside my house. I came to trust and rely on him, and I came to love him. After that first day together, he walked me home every day of first grade, and he kept up the routine almost every day for the next four years of elementary school.

Chief became my therapy dog long before the idea of utilizing a dog for therapy was common and long before the concept of an "anxiety dog" was well-known. With Chief walking by my side, I could slow my breathing and make my legs move. By keeping my eyes focused on him and holding onto his collar, my apprehension and anxiety decreased. Chief comforted me, supported me, and gave me affection and companionship when I needed it.

Chief gave me something to look forward to every day, and his devotion made me feel special. He helped me to change from a shy, timid elementary student to a more confident, courageous middle-schooler. And he wasn't even my dog.

Decades have passed since I took those walks with Chief, but to this day, if I feel stressed or apprehensive, I put out my hand to feel for his collar. And then I sense him walking beside me and I find my courage.

— Billie Holladay Skelley —

A Neighborhood Hero

Dogs have faster reactions than humans and can act immediately when they detect something unusual. This can help scare off intruders or alert you to get to safety.
~Author Unknown

Kaya was a rescue that my husband brought home one evening. Her beautiful eyes and happy demeanor won him over, but I wasn't so easy to please. When I saw the scrappy, black-and-brown dog, I made some demands: First, the dog needed to have a bath, and second, she had better not sleep on our couch.

Unfortunately, I hadn't thought to mention "no barking or howling." And for the first few nights, from around midnight until 3:00 AM, she howled like a coyote and no one got any sleep.

That's actually how we ended up calling her Kaya, a nickname from the word "coyote" because of how much her howling resembled a coyote calling to the moon.

Thankfully, after about a week, Kaya settled in and stopped howling throughout the night. She was already house-trained and wonderful with our kids. She chased them around the house and put her head on their laps for petting during family movies. In a short time, we felt like Kaya had always been a part of our family.

Kaya got along well with our other dog, a Boxer named Zawadi. The two dogs usually only made lots of noise when someone pulled into the driveway or approached our front door.

We lived in a compact neighborhood. Our neighbor's house was very close to ours and we had a shared fence. Both of us mostly kept to ourselves, so we didn't know them very well.

Kaya had been living with us for nearly three months when, one night at four in the morning, she started howling like crazy. I looked outside to see her running up and down along the shared fence. After a few minutes, Zawadi joined her.

Now, there were two dogs, barking frantically at the fence and leaping into the air.

It was enough noise to wake up the neighbors — literally. After about a minute, the neighbor's lights flipped on.

Then, to my surprise, came a shout louder than even Kaya's howling. This was followed by the sound of glass shattering and a door slamming. More shouts and banging ensued, all against the constant background noise of my two dogs.

In the next few minutes, more and more neighbors flipped on their lights, and the shouting continued.

My adult son went outside to investigate, and I did my best to quiet down the dogs. When he came back, it was nearly five in the morning, and the police had just arrived at our neighbor's house.

As it turned out, Kaya had heard unusual noises from the neighbor's house and knew something was wrong. She started barking and wouldn't stop until the neighbors woke up — just in time to catch a burglar trying to break in through their back door!

Our neighbors managed to capture the thief and restrain him until the police arrived. The only loss they could report was a broken pane of glass on the back door.

Kaya's incessant barking had helped capture a burglar in the act.

Ever since the incident, our neighbors aren't afraid to come knocking every once in a while. Kaya is their favorite dog, and she's known throughout our area as a neighborhood hero.

— Ree Pashley —

An Angel in a Fur Coat

Dogs have given us their absolute all.
We are the center of their universe.
We are the focus of their love
and faith and trust.
~Roger A. Caras

As a child growing up, I heard frequent references to a guardian angel. A lost bracelet found when the snow melted. Managing to grind my bicycle to a halt before hitting a car backing out of a driveway. Being ill on the day of the surprise arithmetic test. My guardian angel was with me!

Who or what this guardian angel might be, however, was never considered. It just was.

With time, however, the guardian angel was displaced — rarely mentioned and even more rarely credited.

Once grown, I found a partner who desperately wanted a dog. We adopted a six-month-old rescue puppy and named her Farlie.

Some months after her arrival, at one of our raucous family gatherings, nobody noticed that Buddy, one of my son's dogs, was missing — except our puppy.

Insistently, she bumped against my knee and moved away. Distracted and busy, time and again, I brushed her aside. Finally, I followed her to the laundry room and found a very dispirited Buddy accidentally locked inside.

Buddy was welcomed back, Farlie was praised, and we thought

no more of the event until the day when Fran, my partner, put a container of popcorn in the microwave. Apparently, she set it for two hours instead of the intended two minutes. In another room, Farlie was again nudging me, and again I was slow to respond. Finally, I followed her into the kitchen. It was thick with black smoke — and getting thicker by the moment.

We were taking note and becoming very impressed with Farlie.

Then, one spring morning, my partner and I were working in a room where Farlie was not allowed, so we were surprised to see the dog leaning and craning her head in the door, pressing it forward as far as she could reach. We shooed her away, and Farlie, obedient but seemingly reluctant, moved down the hall.

A moment passed, and again I felt a bump on the back of my legs. Turning to scold the dog, I realized that, yet again, I was being urged to follow. Then, we heard very faint cries for help.

Again, Farlie nudged me, and the three of us proceeded outside where we found the next-door neighbour, a recent amputee, lying on the ground. Her wheelchair had tipped when she was attempting to maneuver out of her apartment.

"My guardian angel!" The neighbour wrapped her arms around our dog's neck.

"A guardian angel in a fur coat," I agreed.

— Robyn Gerland —

Changed by the Dog

Priorities

Never get so busy making a living
that you forget to make a life.
~Dolly Parton

Hunched over my desk, I held the phone in a death grip as one of my editors and I debated how to avoid a nuisance lawsuit from, honestly, a big nuisance. Usually, these fights energized me, but my patience was wearing thin.

We were on a tight deadline to decide what words to publish when my office door opened briefly and then closed again. I turned around and saw a little yellow dog sniffing the floor. She looked up and wagged her tail.

"I have a puppy in my office," I blurted out to my colleague.

Instantly, his voice softened. "Well, you take care of that, and I'll follow up with the lawyer," he said. "Talk to you soon."

As I looked up, I saw my husband's gleeful face in my office window. The guy who was going to "look at a litter of puppies" today. The guy who is a giant puppy himself.

As I bent down to meet the pup, he burst into my office.

"Are you surprised?"

I scooped the dog into my arms and snuggled her fur.

"What are you doing? It's the Tuesday after Labor Day, and the whole world just went from zero to sixty after the summer break."

"Well, she was the only puppy left. Even her mother had gone home," he pleaded as he stroked her fur. "I couldn't leave her there."

Aware that the clock was ticking, I walked into our production area with the dog still nuzzled into my neck. My goodness, she was sweet!

"Guys, it looks like we're going to have to extend our press time," I announced.

As the team turned, they said in unison, "A puppy!" A call to the press generated the same response. "Well, if you have a new puppy there, we will wait!"

With the pressure off, the pup named Puck circulated through the office. Her initial impact would then ripple through my life in unexpected ways.

Two weeks later, the twelve-pound bundle was in my care as my husband went away on a boys' weekend. I was booked to cover a series of events, but I slipped home in-between to let Puck and her tiny bladder outside. Each time, she greeted me with grateful kisses.

Later in the day, I headed to my final assignment: a powwow forty minutes north of my home. It was a hot day, and I parked far from the ceremonial grounds due to the large crowds. As I trekked in, I began to question my priorities.

Here I was, miles from home, among strangers, to take a few photos that would fill part of a page days from now, long after anyone who was interested would have shot and shared their own. No one cared if I was there, but a little dog waited at home for me to enjoy more of this beautiful summer day.

As I rushed home afterward, I felt incredibly guilty about my day's choices. Then, I faced a terrifying night that reinforced my doubts.

Just before bed, we went outside for a final pee break. Something caught Puck's eye, and being a Lab, she pounced on it with her mouth. As she spit it out, her mouth began to foam, and she shook her head to try to clear it.

She had grabbed a toad, which responded by exuding venom. For larger dogs, this wouldn't be a problem. However, for a fourteen-week-old baby, the dose was toxic.

Over the next eight hours, Puck puked, experienced diarrhea, lost control of her bladder, and drooled uncontrollably. Over and over again. I could only give her water and try to comfort her until the poisons left her body.

By daylight, I was covered in sticky bile and saliva, but Puck was still alive. She awoke with her tail thumping and brought me a tennis ball.

Suddenly, the priorities in my life became crystal-clear. I wanted to be home. I wanted to play with her and my older dog. Why was I making the outside world a greater priority every day? Clearly, newspapers could go out into the world without me. Deadlines could bend.

It took the brown eyes of a tiny dog to show me this revelation.

I wasn't the only one she had converted. Our ten-year-old black Lab Maggie had struggled with hip dysplasia for years. When Puck curled up against her on the floor, Maggie heaved herself up and moved to another spot with great pain. Oblivious to this slight, Puck popped up and lay down beside her again.

After a while, Maggie just sighed and gave up. However, within a few weeks, she was enlivened by gentle games of tug of war. Puck would bring her a toy and pull on it without hurting the older dog's joints. After all, the little dog didn't create that much resistance.

Maggie lived two years longer than we expected. And we suspected our sweet puppy had helped Maggie rediscover her love of play, too.

As for me, I started to negotiate my exit plan from my stressful job early in the new year while taking off more personal time. It took a while for the details to fall into place, but I resigned before the following summer.

It felt amazing to clean out my office and turn over my keys. As I carried out the last box, I turned to look at the spot where I had met Puck. My little playmate. The dog who changed my life.

— Lois Tuffin —

Him and Me

Dogs have a way of finding the people who need them,
filling an emptiness we don't even know we have.
~Thom Jones

"It's time," my kids told me. Three years had passed since we said goodbye to our Golden Retriever, but I wasn't so sure I was ready for another. This dog-owner thing was a big undertaking. At least, it was for me. I shed a tear when our fish died. I felt bad each time I had to kill the ants that ventured into our kitchen.

Was I ready to emotionally invest in a dog again? With our kids grown and us being down to a single cat, we had entered into a cruising phase of sleep-ins and late breakfasts, less commitments and more time for watching the sunset. Things were pretty good.

Still, our kids insisted. I decided it wouldn't hurt to look. So there I was in front of my computer. I narrowed down my search criteria to Golden Retrievers and Cocker Spaniels. And there he was, somehow looking like both breeds, unless you counted his small stature and his mere fifteen pounds.

He would probably not become the walking companion my husband wished for, and the hill in our backyard might be too much of a challenge for those little legs. But at least he was bigger than a Chihuahua. My husband didn't ask for much, and that was one request I wanted to honor.

When I looked closer, I could see that he was raising his right front paw as if he didn't want to put weight on it. I scrolled past the picture to the description. His name was Crash, named after the car accident he had just experienced. He'd been saved at the last minute by a vet assistant who thought he was worth it. No tag, no chip, but the vet agreed to operate.

And so began a journey of helping a dog heal. The cast around his front leg had been removed, the fleas and ticks were gone, and his matted fur was trimmed, making him look like a scholar of sorts. Within days, the dog we now called Nathan was beginning to put weight on his healing leg. With lots of room to explore, he soon began to build muscle strength.

His physical injuries improved with lightning speed, but his mental scars were more of a challenge. He'd spent six weeks at the vet and a week in foster care, and he showed signs of having been abused. He didn't trust humans, especially men. Any sudden movement would make him freeze or squeal in fear.

To build trust and keep him from reinjuring his leg, we spent most of our time on the floor during those first few weeks. At night, Nate and I shared our son's low-to-the-ground teenage bed. It worked wonders. Soon, it was him and me. Me and him.

Looking at the tiny, warm bundle curled up by my side, I couldn't help but wonder about his back story. He was eager to please. He preferred to sleep in until nine. He didn't bark unless he absolutely had to.

He was the perfect dog. What kind of person would want to harm him? What made him run in front of a car late in the night? That I felt a strong urge to protect him was clear, but there were more layers to the feelings I experienced when looking at him. There were reasons why I chose this dog, and some of them were self-serving. Not only did I want to heal him, but I wanted to heal myself.

I was born ten weeks premature with a right leg that is shorter and weaker than the other. Although I went through an operation at the age of five, I had to struggle with things that others took for granted. I worked hard to gain strength and improve my balance. I watched every step, was careful not to fall, and walked as gracefully as I could so others wouldn't notice or, even worse, feel sorry for me. I hated pity in all its forms.

There's a big difference between pity and compassion, however—one that I failed to see. As my need to improve increased, my self-compassion decreased. And, somewhere along the way, I became my own worst critic. This became clear to me while watching my dog struggle. We had so much in common, my dog and me, except he got the encouraging, accepting me while I got the self-critical me. One of us was getting emotionally stronger while the other was not. Imagine that!

Here I was praising my dog, showing him that he was more than enough just the way he was, accepting him, and maybe even loving him more because of his shortcomings. But how did I speak to myself? My internal voice was often harsh, demanding, sometimes even demeaning. Instead of feeling self-compassion each time I failed, I often felt shame.

It took a traumatized rescue dog with a metal plate in his leg for me to see all this, to understand how destructive my habits had become. The only good thing about being one's own worst critic is that the power to change is one hundred percent in your control. I had to question my own internal dialogue and trust the supportive voices of those who knew and loved me.

I no longer had to be perfect. I would walk whatever way came naturally to me. And I would speak to myself the way I spoke to my dog.

It was liberating.

Now, six years later, I've become better at accepting my limits and imperfections. Oh, sure, there are times when I slip back into my self-critical way of being. When this happens, I stop and look at my dog. With seven dog beds strategically positioned throughout the house, he's usually close by.

It's still him and me. Me and the dog who found his way back from his own trauma. The Poodle, Doxie and, as it turned out—mostly Chihuahua—mix who helped me discover a less perfect but better version of myself.

—Anna I. Smith—

Eating Rocks

You see, sometimes in life, the best thing for all
that ails you has fur and four legs.
~Mark J. Asher, All That Ails You

"Why not let him eat rocks?" I asked Abara, a sixteen-year-old trauma survivor, when she placed her hand inside the mouth of a seventy-pound Golden Retriever.

"What?" she responded, pulling a small stone from Gus's mouth.

"He wants to eat rocks. Why not let him?" I asked, knowing the answer.

"Uh, because he'll die," she replied in a sarcastic tone that I, her trauma therapist, had grown to appreciate.

Gus was a two-year-old therapy dog who worked at a residential treatment center for adolescents who had experienced childhood trauma. He was one of forty dogs born, raised, and trained on-site. The dogs were available for adoption when a teenager was ready to return home.

Therapy sessions often occurred in the presence of at least one of these furry co-therapists. They would lie stretched out on carpets, peek at us from under coffee tables, and doze off in available laps. Whenever they were needed, they knew.

It was typical for a sleeping dog to wake, walk to the other side of a room, and plant itself in the lap of a silent adolescent who needed emotional support. The dogs always knew.

"Maybe, but doesn't Gus know what's best for himself?" I asked.

"No, he doesn't," Abara replied. "Rocks could get caught in his stomach. He might not be able to poop them out, and he'd have to get a surgery. Trust me, he could die."

"I know, but Gus seems fine with taking that risk. He constantly tries to eat rocks, and you always stop him. Doesn't it get tiring?"

"Yeah, but I'm not gonna stop doing it." She leaned down and kissed Gus on his broad head. He looked up at her, opening his mouth as if to show her it was empty.

Whenever he was outside, Gus tried to consume as many stones as possible, a pattern that started when he was a puppy. Abara would redirect him or remove the rocks from his mouth. Unlike her peers, she was so consistent with him that the Canine Therapy Director mandated that only Abara accompany him outside. Gus never consumed a single stone while in her care, and she was determined to adopt him.

"There are easier dogs. Why are you so determined to stick it out with Gus?" I asked.

"Because I am responsible for him, and I know what's best for him."

"Why you?"

"I'm going to adopt him; he'll be my responsibility," she said, lowering her forehead to rest upon his. "There isn't anyone who loves him like I do."

"Who do you sound like right now?"

She was silent as if a part of her struggled to accept it. "My adoptive parents," she said in a whisper.

"Yes, you sound just like them."

At age three Abara witnessed the murder of her entire family when her village in Sierra Leone was destroyed during the Diamond War. She lived in an orphanage for two years until an American family adopted her. She learned English and transitioned well into her home in Connecticut. At twelve, when she started puberty, she developed symptoms of Post-Traumatic Stress Disorder. Her parents were confused.

"She was doing so well," they said. "Why is this happening now?"

It's not uncommon for children to develop trauma responses during or after puberty when their brain chemistry is changing drastically, and they are attempting to figure out who they are apart from their family of origin. This pivotal developmental stage is often more complicated for adopted children.

Abara started having nightmares, refused to sleep, and was defiant at home and school. During therapy, she discovered that she was attempting to push away her parents. She did not want them to love her and was determined to have her adoption reversed. When she turned fourteen, the family received a recommendation for trauma-focused therapy with an emphasis on canine-assisted therapy, as Abara had always loved dogs.

"He's just misunderstood," Abara told me when she first met five-month-old Gus, who was a handful. He refused to follow simple commands, and all attempts to train him failed. While her peers preferred the more obedient or docile puppies, Abara gravitated to Gus. She moved his crate into her room so that she could take charge of his training.

"You have to be consistent with him, and you can't give up," she said. "He's not bad," she clarified. "He's waiting for you to give up on him."

"Sounds like someone I know," I replied as she rolled her eyes.

For two years, Abara trained Gus with the support of the treatment center's staff, her peers, and an Animal-Assisted Therapist. She always brought him to her therapy sessions, and I had a front-row seat to observe their progress. Abara, who had refused to participate in family therapy, was now asking her parents vulnerable questions about her adoption and their relationships.

As Abara improved so did Gus. Formerly unreceptive to training, he had become one of the most successfully trained dogs in the pack. He went from jumping on my furniture and knocking over lamps to quietly sitting at her feet when she was happy and climbing into her lap when she cried. Her PTSD symptoms diminished, and she became better able to express and manage her emotions.

"Do you think my parents feel the same way about me as I do about Gus?" she asked, petting Gus.

"What do you think?" I asked.

"I think they do. It's like I can do anything, and they still put their hands in my mouth to take out the rocks that I try to eat." She laughed. "So, I'm Gus, and my parents are me?"

"That's right."

"I'm not going to be able to get rid of them, am I?"

"Can Gus get rid of you?" I asked.

"No, he's stuck with me no matter how many rocks he tries to eat."

"Now, you really sound like your parents," I replied as she rolled her eyes again.

Abara completed her treatment three months later, adopted Gus, and returned home. Five months later, she emailed me:

Hey Amanda,

Guess what? Gus FINALLY stopped eating rocks! I think he just needed to be at home with his family.

Also, I'm gonna visit Sierra Leone in the summer. We found out where my village was, where my orphanage still is, and we're going to visit them. I didn't think my parents would let me, but they really liked the idea, and now we're going.

Things are good at home, and whenever I'm tempted to eat rocks, I remember that my parents love me like I love Gus, and eating rocks is just a waste of time 'cause I'll never gid rid of these crazy people.

Love,
Abara

—Amanda Ann Gregory—

Old Dog, New Tricks

Our perfect companions never
have fewer than four feet.
~Colette

It was going on sixty minutes since we had started our journey around the block. My husband Jim and I were walking our twelve-year-old dog, whose heart was slowly giving out.

Ogie is a Labrador/Hound mix, the stubbornest of stubborn, and the heart of our family. We rescued him from our local humane society when he was eleven weeks old. He was an energetic and curious pup who pounced on giant ants on the front porch that summer and ate "something dead with a tail" off the sidewalk before he could be stopped. That was our first trip to the emergency room with him and what started our long-standing relationship with pet insurance.

Recently, he had started to wheeze when he tried to stand up, and he could only walk a half-block before needing to lie down on the grass in someone's front yard. His back legs weren't working very well, either.

"Let's take him to the vet," my husband said. "Maybe there's something they can do for him, to help him walk better."

We scheduled an appointment with Ogie's doctor, whom he loves, even though he gets frantic when we pull into the parking lot of the clinic. Vet visits are Ogie's nemesis after a particularly traumatic episode when he swallowed a tennis ball.

"The reason Ogie has been wheezing and having trouble on walks," the doctor said, showing us the X-ray, "is that his airway appears to be constricted. You can see here," she pointed, "this is his heart. It's enlarged. I am so sorry to bring you this news, but Ogie has congestive heart failure."

We were devastated. This was not what we were expecting at all. Heart failure?

"What happens now? What do we do next?" we asked.

"Unfortunately, there is a six-month wait for a canine cardiologist. We can try to admit him to the hospital overnight and see if we can get him in faster that way."

Jim and I wouldn't be allowed to stay with Ogie. That would mean our pup would be alone the whole night in an unfamiliar place.

"And if we don't do that?" we asked.

"We don't know how long he has. It could be days. We can try medication."

Still stunned, we decided to bring him home with us and start him on a regimen of multiple medicines. We resolved to do all we could to make him comfortable. He was so unlike himself that day, and we were afraid it was the last one we would have together.

But Ogie rebounded by the next day.

Thankful, we settled into a routine. Breakfast and medicine, then a morning walk. The walks took a long time, and it was a hot and humid Midwestern summer. We brought along a water mister to help keep Ogie cool.

And so, here we were, on a walk around the block that had already clocked an hour. We were starting to get impatient.

"C'mon, Ogie," I said, "it's time to go." I had things to do. Deadlines looming, calls to make.

Then, I stared into those deep brown eyes. Something clicked. "You know what? I get to do this with him today," I said to my husband.

He nodded. "What do we have to rush off to, anyway?"

So, we stood with our dog and waited. We looked at the trees, and he sniffed the grass. Then, he rested, and we rested. We all moved a few steps toward a patch of shade and then rested again. We watched the birds, and I thought, *I've got to check the bird book when we get home to see if that might have been a chickadee.*

Each day now is different. Some good, some bad — most, a little of each. But we wouldn't trade them for the world because Ogie is our world, for better or worse. And, sometimes, Ogie still lunges toward a squirrel or eyes a rabbit as we walk by. And he always, always barks at cats. Or delivery trucks.

Because of this stubborn, lovable, one-of-a-kind Hound, I am finally learning how to slow down and be patient. My sweet, old dog is teaching me new tricks. How did I get so lucky?

— Kristin Evans —

Great Expectations

Sometimes the best therapist has fur and four legs.
~Author Unknown

I hadn't had a dog since I was ten, but after taking care of my son's dog Skyler for six months, I knew I needed a dog in my life. Once I decided to get a dog, I knew I wanted the same breed as Skyler, a long-haired Dachshund.

My son, who lives in Oregon, contacted his breeder and learned that Skyler's parents had recently had two puppies: a black-and-tan and a red. I was thrilled and made plans to return Skyler and bring home one of the puppies.

As soon as I saw them, I was drawn to the red one. Technically, he was "red with a black overlay," which means the nose and eyes are black, but this puppy's eyes were uncharacteristically brown, a brown so deep and soft that they looked like velvet. The minute I held him I knew he was meant to be mine.

A couple of days later, I flew back to Omaha with my new puppy (whom I named Oscar Meyer, the perfect, if unoriginal, name for a Dachshund) nestled peacefully in my lap. The ride home was an easy entry into our new life together, while I was still blissfully unaware of what awaited me.

Though I didn't know what to expect, I never could have imagined that one tiny, four-pound bundle of fur could turn my orderly, peaceful world totally upside down.

Those first few weeks were chaotic. Like any new mother, I was sleep-deprived, exhausted and overwhelmed. Oscar often cried during the night, and my efforts to calm him proved futile. I placed a loudly ticking clock in his little bed. I took him out for middle-of-the-night potty runs. I purchased a waterproof mattress cover so I could bring him into my own bed, hoping the beating of my heart would lull him back to sleep. Nothing worked.

The days were even worse. His primary activity was to chew whatever was within reach. His favorite thing to chew, aside from my fingers and shoes, was the carpeted bottom step of my living room staircase, which he chewed right down to the wood.

I was afraid to let him out of my sight. My daughter still laughs about the dramatic greeting I gave her one day when she came to visit: "Thank God you're here so I can take a shower!"

I began to fear that this adorable, innocent-looking puppy was actually a wild beast in disguise who would never be calm, loving or obedient. I was so distraught that I even called his breeder to let her know I might have to return him.

At some point during this turmoil, I had a surprising new thought. What if there was nothing wrong with Oscar but something wrong with my expectations of him? What if it wasn't his behavior that was wrong but how I interpreted that behavior?

I thought about other situations. How many times had I expected a specific behavior from someone in my life (mostly my children) and been disappointed when they behaved differently? How many times had I interpreted that behavior incorrectly, often taking it personally when it had nothing to do with me?

I realized that Oscar wasn't a wild, mean-spirited dog. He was a puppy, exhibiting normal puppy behavior. My new understanding of him changed us both, in the way I related to him and in the way he responded to me. From that point on, we bonded in ways I never could have imagined.

He quickly became not only my best friend and confidant but my "significant other." As a divorced woman living alone, I began to think of him as my "Plus 1." We often went to Dairy Queen to share a "Pup Cup." When I shopped for groceries, I bought a steak or piece of salmon big enough for two. Though he didn't sit at the kitchen table with me, he would push his food bowl across the floor to be closer to me while we ate dinner.

Oscar is almost seventeen now, and I treasure him more than ever, knowing our time together is nearing its end. His advanced age has brought many physical limitations, including hearing loss. He sleeps most of the day, and when awake, often seems in his own little world. But when I hold him, he snuggles into my arms and gives me sweet kisses. Even though those velvet eyes are partially clouded with cataracts, I can still see the love and trust within, for he knows I will take care of him to the end.

These days, Oscar has a new lesson to teach me, perhaps the most valuable one yet. I watch with amazement how easily he accepts the challenges of old age. Like all dogs, he lives in the moment, adapting to whatever life presents to him. I imagine that he doesn't yearn for the past, depressed about things he can no longer do, or worry about the future, wondering what's in store for him.

As I watch him, I try to do the same. It isn't easy, but as we face the uncertain future together, I'm just grateful that I've had such a wonderful teacher and best friend by my side all these years.

Author's note: Shortly after writing this, I had to accept that Oscar was suffering. My wonderful vet came to my home, instructing me to tell her when I was ready to let him go. As I held him in my arms those last precious moments, I thought, *I can't do this. I'll never be ready to let him go!* Just then, he turned to look up at me, the trust in his eyes telling me it was okay. It was then that I was able to keep my promise to take care of him to the end.

— Sandra Martin —

Their Best Day Ever

A good man will take care of his horses and dogs,
not only while they are young, but when old
and past service.
~Plutarch

His name was Brady. He was a twelve-year-old chocolate Labrador. He liked to hike and swim, but his eyes and arthritis started to take that joy away from him. He liked belly rubs and riding in the Jeep with the top down. He was the best friend to Irene, an eighty-year-old widow who loved him as if he were her child. In reality, he probably was. I had never met either of them before, but they had an impact on me that changed me for the better.

I'm your typical sixteen-year-old boy. I like football, video games, and hanging out with friends. My mom is my biggest fan, but I can be annoying because I don't stick with things too much. I don't have much family: no siblings, grandparents, or cousins. But I do have dogs. They are my family and my best friends. They are my one constant and have made me who I am. They were also my inspiration for my charity, Their Best Day Ever, the one thing I have stayed dedicated to.

I came up with the idea after watching a program on a wounded warrior who wanted to do something special for his therapy canine but couldn't. So, I figured I could help. My idea was to assist elderly dogs for one special day. I made a page on Instagram and did not think anyone would care. It was just an idea. But then, one day, I got this message.

Dear Alex,

My name is Irene. I came across your account while googling things to do with your senior dog. I am a widow with no family in the area, and my Brady is 12 years old, and I can't do things with him like I used to. Would you be able to help him?

Irene offered to pay me, but that was not what the charity was about. So, I wrote her back and was determined to find a way to give Brady the best day of his life. He would be the first of almost one hundred and counting recipients of Their Best Day Ever, but he will always hold a place in my heart.

I met Brady on a Saturday in May. Despite his years — his eyes weren't as sharp as before, and his coat was turning gray — he still had the spirit of a puppy. Most Labradors never lose that. I spent a couple of hours getting to know him and figuring out what he would enjoy most and what wouldn't be too tiring. We decided on a day at the lake.

Honestly, I was not sure this charity would matter to anyone and didn't think it would make a difference. But I was willing to try it, and Brady would be the first beneficiary.

I can't drive yet, so I must rely on volunteers to help me. On Brady's day, we picked him up in a Jeep with the top taken off, just like he wanted. We drove to the Poconos.

The minute we pulled up, it was as if all the limitations of his age had magically disappeared. Brady flew out the back of the car and dove without hesitation into the water. I attend a Catholic school, so I guess the water was like Lourdes to him. Brady was energized. Splashing and diving, catching Frisbees, and then taking a quick breath and jumping back in. He did this nonstop for at least an hour.

When it was time to go home, he climbed into the back of the Jeep and put his head on my lap. I don't know why, but I felt a lump in my throat. I guess it's because, for the first time in my life, I felt like what I did mattered. I had a purpose, and even though I don't have a lot of blood relatives, I could make my own family through the people and pets I meet on Their Best Day Ever.

Brady isn't with us anymore, but I bet he is probably swimming and jumping anytime he wants now. Since that first memorable day, there has been an afternoon sailing for Winston, a retired police dog; a day at the pool for Paxton, a blind black Labrador; a hike to the waterfalls at Bushkill for Sienna, a PTSD therapy dog; and a shopping spree at Petco for Rigsby, a fourteen-year-old retired therapy dog for a kid with epilepsy, and many more.

Their Best Day Ever has given me My Best Year Ever.

— Alex Flowers —

Editor's note: To learn more about Alex's great work on behalf of dogs, check out his Instagram account at "Their Best Life Ever" or his website at theirbestdayever.org.

I Owed It All to Lilly

Some people see an unfortunate dog sitting in a shelter.
I see an angel that someone threw away.
~Author Unknown

We adopted Lilly, a two-year-old Beagle/Chihuahua mix, in June 2020. She was rescued from a hoarder and had spent most of her early life outside with very little food and water and no medical care.

When we met Lilly, she had a broken tail, was malnourished, and had just weaned a litter of puppies. I cradled her in my arms while she showered me with wet kisses.

Lilly was in rough shape due to the humans who had let her down, but while the world had treated her badly, she was grateful for us and trusted us completely. Upon arriving at our house, Lilly cuddled up on our couch and slept like she had not had a good night's sleep in her entire life. She knew she was home.

Lilly brought our children, then ten and thirteen, much comfort during the pandemic. She helped me in ways I would never have imagined. In the first six months that Lilly was with us, I lost a friend to suicide, and my parents lost their house to a tornado.

Lilly was instrumental in helping me with my grief after the loss of my friend. As for my parents, she spent countless hours comforting them while they rebuilt the home they had lived in for forty years. In those moments, I was so grateful for her, and I realized that Lilly could bring comfort and hope to others the way she had for my family. I decided to sign up Lilly and myself for therapy-dog classes, and she passed her tests with flying colors.

When Lilly became a certified therapy dog, I began bringing her to the middle school where I teach. She visited my classroom for one day each month. I immediately noticed that she had a way of getting the students with the most difficult circumstances to open up. One student had just moved to the United States from Ukraine. His name was Elie.

The only information I was given about Elie was that he had moved because of the Ukrainian war. Elie avoided eye contact, laughed when other students got hurt, and yelled swear words across the classroom. He paced when I was teaching and refused to pick up a pencil or write anything down. He tripped other kids at recess, and one day he pulled a chair out from under another student during class. Some of the other students laughed at him and seemingly encouraged this behavior. Other students avoided him completely.

It was clear that Elie was unhappy. He had no friends, and I was unsure of how I would educate a child who refused to engage in class. I was at a loss. Then, I brought Lilly to school for her first visit.

Elie immediately ran up to Lilly and nuzzled her fur against his cheek. At that moment, his face broke out in a smile, and he looked at me and said in broken English, "I like dog. I like dog here. I have two dog. They in Ukraine." I stood there in shock. Elie actually looked at me, spoke to me, and shared something about himself with me. He sat on the floor under his desk with Lilly for the remainder of the class period, and I let him.

While I taught, Elie watched me intently and snuggled happily with the dog. There was no swearing, laughing, or pacing. No devious mischief. Just a quiet boy enjoying his time with a furry friend.

Eventually, Elie began to open up to me more. He loved to look at pictures of Lilly and ask questions about her. His English improved through our conversations. He awaited her monthly visits. Elie eventually shared with me that his father and brother were both in the Ukraine fighting in the war. He'd had to leave behind his two beloved dogs. He had lost friends and loved ones due to the bombings in surrounding towns. And, of course, he worried constantly about his family and friends who were still in Ukraine, especially his father, brother, and pets.

With Elie's permission, I shared with his classmates that he'd had to leave family and friends behind, that he had lost people he loved, and that he missed his dogs who had to stay in a war-torn country. The students expressed a profound sense of empathy. Two girls in my class approached me at the end of class to ask if they could help Elie with his schoolwork during study hall.

Eventually, I noticed that Elie was invited to play soccer with a group of students at recess. He began staying in his seat during class and attempting assignments because he now had students who were helping him and cheering him on.

I can't say that everything was perfect from that moment on. There were still many bumps in the road. At times, Elie still said or did something unkind. Some students still laughed at him and his antics. Many excluded him. However, Elie had friends, and students began to stand up for him. His friends reminded him of expected behaviors and helped him with his schoolwork. It was not always easy for me to reach Elie, but there was no question that he had grown by leaps and bounds.

As the end of the school year approached, a parent-teacher conference was scheduled with Elie's mother. The school hired a translator. Through the translator, Elie's mom thanked me for treating him like one of my own children. She said that he spoke of Lilly all the time, and he actually looked forward to coming to school to be with his friends and learn in my class. And then, she began to cry. For the first time since leaving their home country, Elie was happy. With that, we both cried. Here we were, two moms from a world apart, speaking different languages yet sharing our love for the same boy.

When that school year came to an end, the hug I got from Elie on the last day of school said it all. I knew then that the confidence he had gained and the friendships he had made had set him up for a hopeful future. I owed it all to Lilly. When he arrived, Elie was in rough shape due to the humans who had let him down. But while the world had treated Elie badly, he was grateful for us and trusted us completely — thanks to his love for a dog.

— Laurie Dell'Accio —

Single Dog-Parenting

The whole glorious history of animals with people is about joy and connection. It's about loving this creature and letting this creature love you.
~Jon Katz

When my husband died suddenly at age sixty, my entire world was shaken to its core. How would I ever manage to do everything on my own while weathering the paralyzing waves of grief?

Our Miniature Schnauzer, Theo, was four years old when my husband passed. A gorgeous, milk-chocolate brown with striking blue eyes, Theo had been deeply attached to my husband, who was always quick to scoop him up in his big arms when he got home from work. It always put a smile on my face to see the two of them cuddling on the couch or lying side by side on the floor, playing contentedly while I made supper.

I couldn't bear to imagine what Theo must have felt when he realized that his dad was never coming home again. For weeks after my husband passed, Theo would sit on his gray, velour perch and gaze out the front window, sweeping his head from left to right and back again. Occasionally, he would turn around and look at me with mournful eyes.

"Daddy's gone bye-bye, baby," I'd say, as tears welled up in my eyes.

Not long after my husband's passing, I was sitting at my dining room table having supper when I felt Theo nudge my leg. I looked down to find him standing at my feet with his head bowed.

I murmured, "Sorry, baby, I don't know what you want."

Then, it hit me. My husband always caressed Theo with his left hand while he was eating. Theo was waiting for his only remaining parent to fulfill what his daddy now couldn't. I reached down to rub his head and chest — a routine we continue to this day.

This prompted me to look for ways to bond more closely with Theo that would also honour his special relationship with my husband. My husband was always so gentle with Theo when he dressed him for inclement weather, running his hands lovingly over Theo's legs as he put on Theo's boots. It inspired me to slow down and channel that care and tenderness he so aptly displayed instead of always being in a rush to get out the door.

Now, when I do yardwork — something I rarely did when my husband was alive — I bring Theo outside with me, taking time out of my chores to run around and play fetch with him just as his daddy did. Now, I'm the one who lies on the floor and plays with him. Now, I am the one who snuggles with Theo on the couch while dinner is baking in the oven.

There's no question that single dog-parenting has its challenges. Taking Theo out for daily walks falls squarely on my shoulders even during the most frigid temperatures. I am the one taking him to the emergency room in the wee hours of the morning. I am the one nursing him after surgery or while he is sick. I am the one making all the decisions about his care. Single dog-parents may get all the kisses and cuddles, but we also have all the responsibility.

Still, I wouldn't trade having Theo in my life for anything. It is beautiful to feel unconditionally loved by a little creature with incredibly expressive eyes. Theo has helped fill the gaping hole in my heart. I love pulling up my driveway and seeing his little face peering out the window, waiting for me. He keeps me company on those long, lonely nights. My heart flutters as I watch him run in that slightly off-kilter way he does down the hallway, tail wagging in anticipation of our bedtime snuggles. These are things I treasure.

Never in my wildest dreams could I have imagined I would become a single dog-parent. It hasn't been easy, especially while wading through such tremendous loss, but when I focus on the blessings that my canine cutie brings, everything seems easier to bear.

— Sally Meadows —

Unexpected Lessons

Life is what happens to you while you're
busy making other plans.
~John Lennon

When I was thirty-seven, the breeder handed me my very first dog — all one-and-a-half pounds of him. He looked more like a giant rat than a dog.

We named him Bandit because he kept stealing and hiding things, mostly slippers. A Yorkipoo, he looked like a Yorkshire Terrier but with curly, soft, brownish-gray Poodle hair.

To say Bandit rocked my world is an understatement. Having never owned a dog before, I was completely clueless. Poor Bandit was my first test subject, and I made many mistakes.

"Socialization," I kept reading, was necessary for puppies. So, I set out to expose Bandit to as much life and variety as I could.

We took him on trips and got him out and about as much as possible. I even took him through a car wash, which I think traumatized him for life.

However, in my quest to socialize him, I overlooked a few things — most importantly, the fact that he got carsick. Every single car trip was a disaster. Plus, he was very anxious and he craved routine and familiarity, not adventure and long car trips.

Funny thing about dogs, though. In my many hairbrained attempts to expose him to life and all its complexities, he was actually changing me more than I was changing him.

The changes were slow and subtle. I knew something was up when I was out for a morning run. I thought, *I really should be cutting down on my runs so I can spend more time with Bandit before work.* Then, I started worrying that I wasn't bonding enough with him. Before I knew it, I was head over heels, crazy in love with my pint-sized fur baby.

Then came the real shocker: My fur baby got me thinking about having a real baby. Not that I didn't want children necessarily. I had just never been in a hurry and had always taken a wait-and-see approach. I was hardly the maternal type, or so I thought. I craved independence, freedom, my own space. Or did I?

Apparently not, because two years later I had not one, but three, babies: two fur, one real.

I am not sure what would have happened if Bandit hadn't come into my life. He seemed to take everything I thought I understood about myself and flip it upside down and inside out. I was never a huge fan of animals until he came along, but he showed me the amazing bond that can happen between humans and animals, and the depth of my ability to love and care for others.

All these big lessons from such a little dog. But, as the saying goes, "Good things come in small packages." Or, in my case, in a furry giant "rat."

— Aimee C. Trafton —

Unleashing Confidence

I was always looking outside myself for strength
and confidence, but it comes from within.
It is there all the time.
~Anna Freud

When I first adopted Pepper from the local animal shelter, I had no idea how much she would change my life. As a shy and introverted person, I was content to keep to myself and avoid talking to strangers whenever possible. But Pepper had other ideas.

From the moment I brought her home, Pepper made it clear that she was not going to sit around the house all day. She wanted to explore the world, meet new people, and experience everything that life had to offer. And, as her human, it was my job to make that happen.

At first, I was hesitant. I would take Pepper out for walks around the neighborhood, keeping my head down and avoiding eye contact with anyone we passed. I just wanted to keep to myself, but Pepper wasn't going to settle for that. She would tug on her leash, eager to go say hello to everyone we met. And I mean everyone.

I resented this initially. I didn't want to be bothered with idle small talk, and I certainly didn't want to put myself out there and risk an awkward conversation. But Pepper was persistent, and eventually I realized that her outgoing nature was actually a gift.

As we continued to explore our neighborhood together, I noticed things that I had never paid attention to before: the friendly neighbors, the local shops, and the little things that made our community unique. It was like I was seeing my neighborhood for the first time, but this time with a friend by my side.

And as Pepper led me from one person to the next, I began to realize that I was making even more friends. I was learning about their lives and their stories, and finding common ground. Frank, a kind man from Italy, would chat with us every evening at 7:00 on the dot no matter the weather. And Bethany, a mom of five, would always wish me a good morning as she packed her kids into the car before school.

At first, it was a little uncomfortable getting to know these people. I would stumble over my words and feel awkward as I tried to make small talk with people I had never met before. Even as an adult, this was something I had always struggled with. But as I continued to push myself out of my comfort zone, I started to feel more confident.

Pepper was always there to cheer me on, wagging her tail and giving me a nudge whenever she seemed to sense that I was feeling nervous. And, as I started to realize how much I was gaining from these interactions, I found myself looking forward to them.

Eventually, I began taking Pepper on longer walks, exploring new areas and meeting even more people. I felt myself growing more and more sure of myself. Before long, I was striking up conversations with people at the grocery store, chatting with other dog owners at the park, and even attending local events and meetups. It was like I was a completely new person—even friends and family pointed out these changes and encouraged me to continue.

It was all thanks to Pepper. Her outgoing personality forced me out of my shell and gave me the courage to explore the world around me. And while I was once frustrated by this and even resented her for it, I now see it as a blessing.

I don't think I would have been proactive enough on my own to make these changes, and I can't thank her enough for the new life she has allowed me to experience.

Pepper is getting older now, but we still have several more years ahead of us. And I promise that I'll continue to let her lead me around the neighborhood for as long as she can walk.

—Anne Taylor—

Meant to Be

Double Rescue

When I look into the eyes of an animal I do not see an animal. I see a living being. I see a friend. I feel a soul.
~Anthony Douglas Williams

"I'm telling you guys for the last time, don't ask me to get the first dog we see. We are just starting to look for a dog, and it takes time to find the right one. So, please don't rush me, okay?"

I can still remember that cool May morning when I said this to my kids as we were getting ready to see the first puppy that we were checking out. We had been submitting adoption applications for weeks, but puppies kept getting adopted before we could schedule a visit.

The decision to get a puppy was a family decision, as we felt that my daughter would be happy to have a companion when my son went off to college in the fall. A smaller part of the decision was my newfound desire to care for nature and animals, as they had helped me heal my heart after recent difficult times.

So, on the May morning in question, we drove up to a home and waited for the foster parent to come out with the puppy so we could meet him.

My head was going in all types of directions as we waited for her to come out. *What if the kids like the pup and want it?* I thought. I had warned them several times to not get attached to the first dog they saw. *Am I ready to commit to taking on the responsibility of caring for a pet? What am I doing?*

The front door of the house opened, and an energetic, brindle puppy ran straight to me and jumped into my arms. As I put my hand under his chest to hold him, I felt his heart and my heart beat at the same time, and tears rolled down my face.

That is it. He is my dog, I thought. No matter who said what to me, my mind was made up. He was my baby, and nothing was going to change that.

As the kids approached me, I suddenly felt ashamed of all the warnings I'd given them about not falling in love with the first dog we saw. Also, what if my daughter did not like the dog? After all, we were getting the dog for her, and we had all agreed that her opinion would carry the most weight.

I tried to compose myself as the rest of the family got to know the pup a bit. I anxiously watched and hoped they would love him as much as I did. They all played with the dog, but he kept coming back to me. Neither of them got to hold the pup for long because he kept jumping out of their arms and running back to me. Even when the foster mother came to get him, he jumped out of her arms and ran to me again. At that point, I could not hold in my emotions any longer. I held him tightly and started singing to him, something I did with both my kids when they were babies.

Then, the moment of truth came. It was time for the family meeting. I took a deep breath and asked my daughter what she thought of the dog, trying my best to dampen my excitement. She said she liked him. My son was more reserved and not sure if we were serious about the adoption.

The next step was a house inspection and the adoption paperwork. For the six days that followed, I was on pins and needles as we got the house ready and bought puppy gates for the kitchen and stairs. I worried every day about losing the puppy to another family, as the woman had said that someone else was interested, too.

Finally, the day came, the house passed inspection, and we got our Gino, my baby. It was one of the best days of my life.

Fast forward a few months later after a series of unexpected family deaths, breakups, heartbreaks, and tough emotional times. Gino wiped my tears many times — something I did not know that dogs could do. He still does it. Gino became my car companion as I made the difficult trips up and down winding hills, carrying broken dreams and broken promises in the back of a rented U-Haul truck.

Gino was with me as I isolated myself for months and didn't talk to anyone. Gino was also the one who got me out of the house again. Although it started with trips just long enough to do his "business," he started pulling at the leash and making me walk farther. Short walks became mile-long promenades, which reminded me of the healing power of the sun and nature. The rescue pup ended up rescuing me. His unconditional love allowed me to start opening my heart again — to Nature, to Life, to Myself, and to Love. He is the embodiment of the St. Francis quote: "It's in giving that we receive," for it is in rescuing him and giving to him that my heart got rescued. I am grateful for him and look forward to loving and caring for him for many years to come.

If you ever consider getting a dog, please get a rescue. They will never forget what you did for them and will pay you back with a love sweeter than anything you have ever known.

— Maiya Katherine —

The Eclipse Dog

Dogs are not our whole life, but they make our lives whole.
~Roger A. Caras

A couple of weeks before the total eclipse bore down on Texas, I slept in a little later than usual. When I wandered into the kitchen, my husband said, "We had a visitor this morning."

I raised my eyebrows. "Who?"

"A black dog who followed the car into the garage and greeted me when I got out to go into the house. She was real friendly and sweet."

"Where is the dog now?" I asked.

That's when I learned that he and the black dog had walked around to all our neighbors, asking if the black dog belonged to any of them. She didn't. Finally, he contacted our Chief of Police who arranged for her to be taken to where the town holds dogs until owners pick them up. The dog was checked for a chip, but she didn't have one.

Stray dogs are a big problem in our small town. People are always dumping dogs, either in town or on one of the rural farm roads that lead into town.

"What's going to happen to her?" I asked.

"He said he'd put some notices on local social media and see if anyone responds."

I immediately went into worry mode. Over the next few hours, I emailed local friends and posted a photo my husband took of the dog on our town's social media pages. I figured that between the Chief's posts and mine, we'd find the pup's owner. Several people commented that she had been wandering around our town for the past couple of weeks. My worry meter went up another notch. Why hadn't anyone claimed the sweet girl?

After a few hours, I suggested to my husband that we temporarily foster the dog until the owner could be found. With a big backyard and our own dog to play with, we figured it would be a good alternative. My husband called the Chief, who told him that a city employee had already taken her to the county dog pound.

My heart fell. I'd learned from one of our neighbors that our county dog pound was dangerously overcrowded and had put out a notice that they would have to start euthanizing dogs to make room. It was late in the day. My husband told the Chief that the dog was at risk of being euthanized and asked if he could retrieve her. He was told that the pound was already closed for the night. The Chief would call in the morning. I just hoped it wouldn't be too late. I barely slept that night.

Late the next morning, we got a call from the Chief that the dog had been retrieved from the pound and was on its way to our home. Not long afterward, a police car pulled into the alley behind our house. An officer led a big, beautiful, sleek-coated black Labrador mix into our fenced yard. She ran up to me, bounced up on her hind legs, placed her big paws on my shoulders, and nearly knocked me down while licking my face.

"She's sweet, isn't she?" he commented.

I nodded. "How could anyone abandon this dog?" I asked, trying to fend off the kisses.

"Are you going to keep her?" he asked.

"Oh, no, we already have this guy." I pointed to our dog running circles around the black dog. "And we have two cats that would not take kindly to another dog in the house."

"What are you going to do with her?"

"Try to find her a new home. We couldn't let her stay in that shelter."

The officer looked down hesitantly. "Would you let me know if you don't find anyone? I'd take her."

He pulled out his wallet and showed us a photo of a black dog that could have been the twin of the black dog standing in my yard. Melancholy filled his eyes as he explained that his black dog had recently passed away, and he'd been thinking of getting a new dog. He and the black dog standing next to me exchanged the most adoring, wistful expression.

I didn't hesitate for a moment. "She's yours," I stated.

He looked up at me. "Really?"

I nodded. "There's no reason to look for someone else to adopt her when the two of you have already bonded."

The officer looked up at me, a big grin sweeping across his face.

"Do you want to take her now?"

He shook his head. "I can't take her until after I finish my shift tomorrow. Can she stay here until tomorrow evening? I can pick her up then."

I nodded. The officer reached down and petted her, thanked us, and departed. My husband and I looked at each other. What were the chances of the man who broke her out of dog jail at a "kill shelter" wanting to adopt her? This was one lucky dog.

Over the rest of the day, we discovered that our new guest could jump over our picket fence like it was a small stick. If we put a leash on her, she would automatically heel on the right side. She would sit on command, had a voracious appetite, and was a little afraid of my fifteen-pound dog who weighed at least fifty pounds less than her.

Come evening, my husband set up a bedroom for her in our enclosed breezeway. We couldn't let her into the main part of the house because our cats could smell her and were quite upset. The dog accepted being in the breezeway as long as we kept checking on her and left on the light. But, come bedtime, when we turned off the breezeway light, we discovered her fear of the dark. She barked and cried and whined like a little puppy. We knew that no one was going to get any sleep. I turned on the breezeway light, and she stopped crying immediately.

The next day, we all went back into the yard to play, and just as he promised, the officer showed up after his shift. He and the black dog immediately exchanged that same look of love and adoration.

"See why I fell in love with her when I picked her up yesterday?" he asked.

It was a remarkable thing to witness. Clearly, the officer was her hero for rescuing her, and she was the dog he needed to heal his broken heart. He walked her out to his pickup truck and opened the door to the back seat. Before he could lift her into the truck, she leapt in, sat and was ready to go. She knew.

The officer turned back to us, grinned, got in his truck, and drove the black dog to her new home. A couple of days later, we learned that he gave her a new name, Luna, to commemorate the total eclipse that would soon cast its shadow over Texas.

—Jeffree Wyn Itrich—

A Sweet Ray of Hope

You can always find hope in a dog's eyes.
~Author Unknown

One morning, I came downstairs to find my husband sitting at the kitchen table, staring at his laptop. When he saw me, he turned his computer around to reveal a cherubic golden face with big, brown eyes.

"That's Hope!" I exclaimed. As soon as the words escaped my lips, I realized that my husband had no idea what I was talking about.

"You know I'm not looking for a puppy," I added, but I was already smitten. Golden Retriever puppies may just be the cutest puppies on the planet! I also couldn't help thinking about what had happened the day before when I was out running.

We'd just lost my best friend, Maverick, our thirteen-year-old, ninety-pound rescue mutt, who looked and acted like a Golden Retriever. We'd found Maverick when he was four months old in front of a Petco store, a few days after saying goodbye to our previous pup. There he was, a little, brown-and-black mutt, peering out from inside a shiny metal X-pen set up by a local dog rescue.

I hadn't gone to Petco to get a puppy. I just wanted a puppy fix. We were getting ready to leave on vacation, and it made no sense to get a dog until after we returned. But I had a hole in my heart that I needed to fill, even if only temporarily.

I sat in the Petco parking lot cuddling Maverick for nearly an hour, trying to convince my husband this was our next dog. Eventually, he agreed. We took Maverick home that afternoon.

I worked from home, and Maverick was my constant companion. He was the first dog I became truly attached to, and I often referred to him as my "heart dog." Losing him had left a gaping hole in my heart — a hole I knew only another dog could fill. It was just three days later, when I was out running, that the name Hope and an image of a puppy came to me. I always knew we'd get another dog after Maverick was gone, so I wasn't all that surprised. I'd been perusing the local Golden Retriever rescue website hoping to find a male dog, a few years old so he would be past the challenging puppy stage.

Because Hope is clearly a female name, and I wasn't looking for a puppy, I dismissed the thought, finished my run, and didn't mention it to my husband. Until the next morning when I came downstairs and saw that little golden face on his computer.

"Maybe Maverick sent her," I said, knowing I probably sounded a little crazy. But we agreed it was too much of a coincidence to ignore. So, we got in the car and drove an hour to meet Hope. When we walked into the breeder's house, there she was — the last remaining puppy from the litter — sitting inside an X-pen, peering up at me just like Maverick had thirteen years earlier. And, just like with Maverick, I knew she was our next dog.

What I didn't know was how much she'd live up to her name.

I would get my first glimpse four months later.

***

Dad loved dogs, and he especially loved Hope. He often dropped by my house for an impromptu visit after his weekly softball games. I suspect he wanted to see Hope as much as he wanted to see me.

When Hope was six months old, Dad had heart surgery. After he was released from the hospital, I took Hope over to his house for a visit. His face lit up when he saw her. I can still picture the two of them sitting on the back patio, in the shade of the lattice roof, both of them with big toothy grins.

Those grins inspired me to get Hope certified as a therapy dog. This decision turned out to be a godsend, not only for all the people whom Hope has blessed over the past ten years, but also for me.

***

Burned out in my career and in need of a break, I decided to take some time off work and spend my days doing volunteer pet therapy with Hope. Our visits with veterans in the spinal-cord-injury clinic, stressed-out college students, members of an addiction support group, and the elderly in assisted-living facilities, nursing homes, and memory-care units provided me with a great big dose of perspective. Our pet-therapy work became a necessary and helpful distraction for over a year as I healed and decided what my next career move would be.

As Hope was helping others, she was helping me.

Hope also helped my son through the most challenging few years of his young adult life. In his first year of college, I noticed my son was holing up in his room more than usual. We rarely saw him, and when we did, he had his head down and was scurrying off to work, school, or back to his bedroom. He rarely interacted with us. It was not necessarily unusual behavior for an eighteen-year-old but it was a departure from his demeanor in high school.

When he brought home his first report card, we knew something was terribly wrong. Our straight-A student was failing college. When I approached him about it, he admitted he was completely overwhelmed. He'd stopped going to class because it gave him immense anxiety. Through that conversation and a subsequent visit with a psychiatrist, we learned he was severely depressed.

Hope was never one to sleep on our beds, but she took to sleeping on his. If I couldn't find her, I'd peek in my son's room, and there she'd be, curled up on the end of his bed. Keeping watch, offering comfort, helping him heal.

***

The dictionary defines hope as the feeling that what is wanted can be had, or that events will turn out for the best. That's exactly what I needed when I found Hope. And it's the gift she's shared with thousands of people in her ten years as a therapy dog.

There's just something about her warm, sometimes silly, unconditionally loving presence that makes it nearly impossible to feel anything else.

— Debbie LaChusa —

Rebel Heart

You can usually tell that a man is good
if he has a dog who loves him.
~W. Bruce Cameron, A Dog's Journey

There are some things I'm proud of and some things I'm not. I'm proud of adopting Dixie, my senior rescue dog, but I'm not proud of why I did it.

I was twenty years old, in college, sharing a second-floor apartment with a roommate. Our back windows overlooked a fenced yard and detached garage. Someone was living in that garage, and he was cute. Sometimes, he played bluegrass music loudly, and the notes drifted up to my apartment, where I developed an interest in banjos and mandolins.

Beside my apartment building was a large detention basin. This was a grassy depression, a few hundred yards long and maybe a hundred yards across, meant to catch excess rainwater. I could just barely see it from my bedroom window. And it was there that the cute guy took his dog to run.

I'd catch sight of them in the window and make my way to the basin. Half the time, I'd miss them. When I did make it, I never had enough nerve to introduce myself. But I could hear him call his dog's name, plain as day. The dog was named Rebel. It was a Beagle.

So, I went to the pound and told them I wanted a Beagle. Just my luck, no Beagles. They took my number with a promise to call if any came in.

The following week, I got a call from the pound. Someone had brought in a female Beagle. They'd taken her home to keep her comfortable. After a week, if no one claimed her, the Beagle could be mine.

I went to visit the Beagle. She was old — at least ten years old, likely older, they told me. Her teeth were in poor condition, and she had bad breath. She'd been bred many times. She was small for a Beagle, the smallest kind, and her face was adorable — all smushy rolls of skin and floppy ears.

I named her Dixie. You know, to go with Rebel.

I said I wasn't proud. I'm not proud of the name now, either, since I've thought harder about what such names mean. At the time, though, I just wanted it to match Rebel. Can all be forgiven for love?

Maybe, without my crush as motivation, I wouldn't have gone through with the adoption. Dixie tested positive for stage three heartworms. I took her to the vet for arsenic shots in her back and carried her around afterward — down the steps, through the parking lot, to the basin. She couldn't walk, just pee, and got carried right back home.

She loved to snuggle in my lap. She'd let me hold her like a baby in the crook of my arm. She slept with me in bed, although I had to lift her up and down. In fact, Dixie did a lot of sleeping. I don't know what her life had been like before I got her, but it wore her out.

Her favorite thing was to have a blanket thrown over her, and she'd snort and wiggle, toss and wrestle her way out of it. She'd do it again and again. Once she recovered from the heartworms, she liked to go on walks, and she stayed right with me. Her belly, stretched out from so many puppies, almost met the ground, and her short legs couldn't carry her very fast.

A few times, I made it to the basin with her when Rebel was there. The dogs ignored each other. "Dixie! Dixie!" I called loudly, even when she was right beside me, not needing to be called, just so Rebel's owner could hear the matching name. But Rebel and his owner walked away, oblivious.

But that didn't matter anymore. I adopted Dixie for all the wrong reasons, but I loved her for all the right ones.

— Jessi Waugh —

Message from an Angel

When we open our hearts, angels appear in the form of guiding voices, helping us find our way in the darkness of life.
~Paulo Coelho, Brida

It had been nearly two years since Nellie, my first Westie, had passed away after a long illness. The following Christmas, my husband Paul gave me a handmade gift certificate good for one puppy of my choice. Having been so heartbroken over losing Nellie, and feeling I would be disloyal to her memory, I wouldn't allow myself to consider getting a replacement dog. My gift certificate remained tucked away in my desk.

Deb, a friend from the West Highland White Terrier Society of Connecticut, and I had made plans to attend a book signing. When Deb got into my car, her smile was bright, and her hands were aflutter with excitement.

"Have you seen the email about the puppy that Kathleen's fostering?"

"No."

"There's a Westie puppy up for adoption."

Puppies were exhausting and needed constant attention. Then there were the endless puddles to mop up, not to mention the books, slippers, or glasses that would be destroyed because either my husband or I would forget to move them out of reach. I thought the Westie in our Society's rescue program should be adopted by someone ready to handle a new puppy.

I shook my head. "Not interested, but thanks for thinking of me."

Before I put the car in gear, Deb said, "Would you mind stopping at a psychic fair? We've got plenty of time, and it's on our way."

"What's a psychic fair?"

"It's a gathering of psychics who do tarot-card readings, crystal healing, and offer spiritual advice."

The voice in my head said, *There's a sucker born every minute.*

I shrugged.

"Why not?"

The fair was held in a nondescript function hall. Two meeting rooms were lined with tables and chairs for the psychics and vendors selling crystals, handcrafted jewelry, essential oils, and books.

"Walk around and check it out," Deb said. "There are two psychics I want to see. Let's meet back here in half an hour."

As I wandered around, the heaviness of frankincense and patchouli incense made me long for fresh air. Shadows from candles flickered across the faces of psychics and their eager customers. I eavesdropped on tarot and palm readings, noting the common themes of finances, romance, and health concerns.

I shook my head and thought, *What a bunch of hogwash!*

In the second room, a sign advertising "Angelic Messages" caught my attention. Despite my skepticism, I asked the psychic what an angelic message was and how it worked. This woman, whose soft face was framed in gentle wisps of light brown hair, smiled as she answered my question. "Angelic messages are channeled through me to a person who may be receptive to hearing advice or thoughts from his or her angel."

Despite my better judgment, I asked, "How much?"

"Fifteen dollars."

Fifteen dollars seemed a small price to pay for a story I could tell at parties for years to come.

I handed her the money and sat down. I said nothing, knowing the only obvious thing about me was that I was a woman wearing a wedding ring.

What will she start with? Finances, health concerns, or marital problems?

Instead, she closed her eyes and asked me to do the same. The skeptic in my head continued to taunt me. *This had better be good.*

A few minutes later, she told me to open my eyes. When she asked, "Is your mother on the other side?" I leaned in.

"Yes."

"There's a little white dog standing by your mother's side."

My heart stopped. She had my full attention now.

"She wants you to know that she's fine, and that it's okay for you to get another dog."

This woman knew nothing about me, my mother, or the Westie whose death had left me heartbroken.

I couldn't stop the flood of tears that rolled down my cheeks. She handed me a tissue and asked if I understood the message. All I could say was, "Yes."

I was still crying when I met Deb at the exit.

"What happened?"

As I shared the message I'd been given, her face brightened.

"It's a sign. You have to adopt that puppy!"

"What puppy?"

"The one Kathleen's fostering."

After the author's talk, I called Kathleen. A half-hour later, I was on her doorstep, ready to meet my destiny.

Tucker, a three-pound, furless, white puppy, wore a tiny, blue-striped turtleneck sweater and looked more like a mouse than a puppy. His ears and tail were much too large for his little body. I wondered whether he would grow into them or if they would be the thing people noticed first, like someone whose nose or teeth are too big for their face.

I was instantly smitten by him as he hopped forward and backward in the most peculiar way.

"How did he end up in our rescue program?"

"A couple bought him over the Internet," Kathleen said.

I shuddered. Apparently, they weren't aware of the horrific conditions of puppy mills.

"After retrieving him from the airport, their vet diagnosed him with ringworm and shaved off all his fur. He told them their new pup would have to be quarantined from their other animals for forty days. They couldn't keep him because of the husband's medical condition, so the wife called our rescue program and surrendered the pup rather than pay to board him for forty nights."

She continued, "Tucker was malnourished, but he's got a good appetite now, and his fur will grow back."

"I want him!" The words flew out of my mouth. Then, I backpedaled a bit.

"Of course, Paul needs to see him before we make a final decision. It's just a formality since I have a gift certificate entitling me to one puppy of my choice."

"When will he be home?"

"Wednesday night. I'll have the paperwork ready. If he's in agreement, we'll proceed."

Before leaving her house, I snapped Tucker's picture. Later that night, while looking at his image, I realized that something inside me had shifted and been replaced with an excitement I'd felt the few times in my life when I'd been brave enough to open my heart.

Three nights later, after I picked up Paul from the airport, we stopped at our favorite pizza place. While waiting for our dinner, I handed Tucker's picture to Paul and said, "I'm ready to cash in my gift certificate."

His eyebrows furrowed.

"What is this?"

"This is our new puppy."

He groaned.

After dinner, we drove to Kathleen's house so he could meet Tucker. He wasn't as smitten with our sweater-clad puppy as I had been. Instead, he shook his head and said, "If you're sure..."

"Very sure."

Two days later, Kathleen delivered Tucker to us in a gift bag. That was sixteen years ago. Since then, he has matured into his body and developed an uncanny resemblance to Nellie. When Tucker nuzzles his head against my leg, the way she used to do, it makes me wonder if she's sending me her love through him.

— Amy Soscia —

The Power of Canine Connection

So it's true, when all is said and done,
grief is the price we pay for love.
~E.A. Bucchianeri, Brushstrokes of a Gadfly

Nacho, a Red Heeler Cattle Dog, was living with my husband before we became a couple. When I first met Nacho, he growled and lunged toward me. But after much ball throwing and time spent together, we became almost inseparable.

When Rick and I married, I said to him, "Nacho thinks he's a part of our marriage." At first, Rick didn't understand what I meant, but soon he learned that Nacho thought we were a "throuple"—all equals in a strong relationship, and that each of us had our roles. He was the protector and constant companion. We were the providers for his daily needs: food, water, walks, and lots of ball throwing and beach running. And we all showered each other with unconditional love.

One afternoon, a massage therapist was coming to the house to work on me. She phoned ahead of time and said, "I feel like I'm meant to bring my cards. Is that okay?" She possessed a stack of angel, tarot, and other cards from the divine realm.

"Sure," I said, a bit skeptical.

When she got to our home, she set up her massage table in our game room and put the cards in a pile on the table. Nacho immediately jumped onto the table, sat and looked at her.

"Weird," she said. "I think I brought the cards for him, not you. Nacho, pick a card that shows how you feel about Jill."

He moved his paw and hit the stack. Then, he placed one paw on a card that was facedown.

We watched, amazed.

She flipped over the card and said, "Huh. Happiness."

I couldn't believe what I saw.

The card featured three dolphins forming a circle and the word "happiness" above them.

"Does the rest of it mean anything to you?" she asked.

"Yes," I said, teary-eyed. I lowered the waist of my pants and showed her my dolphin tattoo. "I can't believe he picked a card at all, but especially that one. He believes our marriage and this household are the three of us. He's one special dog."

"He is. Old soul. Otherworldly," she said.

Fast forward four years, and Nacho grew ill. The vet suspected cancer, but the only way to confirm was exploratory surgery, which we didn't want to put Nacho through. We did everything we could to keep him comfortable and bring him joy.

But after more than a year of slowing down, fewer trips to the beach, much shorter walks, and little interest in ball chasing more than one or two throws and runs, Nacho's life on earth was ending. I told Rick that Nacho would let us know when it was time for him to go. And I was also sure that, after the fact, he'd send us a dog when it was time. I wasn't sure when or how, but I just knew it would be that way.

When Nacho left us we felt like part of us had gone with him. The silence in our house was deafening; I missed hearing the click-click of canine nails on the hardwood floors. But we weren't quick to rush into finding a new companion. Nacho was irreplaceable, and our pain was great.

However, two and a half weeks after Nacho died, I received an email from one of my clients who had unexpectedly lost his wife a couple of months before. The subject line of the email said, "My Angel Doing What She Loved" and the name of a foundation I had never heard of.

I opened the email and there, instead of words, was a photo of his wife holding a puppy. My breath caught. What was this foundation?

I searched on Google, and the foundation website was the first hit. Its mission was to rid the world of homeless pets. And there was a newly adoptable female Red Heeler Cattle Dog—a rare breed in the area where we live.

I called out to Rick. "I think Nacho sent us our next dog."

With tears in his eyes, he came into the room. "I'm not ready," he said.

"I understand."

"Let me see anyway," he said. He looked at the brown-and-white dog who the shelter had named Jenna. "She's beautiful. But I'm not ready."

"Okay," I said, knowing that if Nacho had really sent her, he'd let Rick know.

I'm not sure what happened during the following hours, but the next morning Rick said, "That dog you showed me yesterday… Can I see her again? I'd hate to pass up a really good dog. Can you call about her?"

I did, and when we met her, she walked up to my husband and slurped his cheek. That made us both teary-eyed. We knew that Nacho had brought us together.

And that's how we met, fell in love with, and became a family with Coconut the Cattle Dog.

—Jill L. Ferguson—

The Rescue

Destiny doesn't make mistakes.
~Dustin Poirier

The late autumn morning was crisp and clear. Rust and gold leaves appeared in little mounds along the sidewalk, and since no one was looking, I delighted in kicking my way through them as I walked along. The street was almost empty except for my roommate, Anne, who was waiting at the corner in her car.

We were headed to the pound to find a dog. Anne and I believed that giving an abandoned dog a home was the best way to go. No puppy mills for us. Altruism and excitement, a heady combo, filled the air as we drove toward the pound.

Upon arriving, we were led to the back part of the pound where all shapes and sizes of dogs were separated from one another in metal cages. There were water bowls, food dishes and scraggly blankets, but only the bare necessities. I did not see a toy anywhere. How could we ever pick one dog from among the barking, desperate, friendly creatures who threw themselves at us against the sides of their cages? I was about to give up altogether when I heard it: the weirdest bark I had ever heard. It was a bass bark that cut through all the others.

When I finally located its owner, I was surprised to see a small black-and-white dog pressed against the enclosure. I had expected a huge dog on the other side of that big bark, but it was a feisty little Border Collie. He captured our hearts, and we took him home.

Our first weekend together was magical! We walked in the park, along the streets, down to the river and back home again. Our dog, whom we now called Prancer, led the way, dancing along on his slender legs. We met new people thanks to him, and many, many dogs. He seemed to be non-aggressive and very sociable. Everything was going better than I had hoped for.

We never thought to ask if he was house-trained, if he would bite, or if he exhibited anxiety, but we would soon find out.

On Monday morning, Anne went to work, and I went on a job interview. Prancer stayed at home and watched our house. But what he really watched was the street below, waiting for us to come home. All through the weekend, we had enjoyed his deep bark.

The neighbors, however, were not amused. That first day alone, Prancer positioned himself at the window and let go with his profundo bass—from 8:00 AM until 6:00 PM. I apologized to the complaining neighbors and promised that I'd keep the windows closed the next day.

When we arrived home the second night, the stuffing from the sofa cushions was scattered from one end of the apartment to the other. The cushions—what was left of them—had to be thrown away. We folded blankets to place on the couch so that we could watch TV that night.

Now I was afraid to walk into the apartment for fear of what I might find. I had purchased a coat in Italy the year before. It was soft, brown suede and was the best piece of clothing that I owned. I was told that I looked terrific in it.

Surprise, surprise! When I walked through the doorway on the third night, part of the collar of the coat lay on what was left of the sofa. I rushed to the closet. I was sure that the closet door had been tightly closed when I left the house. Hanging in strips was my beautiful suede coat.

And yet, he was a sweet dog. He showered us with kisses and snuggled between us as we watched TV. He seemed to be house-trained. Twice a day, we walked him, and he cooperated without too much fuss when we returned home.

His most memorable feat was pulling a cast-iron frying pan off the stove. It was full of bacon drippings for cooking. When I discovered the pan, there wasn't a drop of bacon grease left in it. There were, however, pools of puke all over the house, bed, and sofa.

Something had to be done. We were at our wits' end, and Thanksgiving holidays were almost upon us. Anne's family was waiting for a promised visit, and we had no choice but to bring Prancer with us. Anne's father owned a small ranch near Dallas. The four-hour trip ahead of us did not look inviting.

After many attempts to climb into the front seat of the car, Prancer lay dejectedly on the back seat, intermittently whining and throwing up. The trip was hellish for us all. Whenever we stopped to eat or take a bathroom break, one of us had to remain in the car with Prancer so he wouldn't throw himself through one of the car's windows in a bout of hysteria.

It was a great relief when we finally arrived at the ranch. In the distance was a pasture full of grazing cattle. Anne's family came out to greet us, and Anne approached her father to discuss Prancer and where we should put him. As it turned out, it was a moot point because Prancer had already slipped out of the car and was racing toward the herd of peaceful cattle.

"Prancer!" I screamed.

"Come back, Prancer!" Anne yelled as she and her father raced for the pasture. The dog ignored our cries and snaked under the barbed-wire fence and into the forest of bovine legs. He was a fireball of yapping, threatening teeth. Before the cattle realized what had happened, they had all been rounded up and pushed into one tiny corner of the pasture.

Anne, her father, and I stood with our mouths open. Prancer danced up to us for his reward. He received his strokes and then raced back to guard his charges. Who could have known where his talent lay? My guess would have been a demolition expert.

Prancer became the celebrated guest of the weekend. Anne's father, who never said much, said one thing loud and clear: "He stays right here!"

So, I guess our altruism paid off. We returned home to our dogless, wrecked apartment, and Prancer started his long and happy life guarding cattle on a tiny ranch in the middle of nowhere.

—Judy Kellersberger—

The Interview

Protecting yourself is self-defense.
Protecting others is warriorship.
~Bohdi Sanders

"And that's why I think I'd be good for this job," I finished typing, and then I smiled before remembering that my potential employer could not see me. We were talking online, via social media. We had not met in person yet. We had not gotten that far. But from what I had read of her requirements for a personal assistant, I knew I wanted the position. She even had a little Cockapoo who had the final say on any applicants. "Your puppy sounds so cute," I added. "I love dogs." Then, I started to worry that typing that was too much at this early stage and moved my fingers away from the keys, stopping myself from adding anything more.

The bubbles appeared on screen, showing that the lady was typing something in response, when there was a knock at the front door. My mother was in, and as I was in the middle of an interview, I left her to answer it. I heard a lot of muffled noise. I was already turning from the computer when my mother called my name. She sounded upset. I hurried downstairs.

"What's going on?"

Our neighbour was in our entrance hall, clutching her little Shih Tzu. Tears were streaming down her cheeks.

"We were attacked," she wept. "Big dog. It bit Marley."

Marley was quiet in her arms but alert. Thankfully, there was not much blood.

"Sit down," I said, guiding her to the living room sofa. "Are you okay?"

She nodded shakily. "Yes. It didn't go for me. But Marley is hurt."

"Okay. Then let's take Marley to the vets, yes?"

"I'll drive," my mother said. She hurried outside to start the car.

"I'll be with you in a moment." I took the stairs two at a time. I was supposed to be in the middle of an interview. There was more writing from my potential employer on the screen, but I took no time to read it. I quickly wrote: "So sorry. Have to go. Neighbour's dog hurt, taking to vets." Half the words were probably jumbled, but I clicked send and did not wait for an answer, just snatched my bag and ran back downstairs.

Our neighbour was waiting by the door. "I don't think I can keep holding him," she said. "Can you carry him for me?" I gently took Marley from her.

The trip to the veterinary hospital was quiet. My neighbour silently wept in the front passenger seat while my mother drove and I clutched Marley in the back, trying to comfort him with gentle strokes and sympathetic sounds as best I could. He made no noise, just quietly shivered in my arms, looking at me with his forlorn, black eyes.

A broken front leg was the diagnosis. And shock. But he was in good hands, and the veterinary staff was lovely, bringing cups of tea and a box of chocolates to my traumatised neighbour and handling Marley with care. Aside from the break, his other injuries — puncture wounds from the other dog's teeth — were superficial, cushioned by his thick coat of fur. And, after some treatment, it was determined that Marley was well enough to take home.

It was late when we got back, and I was emotionally worn out as I climbed the stairs to bed. A cursory glance at my laptop showed a number of messages from my potential boss. *Potential nothing now,* I thought. No boss would hire someone who ran out of an interview.

I did not regret it, though. Given the same choice again, I still would have helped Marley and my neighbour.

But, as I scrolled through the messages, I saw that she had continued to write for a while after I had gone — up until only five minutes ago. She was anxious to hear how the dog was doing. I could see she was still online, despite the late hour, so I typed a quick message, assuring her that all was well. I was about to shut down the computer when another message pinged.

"You got the job!"

I blinked at the screen. "What?" Maybe she had mis-typed.

"You got the job," she repeated. "Anyone who's willing to rush away from a job interview to help an injured dog is someone I want working for me and my puppy."

— Nemma Wollenfang —

Pawprints on My Heart

I feel sorry for people who don't have dogs. I hear they have to pick up food they drop on the floor.
~Author Unknown

"Maybe this was a bad idea," I said as we sat in the parking lot, waiting to meet the breeder I'd contacted online. With my foot tapping out a rhythm to the music playing in my husband's car, I scanned the parking lot for the correct car.

"We can always change our mind," he said. I bit my lip, looking out the window as I wished for a sign that this was what he would have wanted.

It had only been two weeks since that devastating day when I said goodbye to my soul dog, our Mastiff, Henry. He was only six but had health issues. We'd said goodbye on a horrible Tuesday when his hips failed for the last time and there was nothing else to do for him. It had been an agonizing day, filled with tears and realizations that the goodbye always comes too soon.

I'd spent that blustery winter day holding him on our living room floor as my husband made preparations I didn't want to face. I reminisced about our favorite memories as I stroked his ears just as I had so many times in our six years together. I looked into his soulful eyes and begged him to understand how much I loved him. Then, as the final hour drew closer, I pulled myself away to run an errand to McDonald's.

For all the years that Henry and I had spent together, chicken nuggets were one of our "things." He loved chicken nuggets from the drive-through, and it was always his special treat. When he got older and couldn't get in the car, I would stop on my way home from work on a day I thought he needed a pick-me-up. He always perked up when he saw the familiar cardboard box.

I was sobbing when I drove through that drive-through and placed my order on his final day.

Henry ate those chicken nuggets happily. Looking in his eyes in those last moments, I knew that, in a strange way, those nuggets were a sign to him that I loved him. We said farewell an hour later.

It was a dark couple of weeks. My husband worked evenings, and I often found myself at home alone, staring at the spots that used to be Henry's. I'd come home to a shell of a house, empty and quiet. I sobbed in the shower, wishing for a sign from Henry. I'd cry myself to sleep.

And then, on a Friday less than two weeks later, I saw a photo on social media of a black Great Dane puppy who needed a home. The last of his litter, he was only a few hours away from our home. Instantly, I felt like he had to be mine.

My husband was at work when I made the arrangements. He found out through a string of texts explaining all about the puppy. When he read to the bottom of the messages, he learned the news: The puppy was ours.

On a cold February day we drove through Pennsylvania to buy the puppy. We were meeting in a parking lot, and it all felt a little scary. In truth, as we were sitting there waiting, I knew that the scariest part of all was how I was still grieving Henry. I knew deep down that the puppy wouldn't alleviate the pain and could never be Henry, even though I desperately wanted him to be. Worst of all, I was worried that maybe it was too soon. Was it right to move on so quickly? Henry had been my best friend. Would he be upset that we were "replacing" him only two weeks later?

Before I could change my mind, a car pulled up. I saw a black puppy in the front seat. My heart beat wildly as we got out of the car. We approached the breeder and talked for a moment.

"I'm sorry we're a minute late. I had to stop and get him a treat," she said. "Now, I don't feed them people food, but it's a big day, and he was so good in the car. So, I stopped and got him some McDonald's chicken nuggets. Would you like to feed him a bite?"

The tears immediately streamed down my face to the point that I couldn't talk. My husband gave me a knowing smile as he explained to the breeder that our Mastiff's favorite food in the whole world was McDonald's chicken nuggets, and they had been his last meal.

I fed that Great Dane puppy a chicken nugget. I would later learn he was terrified of all strangers—but he wasn't afraid of me at all. He took the nugget; I petted him and I fell in love. We took him home, the chicken nuggets alleviating so many of my fears.

It wasn't all sunshine and roses, of course. Edmund, as we named him, had a lot of anxiety and was a ton of work. He was not the lazy Mastiff puppy that Henry had been, and he had a lot of differences. Henry loved to play in the sprinkler and his pool; Edmund hated water. Henry loved to snuggle on the couch; Edmund never sat still. There were dozens of differences and dozens of times I cried over my beloved Henry. I was still in a cycle of grief, in truth, when we brought that puppy home.

But slowly, over time, Edmund helped me shrug off the cloak of grief. He reminded me that life is for living. He helped me laugh again at a time when I didn't think I'd ever find joy. And over the years, Edmund has become my best friend, a dog I know Henry would be happy I found.

I don't know what happens to our beloved pets when they die, but I do believe this: Henry knew I needed a sign that freezing day. And to me, those chicken nuggets were the exact sign I needed to know that Henry was still with me—and he wanted me to love another dog again.

—Lindsay Detwiler—

The Boomerang Dog

The bond with a true dog is as lasting
as the ties of this earth will ever be.
~Konrad Lorenz

She was here—and then she wasn't. The only physical traces left behind were nose smudges on the patio window and superficial scratches on my beloved hardwood floors.

For years, our two sons bemoaned their lack of a real pet—aka "one with fur." As much as they adored Wiggles, Finn and Bubbles, betta fish were not the cuddliest of companions. Touché. Furthermore, the ten-second thrill of sprinkling a few rust-colored specks of food into the bowl and then watching them sink to the bottom had lost its thrill long ago.

As our boys' limbs grew taller, voices deepened, and emotions stretched wider, so did their capacity for love.

Hence, my husband and I had reluctantly agreed to foster a dog. And *foster* we meant! None of this #fosterfail nonsense, no matter how lovely a pet it turned out to be! This was not an experiment to learn if pet ownership was for us; adoption was simply not a commitment we were willing to make. With any luck, it would be an overall positive family experience, like a camping expedition with an occasional mosquito bite but hopefully no fire ants.

Layla, an elderly Corgi, had such exemplary manners and discipline that I suspected she was Emily Post's reincarnation. When we said "Stay," she obeyed. When we said "Come," she followed. When my husband grilled bacon-wrapped filet mignons, she showed as much interest as my vegan friend Lisa would. Furthermore, she didn't bark, jump on furniture or people, veer into the neighbor's yard, or chase the baby bunnies hopping about our neighborhood. When the boys dressed her in a Clint Eastwood poncho, Ozzy Osbourne baseball cap and Green Bay Packers jersey, she wagged her tail. Her urine didn't even burn our grass; in fact, the lawn magically flourished like Chia Pets wherever she peed.

Oblivious to the fact that she was brought into our household for the benefit of the children, it was me she became fixated on. In the mornings, she sensed the very moment my brain morphed from dreamland into semi-consciousness, and her tail thump-thumped on the carpet like a heartbeat before I was ready to open my eyes. When I moved from one section of the couch to another, she relocated her position on the floor. When I showered, she nosed her way into the bathroom and stared at me through the glass door. When I sat on the toilet, her face pointed squarely in my crotch. She was always just "right there," which admittedly I found somewhat annoying.

But then Covid-19 hit hard and fast, and, yep, she was right there. When my youngest son struggled with distance learning and sobbed, "I'm not the same boy, I'm not the same boy," over and over and over. When my oldest son slammed his room door for the umpteenth time, angry from missing his friends, parkour, and band practice. When my husband's job was put on furlough. When I lay in a heap on the floor and shrieked like an injured animal from the raw pain of an indefinite separation from my mother in her memory-care facility.

During those excruciating lows, Layla placed her paw upon our bodies like a minister's palm on a parishioner's shoulder during prayer and waited for our storm to pass.

At the seven-week mark, we got the call. "Can you bring Layla to meet her new mom tomorrow?" New mom? Tomorrow? I did not like the sound of either of those things.

Yet, we were not adopting a dog! As I said.

I typed up more careful notes than I did with our first babysitter: *Layla does not tolerate the heat well. She needs to sleep with a nightlight on.*

She loves Beethoven's Ninth Symphony, ice cubes, car rides, Crime Junkie podcast. Don't hesitate to call with any questions day or night.

We said goodbye at a suburban Chuck & Don's pet-supply store. Never in their lives have the boys cried so hard or so long.

In the weeks that followed, they talked about Layla constantly and obsessively. Remember this? Remember that? Remember when? Every single night, she took center stage in their prayers and dreams. Our sons were still smitten with their beautiful first love.

Several weeks later, as I Windexed her nose smudges off the windows and attempted to buff her nail scratches from the hardwood floors, I, too, romanticized about the one who got away. I texted her new mom. "How's our girl doing?" *Our.* Verbally marking my territory, as if she still belonged to my family.

Although Layla was very much loved and exceedingly well-cared for in her new home, the new mom inexplicably felt that another fate was in store for her. And, it turned out, she was 100-percent correct.

Exactly one month to the day that we said goodbye to her, Layla returned home to us — for good.

— Jillian Van Hefty —

A Dog's Purpose

Iggy

Be here now. That's a dog's purpose.
~W. Bruce Cameron, A Dog's Purpose

Iggy was our first empty-nest dog. We met her at a local animal shelter. She was a twelve-week-old, black Cocker Spaniel/Terrier mix. She sat in the back of her pen thumping her tail when we paused to look her over. She didn't bark at all, which persuaded us to pick her over all her yapping, barking, or growling shelter mates. When the shelter staff put her in my arms, she licked my neck and I was hooked.

We named her Iggy because the name seemed to fit her sassy, playful personality. In retrospect, Houdini would have better suited her. Iggy never met a fence she couldn't get over, under, or through.

When Iggy was about six months old, we moved into a small house at a seventy-seven-acre summer camp and retreat center, where I assumed the role of Executive Director. Iggy adored the children who came in batches of a hundred or so every Sunday afternoon. The college-age staff loved having her visit them in the staff house on their breaks. On Saturday afternoons, she rode with me in a golf cart to check on the cleanliness of cabins after the campers went home.

One day, she jumped off the parked golf cart and ran under the barbed-wire fence that separated our camp property from the ranch behind us. Although she only weighed fifteen pounds, she barked at a cow that probably weighed a half-ton. The cow nibbled on grass and ignored her. Iggy moved closer, ignoring my efforts to get her to come to me. The cow glanced up. Iggy moved closer, barking all the time. When the cow had had enough of this pesky pooch, she bellowed her disapproval. A herd of cattle appeared from over the hill, slowly walking toward Iggy. She scooted backward under the fence, turned, and ran all the way across camp to our house.

Our daughter lived about ninety miles from the camp and had two young children. One day, I took Iggy with me to visit and put her in the fenced-in backyard with the children. We could watch them through the kitchen window. Carol, thinking it was too quiet in the yard, said she could no longer see the children. That was because they were not in the backyard. The meter reader apparently failed to properly latch the gate. Either one of the children or Iggy figured out how to nudge it open.

We found them in the driveway. As soon as Iggy saw me, she bolted across a busy street, miraculously managing to dodge the cars. I went after her, but she ran and disappeared. I looked for her for a half-hour before I gave up and called Animal Control to report her missing. Upset but out of options, I returned to camp without her. Three days later, I got a call that someone had found her five miles away. Though she seemed contrite for a while, that was not her last escape caper.

When we moved into town, we bought a home with a dog run set under several trees for shade. The pen had a concrete floor and was enclosed with a four-foot-high chain-link fence. On pleasant days, we left Iggy in the run with toys and water when we went places where we couldn't take her. More than once, we'd come home to find her sitting by the back door, waiting to be let in. We asked the neighbor to watch to see if he could determine how she was getting out.

"She won't do anything while I'm looking, but I think she must be climbing the fence!"

Our next home came with a screened-in porch. One evening, I left her on the porch when I went to a meeting, confident she would not be able to get out. I came home to an empty porch and no clues as to how she had escaped. I grabbed my flashlight and started walking around the neighborhood, calling her name. I heard her barking a block away where I found her chained in someone's backyard. Sheepishly, I rang their doorbell and retrieved her.

Another year, another home. This home had a fenced-in backyard with six-foot-high wood planks set so there was virtually no space between them and the ground. The family next door had two grade-school-age boys. They didn't have a dog, so we invited them to walk Iggy whenever they wanted. We left her outside, optimistic that at last we had a yard she couldn't escape. We came home to find the boys walking Iggy toward the garage.

We thought it was sweet that the boys had taken her for a walk until their father explained that it was the third time that day they'd found her wandering around their backyard. Apparently, she figured out how to jump up and push up the gate latch to escape yet again.

Eventually, I retired and no longer had to worry about what to do with Iggy while I was away for hours. But then another challenge came along. I had a chance to go overseas for an extended period of time. Iggy was now fourteen years old. Even if I could have taken her with me, she'd have to be quarantined for ninety days. I couldn't put her through that. Instead, I found Lisa, a dog-shelter volunteer, who agreed to keep Iggy while we were gone.

Iggy and Lisa's blind ten-year-old Poodle bonded quickly. Iggy became the Poodle's seeing-eye companion. When I reclaimed her several months later, Iggy sulked, barely ate, and had none of her usual playful energy. I asked Lisa if she'd consider taking Iggy back. She said she'd actually been reluctant to let me take Iggy home. I hated to let Iggy go, but she was happier with her Poodle buddy.

Though I missed Iggy, she was where she needed to be for her final senior years. She lived to age sixteen. Lisa told me that she never once tried to escape. Perhaps Iggy accepted her role as a seeing-eye companion to Lisa's blind Poodle. After years of figuring out how to escape from any place, she seemed content to stay where she was.

— Kathryn Haueisen —

Otis

Because of the dog's joyfulness, our own
is increased. It is no small gift.
~Mary Oliver

Otis was not an ordinary dog. Neither rain, nor snow, nor sleet, nor hail kept him from his mail-delivery rounds. I suspect that very few pets from Montrose, Pennsylvania were the topic of articles in the *Montrose Independent*, *The Philadelphia Inquirer*, and the *Des Moines Register*.

He joined our family in 1968 on my sister Ellen's twelfth birthday. This cute pup, the runt of the litter, was no high-class purebred. Pepper, his mother, was an English Setter and lived with our friends, the Donovans. Otis's dad was a stray mutt. Otis had somehow inherited a way of lifting the side of his mouth, creating a very appealing smile. He was basically white with some brown patches, and topped out at about fourteen inches high.

Otis joined our family at the beginning of summer and there were lots of people to keep him company. But things changed when the school bells rang. Not only had our dad gone to work, but our mom was a teacher, so on school days no one was home during the day.

Since Otis had previously befriended Art Wilcox, our mailman, he decided to walk up our street and greet him. Art allowed Otis to accompany him as he delivered mail on our block.

As time progressed, so did the relationship between Otis and Art. Gradually, Otis extended his participation in mail delivery and joined

Art about 200 yards from our home. Soon, the two met near our town traffic light. Ultimately, Otis left for the post office minutes after we left for school, and then he and Art did the entire delivery route together.

By the time Ellen was in high school, Otis was well-known in our town. Some citizens offered him treats or enjoyed petting him for a few minutes. When Art stopped for lunch, a suitable dog lunch appeared for Otis. Otis was so familiar with the route that substitute mail carriers were simply instructed to follow the dog's lead. Dogs along the way were distracted by Otis and rarely bothered the mail carriers, so his presence was always welcomed.

As Otis aged, he sometimes went home with Art. Otis had become lame. He spent many weeknights at Art's home. It was an amicable arrangement because Art could give Otis a ride to and from "work." By then, members of our family were engaged in after-school activities and did not have much time to enjoy Otis before he went to sleep.

Eventually, a schedule developed. Otis returned to our family home on weekends but boarded at Art's on weekdays. We suspected that local church bells served as his calendar and clock.

Like many working males, Otis relaxed on Sundays. One Sunday, my husband Larry decided to see how long Otis, who enjoyed being petted, would remain in one place. During a football game, Larry took a seat in the preferred television-watching chair with Otis at his side. The petting began as the game started. Hours passed, and the game ended. Otis was still enjoying the petting experiment, but my husband decided to stop the experiment and consider it inconclusive.

One weekend, Otis was not at our house. We assumed that he was at Art's. To be sure, we phoned to confirm. Art said Otis was not there. We searched high and low in our neighborhood, and Art did the same in his. The search spread to the whole town, with many volunteers. Eventually, it occurred to Art to check inside the post office. Somehow, Otis had been shut in when the post office had closed on Saturday night.

Not many weeks after that event, Otis lost his life while crossing the road near the town traffic light. He was too lame to finish crossing before the traffic light changed, and a turning car hit him. Our mother was called. She gently notified each family member. Many citizens in the town, however, learned of this death while driving by the Bartron Funeral Home where the death of Otis had been posted on the lighted memorial board, a place generally reserved for humans.

The final resting place for Otis is at our old family home. His memory lives on in our town and in the many newspapers where he was featured.

—Judy Kelly—

Charlie's Playground

I think dogs are the most amazing creatures;
they give unconditional love. For me,
they are the role model for being alive.
~Gilda Radner

A few years ago, I took my Golden Retriever, Charlie, on a walk through the park. It was a warm spring afternoon, and the sun was shining so brightly it felt like the whole world was glowing. All of a sudden, Charlie took off. His tail was wagging so hard I thought it might fall off, and his tongue was flapping all over the place. "Charlie!" I yelled, running after him. I didn't know what he saw, but I was curious (and a little worried) to find out.

When I caught up to him I saw something that made me halt. Several kids who had disabilities were playing on the playground. They were hyper and were completely engrossed in their games. A few were swinging on swings, climbing the monkey bars, or on the merry-go-round. Their giggles filled the air like the most cheerful music ever. Then I noticed one boy sitting off to the side. His name was Timmy, and he was in a wheelchair. He was smiling as he watched the other kids, but he also looked a little sad, like he really wanted to join in but couldn't.

Charlie decided to do something extraordinary. He walked up to Timmy and wagged his tail as if it was the best day ever. Timmy's eyes opened wide and he beamed. He extended his hand towards Charlie to pet him, and Charlie sat beside him, leaning in. It seemed that he already was sure that Timmy was his new best friend. Timmy laughed and rubbed his hand through Charlie's fur. They were the perfect pair.

Before long, other kids came over, curious about Charlie. Instantly, Timmy was part of the group, laughing and playing with everyone else. Charlie made it all happen.

The whole afternoon was like a dream. Charlie ran around making every single kid smile. He was like a furry superhero spreading happiness everywhere. Timmy looked so happy, and I could tell he didn't feel left out anymore. When the sun started to set and it was time to head back home, Timmy leaned over and gave Charlie a huge hug. "Thank you, Charlie," he said, grinning from ear to ear. It was the sweetest thing ever.

Walking home, I couldn't stop thinking about what I had just seen. Charlie showed me how a small act of kindness, like just being there, can make a huge difference. I'll always remember that day, the way the sun felt on my skin, the sound of the kids' laughter, and how Charlie made everything better just by being himself.

— Genesis F. —

Magic Potion

I have found that when you are deeply troubled,
there are things you get from the silent devoted
companionship of a dog that you can get
from no other source.
~Doris Day

Fifteen years ago, a Goldendoodle with big eyes, fluffy fur, and a yellow ribbon around his neck arrived at our Cape Cod home from Georgia. Most people thought I got a dog for my five-year-old, Emily, who'd just finished treatment for cancer. But really, the handsome pup who hid behind the couch was for my seven-year-old daughter, Isabelle.

Isabelle had spent a year and a half being shuffled to friends' and family members' houses with little structure and a lot of unknowns. She didn't want to talk about her feelings. Instead, she bit her nails and had a few accidents at school.

Isabelle watched Emily lose her hair, weight, and the strength to play outside. At school, her peers had no idea what she was going through, nor did the adults who couldn't fathom what it was like to be a little girl who was afraid her sister might die.

My husband and I did the best we could to meet Isabelle's needs, but most of the time we were distracted and overwhelmed. Only one of us was home at a time, while the other was at the hospital with Emily. Isabelle lost herself in television shows and chocolate pudding; she retreated to a detached version of herself.

When Emily's eighteen months of treatment were over, it was time to focus on Isabelle's wellbeing. The eight-pound pup, whom we named Obi—a nod to my husband's love of *Star Wars*—was "hired" to help Isabelle heal. It was a job that the adults in her life, including myself, were failing at miserably.

Initially, Isabelle was afraid of him. He snatched food from her hands and jumped up on her. I considered dog-training classes, but post-cancer appointments didn't leave much time for that. Within a few weeks, though, Isabelle taught Obi to sit. He learned there would be a "treat" if he came back from running after a squirrel. He learned the meaning of "no" and "paw."

Every afternoon, Obi trotted to the end of the driveway with me to get the girls off the school bus. Isabelle played with him in the leaves or the snow. Afterward, he sat with her on the couch while she did math homework and spelling worksheets. He asked for nothing except belly rubs and an occasional carrot or piece of red bell pepper, his favorite.

Obi became a welcome distraction from the world of cancer treatment and its aftermath. We took him to the beach and played catch in the backyard. He didn't like the water or fetching a ball, so most days we threw the ball to one another while he watched and gnawed on a stick. On Sundays, we went for ice cream. Emily got vanilla, Isabelle chocolate, and Obi scarfed down vanilla on a dog biscuit.

Isabelle's canine companion gave her back the attention that Emily's illness had taken from her. He didn't try to justify to her why Emily's needs took priority or insist on knowing the "real reason" why she was upset. He just made her feel better by throwing his body next to hers and repeatedly placing his paw on her hand when she stopped rubbing behind his ears.

Every night, she fed him and took him out to pee. She cleaned his water dish and brushed his sandy coat, which resembled human hair more than Poodle fur. Not once did Emily protest about Isabelle taking charge. Emily loved Obi, but she had no interest in taking care of him. Even a prompt from him for a rub made her roll her eyes. He was truly Isabelle's.

Life with Obi was a trade-off. He was expensive, messy and always eating something he shouldn't, like a new L.L. Bean dog bed. The bills for his grooming, vet visits, and food were higher than what I spent on the rest of us. "Just think of all the money you're saving on therapy," my sister said.

Obi was indeed therapy. Every day, Isabelle softened a little more. Her shoulders dropped, her tone lightened, and the sparkle in her eyes returned. She giggled while dressing Obi in costumes for a talent show with Emily in their bedroom. Most of the time, Obi emceed the show.

Middle school tested Obi's ability to navigate mean girls and drama, yet he did. His warm eyes followed Isabelle around the room, calculating when to rest and cuddle and when to do his jig at the slider door and insist they play outside.

On a weekend night when Isabelle wasn't invited to a birthday party, she and Obi ate popcorn and watched movies. He jumped in as her nursemaid when she was home sick from school, easing the guilt I felt that she was alone.

Deep into the pandemic, Isabelle's senior year of high school was spent on a computer screen in the basement. The two of them lay on a mattress eating peanut butter off spoons and bingeing Netflix series. Obi didn't say annoying things like "You'll never forget this year" when her prom was canceled or Senior Week was virtual and "lame."

In the fall, before Isabelle left for her freshman year of college, she sobbed at the mudroom door. "I'll be back soon, buddy," she said.

Six weeks later, Obi stopped eating. We thought he missed Isabelle. I made him chicken and salmon. When he refused to eat what he normally would have inhaled, we took him to the vet. Obi, now twelve, had cancerous tumors all over his body. I called Isabelle at college and flew her home to say goodbye.

When Isabelle walked through the door, Obi's tail swept back and forth for the first time in weeks. Tears fell from her face onto his fur. She said nothing. He rallied and stood up, a newborn colt steadying his wobbly legs. All weekend, she sat on the floor with him, working on her college assignments in the same spot where they learned to read and multiply.

On Sunday, a few hours before she left, Obi buried his head in Isabelle's lap in the backyard. She stroked it and watched my husband and Emily play catch. The sun was warm. It was almost a perfect day to get ice cream.

It's hard not to believe that Obi knew his job was complete. He had listened and loved. He had kept Isabelle's secrets and encouraged her to be brave. His unconditional love was magic, a potion that healed Isabelle.

— Amy McHugh —

Mother Merlin

You know, a dog can snap you out of any kind of bad mood that you're in faster than you can think of.
~Jill Abramson

Merlin was a hazard of my working at a shelter. The six-week-old Collie stole my heart and joined my household of rescues and adoptees. He grew from a fluffball to a handsome, sensitive dog, with a variety of bad-breeding health issues and without any "Lassie" brains. He was a lovable doofus.

Merlin doted on the wildlife babies I often cared for as a licensed rehabilitator. He would avidly watch their feedings and cleanings, staying as close to these orphaned and/or injured babies as allowed. Of all the species, he adored possums most. His favorite batch was a litter of eight possum babies that he obsessively watched over. "Mother Merlin" became his nickname.

When they were old enough, the possums graduated to a heavily weighted-down outdoor cage during nice weather. No bottom on the cage allowed them to learn to forage in grass and dirt and safely experience the sights, sounds and smell of nature. Mother Merlin always lay next to the cage, supervising their every move.

One day, Merlin's insistent barking brought me running. He'd tipped over the cage, freeing eight possums who were too young to be out on their own. The yard was fenced, but the babies could easily fit through the chain link. And possums can move fast.

True to his mothering nature and herding instincts, Merlin tried to corral the escapees. Chastising him for creating this situation, I exhorted him to "find them." One by one, he led me to a baby. Seven of them.

Frantic to find the last one, I kept searching and repeating "find them" to Merlin. He stood by the now-upright cage with the seven possums in it, hanging his head as if ashamed at what he'd done. But he refused to continue to search.

I frantically admonished him and told him to find that last baby.

Merlin hung his head lower and began to lick at his white chest and ruff. After a few more choice words from me about being a useless helper, he ignored me. He stayed by the cage and continued to lick at his ruff. I decided to move the seven babies inside the house, hoping that, without them in sight, Merlin would resume the search for number eight.

Merlin never left his self-appointed post, though. Head down even lower, his licking had soaked his fur. It was totally abnormal behavior for him. Curious, I moved his head up to get a better look at his wet fur. Then, I saw it: a pink tail! I parted the fur and there was baby number eight, snuggled under Merlin's chin.

My apologies to Merlin were profuse as I dislodged the baby and praised his "find" while exhorting him to never do this again as my nerves couldn't take it.

With number eight safely in my hands, Mother Merlin happily followed me inside to watch the little possum be reunited with its siblings. Merlin lay down by their cage, content with a job well done as far as he was concerned. He promptly fell asleep. Apparently, possum motherhood was exhausting.

— Linda Mihatov —

The Great Dog Cure

Even dogs know how important it is to hear
somebody else breathing.
~Benjamin DeHaven

Early in my career as a child/family psychologist, I spent one day a week at an elementary school in central Maine. The school's principal had assigned me a windowless, closet-like room with a small table and two chairs. I carried a large cloth bag with art supplies, books and small toys that were essentials for child therapy.

Despite the simplicity of my workspace, the situations referred to me were complex. My training had been rigorous, and I felt well-prepared most of the time. But every now and then a traditional treatment plan didn't work.

I always meet with parents first to gather background information and fully understand the reasons for the referrals of their children. One morning in late September, an exhausted-looking young mother, whom I'll call Jenny, arrived for her son's intake appointment. The dark circles under Jenny's eyes were unusual for someone who appeared to be in her late twenties. I learned that her eight-year-old son, a third-grader — I'll call him Rudy — didn't sleep.

Because he had trouble even falling asleep, he would wail when she first left his room, wander downstairs multiple times, and insist on getting into bed with her and her husband after midnight. His wish to continue in the family bed was causing conflict between Jenny and her husband, as he thought Rudy was old enough to sleep on his own.

Even as an infant, Rudy had not been a great sleeper. But as he got older, his insomnia got worse. According to their pediatrician, his health was fine.

I asked the usual questions about family history and trauma, but nothing I learned explained his difficulty sleeping except some anxiety that seemed to be part of his temperament. He was a much-loved only child with a large extended family. He often expressed the wish to have a little sister or brother. But, aside from that, he was generally fun-loving and happy. When asked about his strengths, another typical intake question, his mother talked about his kindness, creativity, and great sense of humor.

I initially suggested the usual solutions.

Did they have a bedtime ritual? Yes, every night before bed, they read picture books and said prayers.

What about monsters? Was Rudy reassured about those? Yes, they looked under the bed and in the closet together nightly. No monsters.

Were all screens off well before bedtime? Absolutely, an hour before.

Was his room dark and quiet? It was.

Had they tried leaving music on for him? Yes. He liked music, but it didn't help him sleep.

Melatonin? His pediatrician had suggested melatonin, and they tried it, but it didn't help.

Had she ever tried talking about dreams he might like to have? Yes. He had a great imagination and came up with vivid dream-stories. They didn't help him get to sleep.

Later in the week, Rudy came for his first therapy session. He would have presented as an adorable, curly-haired boy if his skin wasn't grayish and his eyes weren't sunken with fatigue. I started out, as usual, asking him to do a Kinetic Family Drawing, described to the child as "a picture of your whole family doing something." Rudy drew a picture of himself standing next to his parents' double bed with his mother and father in bed, frowning. This led us into an immediate conversation about his trouble with sleep.

The situation gained urgency when Jenny learned she was pregnant with a second child. In response to my unspoken question, she said, "Rudy goes to his grandmother's some weekends, so we have privacy then." She worried about the exhaustion and crowded family bed with a new baby if Rudy couldn't learn to sleep on his own.

One Sunday afternoon, I woke up from a delicious nap with my Beagle, Maggie, still asleep next to me. I had a new idea, a brilliant one, I thought. But would it work? I've had dogs all my life, and their comfort and companionship have been essential. As a child in a household where everyone yelled and no one listened, dogs were my confidants. And, even as an adult, I'd always loved having a dog breathing gently in the room where I slept.

"Do you have a dog?" I asked Jenny at a parent meeting.

"We do," she said. "Skye." She showed me a photo of their little black Scottie.

"Does Skye sleep in Rudy's room?" I asked.

"Well, no."

"Could he? I think it might help."

"I never thought of that," she said. Then, both because she was desperate and because parents assume that psychologists might know something, she said quickly, "I'd like to try it." Then, more slowly, "But I don't know if Rudy's father would go along."

"Why not?" I asked.

"He's kind of old-fashioned about dogs. Thinks they should be in the kitchen at night, guarding the house."

"Are there robbery problems in your neighborhood?"

"No, we're way out in the country. And, anyway, the house has an alarm system. He made sure of that."

"He wants Rudy to sleep, right?"

"That is so right," she said. "I'll see what I can do."

Jenny called that afternoon to say that her husband had agreed to let Skye sleep with Rudy. He wasn't excited about the idea, but he was willing to try anything.

The very next week, when I met with Rudy, his face looked ruddy and his eyes were bright. He excitedly told me about Skye sleeping at the foot of his bed. During our session, he drew a picture of Skye, and we did some relaxation breathing exercises. His teacher stopped by to say he had been more attentive in class.

The following week, at our parent meeting, Jenny's face was bright, her smile wide.

"It worked," she said. "Skye sleeps in Rudy's room now. And Rudy is falling asleep easily and sleeping through the night."

I have suggested "The Great Dog Cure" many times over the years for children who don't sleep. Of course, it's only workable if the family has a dog. Stuffed animals, while sweet and cozy, aren't substitutes. Neither are cats.

Is there evidence that it works? I would say yes. The evidence to me (considered anecdotal, of course) is that for all the times I've recommended The Great Dog Cure for a child with insomnia, I have never seen it fail.

— Miranda Phelps —

The Seventh Juror

It is amazing how much love and laughter they bring into our lives and even how much closer we become with each other because of them.
~John Grogan

I was driving home from North Miami with my friend Lesley when I saw a German Shepherd dog wandering toward the I-95 entrance. I'm a sucker for stray animals, especially when they're in danger.

We pulled over to the grassy median, and I said, "Go get the dog!"

Lesley looked at me quizzically. "What do I say to it?"

I couldn't just leave the dog wandering onto a busy highway. "Try 'Come here, doggy.'"

Lesley shrugged, got out of the car, and approached the dog cautiously. She put out her hand, speaking softly. "Come here, Lady."

The dog sensed a friend. She wagged her tail, sauntered over, and sniffed her hand. Lesley opened the door to my Lexus. It was as if the dog had known us for years. She jumped into the back seat and looked at us as if to say, "Take me home. I'm hungry, and I'm tired, and I've been lost for hours."

I dropped Lesley off at her car and then went in search of my husband.

It was a Saturday morning, and I knew Tom's ritual of meeting the guys at noon for a beer at Duffy's Tavern, which was one of Miami's famous pubs. Even President Clinton had visited for a beer after a round of golf. I spotted Tom sitting at the bar, talking to his buddies. He was surprised to see me. This was "the guys' hangout."

I beamed and said, "I have a present for you. I found the sweetest female Shepherd, honey-colored, short-haired and gorgeous, probably about a year old. She is super friendly."

His mouth dropped open. We already owned two male German Shepherds, and Tom was devoted to them, but we'd always wanted a female dog. Tom followed me out to the car. Lady sat up in the back seat, wagging her tail, and Tom climbed in and stroked her honey-colored head. She nuzzled his hand. I knew from the look on Tom's face that he was already in love. The next day, we took Lady to the vet, who determined she was probably a purebred and in perfect health, about three years old. We posted ads in all the newspapers for weeks, with no response.

Lady got along with both our other dogs, but their temperaments were the opposite of hers. The males were roughhouse tough, aggressive, and ready to guard our house at any signs of intrusion, whereas Lady was gentle, mellow, and preferred lounging and basking in the sunshine to watch the action. Her main objective was to just be near my husband.

Tom was thirty-seven years old and had been appointed one of the youngest federal judges in the country. Tom and Lady became so attached that Tom decided to take her to the courthouse with him. His chamber was nicknamed The Ponderosa because of its immense size. There were multiple rooms where Lady was permitted to roam freely.

Lady became the canine celebrity of the courthouse. The clerks and the marshals loved her and gave her praise and an occasional dog biscuit. Lady loved the attention. She would follow Tom from room to room, happy to be lying at his feet.

Tom was in trial on a particularly complex commercial case that he knew would be contentious and heated. After the jury selection was completed, he decided to use Lady as a "therapy dog" to help the jurors break the ice and bond with each other. He brought Lady into the jury room and introduced her. He said, "This is Lady, and she loves donuts, especially white-powdered donuts." It worked. The jurors warmed up to each other, competing to fawn over the dog. The next morning when the jurors met in the juror deliberation room, Lady visited them and was greeted by the white-powdered donuts that the jurors had brought.

Tom was sitting in the library concentrating on writing an order when he looked down to see that Lady had returned to his private chamber with a nose delicately powdered with white sugar. He petted her head and said, "That's my girl. You're my perfect human-resources tool."

A few hours later, Tom was racing in his usual hurried manner from his chamber to the bench to resume the trial after a lunch break. He donned his black, flowing robe and entered the courtroom with his usual judicial flourish. As he sat down on the bench, he watched as the six jurors were led by the marshal into the jury box. One by one, they filed in with solemn faces and took their seats. Suddenly, a seventh juror appeared: Lady sauntered in and jumped into an empty juror's chair. She sat erect in her chair, alert and attentive, as if waiting to hear the evidence.

At that very moment, Judge Lenore Nesbitt, a revered federal judge and one of Tom's mentors and cherished friends, passed by his courtroom and stood at the doorway. Lenore was one of the first female federal judges in the country and had championed Tom's appointment to the bench. She stood in the doorway and twirled her long strand of pearls, which she was famous for, and said, "Officially, I don't want to know. But off the record, I am really curious."

Without hesitating a beat, Tom said, "She was nominated spokesperson by the jurors."

The courtroom burst into laughter as Lady was cheerfully escorted by a marshal back to Tom's private chamber. The case was later settled amicably.

Eventually, Tom retired from the bench, and Lady retired from her job as the official courthouse companion. At home, Lady continued to be both Tom's cherished companion and mine. In her later years, she was content to keep me company, lounging by the kitchen door as I cooked. While her diet at home was a strict vet-approved diet, any "people food" rewards were appreciated. Hot dogs were her favorite motivation and necessary to disguise the medication for her severely arthritic hips.

Lady passed away at the ripe, old age of sixteen. After she passed, the courthouse sent home a plaque dedicated in her honor. The plaque read: "Lady, our official canine and officer of the Miami courthouse."

Fourteen wonderful animals have shared the Scott household. But Lady will always be special, both in our eyes and in those of the United States court system in Miami.

—Joyce Newman Scott—

Collie

A dog wags its tail with its heart.
~Martin Buxbaum

My big brother Neil came home one summer afternoon and whispered to each one of us three girls. "Big surprise!" he said in a low tone. "Meet me in the garage!" At eight years old, I was the youngest of the kids and was excited to be included in a secret.

I ran to the garage, stepped inside, and saw a beautiful Smooth Collie waiting expectantly. She had short, silky, brown-and-white fur that looked more like the flank of a cow than the long hair of Lassie the television star.

The dog ran to me and swished her tail back and forth as she jumped up on my legs. I was quite intimidated but soon realized she was friendly and not at all scary. Neil and my sisters burst through the door. Neil said that a friend had given the dog to him because they had to move out of town and couldn't keep her.

All four of us kids knew our parents' thoughts about getting a dog. Hamsters, goldfish or an occasional turtle was the limit on living creatures that joined our family. We knew if Neil asked to keep the dog, the answer would not be positive. We decided to hide the dog in the garage for a few weeks and then bring her out and show how easy it was to care for her. Then, they would definitely say we could keep her.

As kids, we truly thought we could feed the dog, take good care of her, and hide her from our parents. As you can imagine, that worked for about an hour. When my dad came home from work, he went to get something out of the garage, opened the door, and spied the dog, who had just chewed up a cardboard box.

My parents listened to the story and then said a resounding "no" to the new family addition. They did agree to keep the dog for a while until they found her a new home. My brother and sisters and I thought they really meant we could keep the dog, so we discussed what to name her.

"Don't give her a name," my mom said. "We're NOT keeping her."

By default, we called her Collie. She was smart, affectionate and playful. Collie loved a game of tag in the backyard or a belly scratch before a nap in the sunshine streaming through the window. We built a fort in the backyard and buried a treasure box with treats of bubble gum and candy to discover years in the future. The following day, we found Collie in the fort, devouring all the gum and candy she had dug up.

It was a fun, memorable summer, and I truly thought Collie would be with us forever. But forever came to a sudden halt after we had Collie for nearly three months. My dad came home from work and said that a colleague had a twelve-year-old son who had been hit by a car a few weeks ago and was convalescing at home for several months in an orthopedic body cast for his broken hip and thigh. Dad said his friend was thinking of getting a dog for his son to cheer him up. My dad told him about Collie and said they could have her if it was a good fit.

The friend had accepted, and on Saturday we would take Collie across town to her new home. I was devastated. I didn't know if I could handle saying goodbye to our sweet canine companion.

Saturday came quickly, and soon we were welcomed into a modest home that was clean and tidy. We were led to a smiling boy in a hospital bed in the family room. We brought in Collie. She wiggled with excitement, went straight to the boy, and gently licked his nose. She seemed to know that the boy needed special care. She calmly lay beside him on the carpet, only moving to lift her head to check on the boy every few minutes.

We visited for a while, and then it was time to leave. I buried my face in Collie's silky fur and told her I loved her and would miss her. She seemed to sense it was goodbye. She looked straight at me with her dark brown eyes. We shared a quiet moment, and she gave me a sloppy lick on the cheek. Then, she gave each one of the kids kisses and love. When Collie was finished with her goodbyes, she walked back over to her spot by the boy and settled down again.

Perhaps Collie was making this easy on us because she realized this was her destiny. This boy needed her. At that moment, I didn't feel so sad anymore. It was as if Collie was finally home.

As the years passed and I grew up, other dogs shared my life. But from time to time, I still think about that special summer and a beautiful, brown-and-white, silky, sweet dog named Collie.

— Laura McKenzie —

The Brothers

Help your brother's boat across,
and your own will reach the shore.
~Hindu Proverb

There have been dogs in my life for as long as I can remember, and they all hold a special place in my heart. But Scott and Curly Joe made me see just how "human" their thought processes really are. These two little Cockapoos were brothers and my BFFs from the day they were born.

The brothers always seemed to know when I was feeling down. Curly had a favorite toy, an elephant, that made elephant sounds. If he sensed I needed it, he would look everywhere for his elephant and then squeeze it so the sounds would make me laugh. Then, he would give me the toy.

The dogs always knew how to make me feel better. They were therapy dogs 24-7, always on the job whether I was listening to their advice or not.

Ever patient, they would stand by me no matter what stupid thing I tried, through every bad decision I made. They would quietly keep an eye on every person I should not have trusted or allowed to come into my life. They never once said, "We tried to tell you, but you wouldn't listen." They would simply say, "Don't worry. We're here for you. We've got your back."

They were about twelve years old when I first noticed that Scott would come in from outside and go to every room in the house. If he couldn't find Curly, he would ask to go back out. After ten minutes or so, they would both show up at the door, ready to come in. I never gave it too much thought until my father got sick. I went home to take care of him, and Scott and Curly Joe came along to help. Now, when they went out, they were no longer on a 50' by 100' fenced city lot. They were on ninety acres of orchard, forest and open fields with cows and an occasional coyote to deal with.

One morning, I let them out as usual, and as I stood at the sink filling the coffeepot, I spotted something moving in the orchard. Thinking that it could be a coyote, I darted out the back door to find the boys and bring them to safety. What I saw moving through the orchard was not a predator but simply one brother helping the other find his way home. Somehow, Scott knew that Curly needed his help. Did Curly tell him that he couldn't see where he was going? Did he tell him that he was lost and frightened? I don't know how Scott knew, but he definitely knew.

I watched as they made their way through the orchard. Scott patiently moved from one side to the other, focused only on guiding his brother home. Every time Curly began to stray off course, Scott would switch quickly from one side to the other until they were headed directly toward the back door again.

Scott continued to take care of his brother until they were nineteen years old. Then, tragedy hit. Scott had gone to the vet to get his teeth cleaned, and he didn't make it through the procedure. Curly took the news much harder than I did. Day after day, he would wander from room to room, looking for him everywhere until he would get to their bed where Scott's scent was the strongest. It seemed to soothe him. I tried to tell him what had happened, although I'm not sure he understood.

After Scott's passing, I came to understand how much responsibility he had taken on. One morning, I opened the back door, and Curly went out while I poured a cup of coffee. I turned to follow him out, but he was already out of sight. I headed out to find him, but I didn't see him anywhere. I finally found him at the very back of the yard. He was standing with his forehead against a white, five-gallon bucket, thinking that it was the white back door. When I reached down and patted him, he just looked up at me like, "Finally, you opened the door. I've been waiting here for the longest time." I never let him go out alone again.

Scott had left some huge paw prints to fill. He had become Curly's caregiver all on his own. No one taught him how. He simply saw the need and, without a whimper or growl, filled it. Every morning, he had made sure that his brother got out to go potty and found his way back home. When they came in, he would guide him to the water bowl and breakfast, and then they would hit the bed by the fireplace until it was time to do it all again.

It was the following year, just after Curly's twentieth birthday, when Scott came to guide him home one last time.

— Cheri Bunch —

A Natural Therapist

Anything But Ordinary

We give dogs the time we can spare, the space we can spare and the love we can spare. In return, dogs give us their all. It is the best deal we have ever made.
~M. Acklam

Sita was anything but an ordinary yellow Lab. She had the most serene expression I have ever seen, with her amber eyes and calm demeanor. The most agitated person would quiet down just by looking at her face. She also seemed to have a maturity beyond her years. I don't think this gorgeous creature was ever a puppy; she was an "old soul" from birth.

Nothing was known about her early life. She was found on the streets and taken to a kill shelter. The woman in charge fell in love with her and called an agency that trains service dogs. Sita immediately began training in a foster home and the prisons in Ohio to become a service dog.

Meanwhile, I applied to the same agency for a hearing-ear dog after a friend of mine was robbed and severely beaten when he did not hear a burglar come into his home. I have a severe hearing loss myself and could not hear people enter my apartment. I was tired of being startled, even by family members. Hearing-ear service dogs alert us when they hear doorbells, sirens, microwaves, or someone entering the house. They "bump" us with their noses to signify the sounds and then look in that direction.

The minute Sita's leash was put in my hand, I fell in love with her soulful eyes. We bonded immediately and became inseparable.

We flew all over the country together and even spoke at a Hearing Loss Association of America (HLAA) convention, where people with hearing loss gather from around the world to support each other and try out the newest technology. My service dog accompanied me to the classes I taught at a local community college, and the students enjoyed her. She went with me to the private practice where I was a counselor.

My caseload included several foster and abused children. This is where Sita had the biggest impact.

One of "my kids" was in the process of being adopted. His parents called and asked me to tell him that the only father he had ever known, a man who had fostered him for several years, had passed away. After I broke the news to him, he went to Sita and grabbed her fur, sobbing into her side. She didn't have to talk. It was enough that she sat there quietly and was there for him.

Sita had a special bond with her groomer, Sharry, who had taken care of her in the past when I was on a cruise for several weeks. One day, I received a text from Sharry's daughter that she was in hospice. I asked if she needed to see Sita, and the daughter replied that she did.

When we entered Sharry's room, I realized that our good friend was in a coma. The daughter whispered to me that the last thing her mother had said was "I need a dog here" because she was such a dog lover and knew she was dying. Her daughter was able to tell her we were coming right before she lost consciousness.

Sita climbed up on the bed and lay in Sharry's lap, and she comforted friends and family as they said goodbye. When the priest arrived to give the last rites, Sita did not want to leave her friend. I commented to the others that she did not want to go, and one of them wisely said, "None of us want to leave Sharry."

The most amazing story was when I had a client sobbing while she told me about all the abuse she had suffered. Neither one of us was paying any attention to Sita lying quietly under my desk. Suddenly, she came out and reached up to the top of my desk. She pulled a tissue out of the box with her mouth, trotted over to the client, and handed it to her. My mouth dropped open because she had never been taught to do this. She had watched me and knew that when someone was crying they received a tissue. My client stopped crying and exclaimed, "Sita, you made my day!"

I had to maintain a sense of humor when three different people asked me why I had her, and I explained patiently that she was a hearing-ear dog. They then asked me if the dog was deaf.

One time, we stopped at McDonald's for a burger. I took her out of the car, went inside to get the burger, and came outside to sit at one of the tables since it was a gorgeous day. A couple in another car was watching Sita and me intently. I became uncomfortable under their intense scrutiny. Finally, the woman walked over to me and said, "We have been watching you."

"I know," I replied drily.

"We are trying to figure out how you can be driving when you are blind!" I tried to explain Sita was not a guide dog for the blind, but I could tell she did not believe me. All I could do was laugh.

This precious creature lived to be seventeen, and I miss her terribly. I still smile when I think of all the people who were helped by Sita, whose work as a guide dog had an impact way beyond what she did for me.

—Jane M. Biehl, PhD—

Dog with a Loving Heart

Did you know that there are over 300 words
for love in canine?
~Gabriel Zevin

The RV was ready, the retirement funds invested, the route planned, and we were excited. After forty-plus years in the workforce, we were retiring and pursuing our dream of traveling around the United States.

As the final countdown for takeoff began, my husband experienced some medical issues that sent him to his doctor for a quick checkup. After finding no clue to his baffling symptoms, he was sent for a CT scan and was eventually diagnosed with lymphoma. Our trip was put on hold while he went through chemo.

We were usually a multi-dog family, but at that time we were down to one dog—a mild-mannered Weimaraner named Anna. We had put off getting another companion dog for Anna since we knew we would be traveling. We planned to take her with us on shorter trips and leave her with family on longer ones. Anna traveled easily, and it would be no problem handling just one dog.

Anna was placid, content to sleep in a warm spot in the yard or stay by our side in the house, but she was not energetic enough for my husband's needs. He relished a dog who would follow him around the yard, run beside him when he rode his bike, play hours of fetch outside, swim with him in the pond, or jump in the truck for a ride. That simply was not our Anna.

As word spread about my husband's illness, sympathy poured in from friends and family. They knew how disappointed we were that our RV travels were curtailed. We did take a few local RV trips between the treatments, allowing us to temporarily leave cancer at home, but the long days of confinement were hard.

My husband is normally very active and energetic, so the feelings of fatigue and lethargy following treatment were unbearable. Our kids were wonderful about trying to help when they could, sitting with him during treatments and calling often.

We had been wanting another dog but had held off because of our travel plans. But then, our son and daughter-in-law pulled me aside one day and asked permission to look for another dog for their dad. They thought a new pet would take away some of the disappointment and fill their dad's empty hours. They promised to take care of the dogs when we resumed traveling. After talking to my husband to be sure he was okay with the plan, I agreed. The search began.

My daughter-in-law soon sent texted us a picture of a lean and fit dog named Maddie who was a German Shorthaired Pointer (GSP), a breed we had never heard about. After quickly searching the internet, we learned the dogs were bred as hunters and were very high-energy. Maddie's owner, a military man, could no longer manage a dog in his small apartment. Maddie was mostly confined to a crate.

It seemed like Maddie would be a perfect fit for us, so the kids arranged to bring her home. We set up another doghouse on the front porch and purchased a second comfy bed for inside the house. Then, we excitedly waited for the new addition to our family.

When our daughter-in-law pulled up in front of the house, out jumped the sleek, mottled-brown body of a GSP, followed by a huge, chocolate-brown Lab! Our daughter-in-law sheepishly explained that the owner had two dogs needing a home, and she did not have the heart to take one and leave the other. She agreed that the Lab, named Capers, would technically be hers. But since our son and daughter-in-law both worked full-time, we knew we were now the caretakers of three large dogs.

Maddie was restrained by a leash, but we could tell she couldn't wait to run. The first time off the leash, she ran in circles around our yard and then continued right into our neighbor's yard where she ate three of his chickens! We could not let her run free.

Our son, who lived next door to us, paid to have an invisible electric fence installed around both our lots. The purchase included training the dogs to learn their boundaries. Maddie was hesitant to go anywhere near the electric fence after only a couple of warning tones. The fence worked beautifully, and she was soon chasing squirrels up every tree, spooking the frogs in the pond, and loving the freedom of the great outdoors.

Maddie and my husband soon formed a special bond. He enjoyed all the dogs, but Maddie attached herself to him and was constantly by his side. While the other dogs would wander off to pursue their own interests, Maddie was faithful to her owner. They spent many hours together, and my husband was constantly thrilled by Maddie's antics. His feeling-good days flew by as he rescued a snapping turtle from Maddie's grasp, ran out in the back field to find a herd of wild pigs she'd cornered, and responded to her frantic barks when she pounced on a water snake. Life was full, busy and fun, and each day was a crazy adventure with Maddie on the prowl.

The time soon rolled around for another chemo session, and I knew my husband would experience the dreaded after-effects of treatment. I had witnessed the joy he felt with Maddie on his good days but wondered what would happen when he felt sick.

After getting home from the hospital, my husband headed straight for his recliner to sleep off the drugs. Maddie was baffled when he did not come out to play. She paced on the front porch, peeking in the storm door and whining for her friend to respond. When I let her in the house, she pranced in front of my husband, hoping for a romp, but all he could do was pat her on the head. Somehow, she seemed to understand that something was different.

I soon realized how smart and perceptive Maddie was about her beloved owner. The next day, my husband roused himself enough to go sit out in the yard to enjoy some sunshine. I pulled a lounge chair in front of the pond, and he stretched out with all the dogs dancing around him. Capers looked at him with her big, deep-brown eyes, a ball in her mouth, as if to say, “Here’s the ball. Why aren’t you playing?” Anna nudged his hand, looking into his pale face as if to ask, “Why aren’t you scratching my back?”

But Maddie — high-energy, mischievous, and wild — was doing something quite different. While her owner was lying there sick and suffering, she carefully crawled in his lap, put her head on his chest, and simply comforted him. She may have been bred as a wild and crazy hunter, but when needed, she was also a loving dog with a lot of heart.

— Robin Stearns Lee —

From Protected to Protector

Blessed is the person who has earned
the love of an old dog.
~Sydney Jeanne Seward

"Where's my potato?" my mother asked from the hospital bed in the middle of the living room in her independent-living apartment. Her full-time aide and I looked at one another. Potato?

But upon hearing my mother's voice, her grey-white Poodle, Baby, jumped on her bed.

"Oh, here you are," my mother said, putting out her hand. Baby began licking my mom's right palm with great gusto before going straight for her lips.

"That's probably not the best thing," I murmured as I gently pushed away Baby. Baby stretched out next to my mom, who stroked her fur.

When my mom was diagnosed with vascular dementia, I slowly took on the role of guardian. But I was unprepared to see Baby — the elderly Poodle my mother had adopted from a shelter several years before — seamlessly switch roles from "the protected" to "the protector."

The first thing my mom did upon bringing home the little Poodle, originally named Holly, was change her name to Baby. My mother often said, "It's almost as if I gave birth to this Baby." I guess that makes

Baby, in some alternative reality, my little sister. Like my mother, I began treating the dog with great care, although for different reasons. "If anything ever happened to my dog, I would want to die," said my mother. Baby had become my mom's lifeline and, therefore, a priority of mine.

My mom had correctly discerned that Baby needed lots of tender loving care to come out of her shell. In fact, my mom's purpose in life became to help her dog feel happy, loved and protected. For my mom, that involved cutting up slices of rotisserie chicken to mix with dog food. When Baby became disinterested, my mother hand-fed her.

When the vet told her that Baby's howling was separation anxiety my mom cut back on her errands. When Baby woke her up in the middle of the night, my mom played with her until the dog fell back to sleep by her pillow.

Just before my mom turned ninety she rolled out of bed and fractured her hip. While I stayed with her overnight in the hospital, my mother's aide agreed to stay with Baby, who kept her up most of the night by howling.

When my mother came home the following evening, carried on a stretcher, Baby carefully watched while cautiously wagging her tail. From that time on, Baby seemed to make it her mission to help my mother feel happy, loved and protected. After looking at me for permission, Baby jumped into the bed and rested at Mom's side. At least for that time, my mom was consoled.

Baby adapted to my mom's needs and new routine. So as not to disrupt my mom's mealtimes, Baby sat on a pillow at the end of the bed, quietly watching. When one of the aides donned plastic gloves to put lotion on my mother or bathe her in bed, Baby knew to patiently lie on the couch until the work was finished and she could rejoin my mother in bed. Each night, when my mom was turned on her side to sleep, Baby was right there, snuggling up to Mom, ready to console her with licks when she awoke or seemed frightened.

Baby was protective of Mom in other ways. She began to bark each time residents walked or rode their scooters down the hallway past my mom's door. Baby didn't stop barking until we opened the door so she could sniff the hallway for any ne'er-do-wells.

As my mother declined, she often forgot our names. It no longer mattered whether she called Baby her "Potato," her "Seventy-seven," or numerous other creative monikers. Whenever she asked, "Where is...?" and her eyes began to scan the room, Baby made a beeline for her.

If Baby could, I'm quite sure she would have said, "No need to worry. I'm never far from you."

—Nancy K.S. Hochman—

The Dog We Needed

Dogs have a high capacity for empathy.
More than intuiting what we think,
dogs may also feel what we feel.
~Gregory Berns

Sometimes, we don't get the dog we want; rather, we get the dog we need. Case in point: Sunny, part Border Collie, returned to foster care three times before he came to live with us at ten months of age.

Sweet but traumatized, Sunny needed a stable environment. As a typical Border Collie, he was whip-smart and learned quickly, but we were frustrated by his excessive neediness and fear-based aggression.

As humans, we often think we're the only ones able to experience and express empathy. But as we got to know Sunny, we realized he had an uncanny ability to sense grief, trauma and illness. Not only would he sense something was wrong, but he would change his behavior and look for ways to comfort us during our darkest moments. We marveled at his gift.

A year or so after Sunny settled in, I sustained a brain injury that resulted in post-concussion syndrome and post-traumatic stress. I was exhausted, depressed, anxious and scared. My humans couldn't understand my symptoms and were generally unsupportive.

But Sunny taught me that I wasn't alone, and that he'd be there beside me every step of the way. If I was emotionally and mentally depleted, he'd lie beside me or at my feet. When I was bedridden, he would jump up beside me and lean against me or put his head or paw on my legs. I had psychotherapists and other healthcare professionals caring for me, but sometimes I just needed quiet to soothe my mind, and that's when Sunny came to my rescue, acting as doctor, teacher and confidant. He'd spend hours at my side, just being a dog. I sort of learned how to be a dog, too — to clear my mind, to be in the moment, and to be content just hanging out doing "nothing."

His limitless empathy — his ability to know when to provide support — saved my life.

Since then, Sunny has been with us through the loss of friends and family members, illness and upheavals. The love and joy he brought into my dad's life after my mom passed away was incredible to behold. After sixty-three years of spirited matrimony, losing my mom put my dad into a deep depression. His emotional state wreaked havoc on his physical body. He was prone to infection, his kidneys failed, and his heart was literally broken. He had to get a pacemaker.

We encouraged him to stay with us at our home where we could care for him. One day, Dad was sitting outside on our deck, crying quietly. I knew he was there, but I wanted to give him space to grieve.

Sunny had a different healing approach. I heard a giggle, then full-blown laughter, from outside. I walked to the window and looked out to see Sunny, his paws up on the chair, plastering kisses on my dad's face and washing away his tears. My dad was laughing, really howling, for the first time in ages. Job complete, Sunny sat beside him with a look that said, "Okay, what else do you need, Papa? We got this covered!"

Sunny gave my dad a new reason to live, an important role to play as "Dog Papa." He stopped in to visit Sunny when we weren't home, and the two of them played fetch for hours. My dad's mobility and mood improved when he was around the dog. He showed pictures of his grand-dog to anyone who would look.

Did we get the dog we wanted? The jury's still out. But we certainly were gifted with the dog we needed: Sunny, who taught us how to feel joy and share empathy and be in the moment.

— Catherine Kenwell —

Strider's Sixth Sense

When life grows cold, a dog will warm your soul.
~Angie Weiland-Crosby

Our Cocker Spaniel had recently passed away and it was time for our family to welcome another dog. While my family and I were enjoying a weekend in Wisconsin I saw an ad for black Lab puppies in the local paper.

We went to the breeder's and met the eight-week-old puppies, who were adorable. They were running around the yard with their ears flapping in the breeze. It was tough to choose, but we settled on one puppy who kept jumping into the laps of our children.

Strider joined us for the six-hour drive back to Illinois and was immediately a member of the family, which also included four cats and two horses. He loved to tease the cats, and he was also a little rascal with us. He would wake up my husband, pretending he needed to go outside, and then leave my husband at the top of the stairs and jump into his nice, warm spot in the bed next to me.

When Strider was three months old, I was diagnosed with breast cancer. I needed surgery and chemotherapy.

I returned home four days after the surgery and recuperated for another six weeks. Strider was with me the entire time. Then I began chemo and returned to work. I lost my hair after two weeks.

One cold January night, just days after completing another round of chemo, I was having difficulty sleeping. My body ached, and my head was terribly cold. As I stared at the clock, I wondered how I would be able to work in the morning.

Suddenly, Strider did something unusual. He moved from the foot of the bed and began pushing his way between my husband and me. "What is he doing?" my husband asked. I replied that I did not know, but that it was okay. Strider squished between us, and then he lifted his head and curled it up over the top of my head so that his chin was resting on my head. I felt very calm and relaxed. My head wasn't cold anymore. I was able to sleep that night.

A special bonding took place that night. Strider was only eight months old but he already seemed to have that special gift of a "sixth sense."

—Dawn O'Herron—

A Bond

True devotion is motivated by love alone
and devoid of selfish entanglements.
~Rick Hocker

"Katie, it's time, dear," my mother said over the phone through her sobs. I ran to the car and called my Jack Russell Terrier, Devon. She jumped in back, and off we went.

My father was in the end stage of his battle with cancer. I visited often and always brought along Devon. They had a special friendship as she and Dad had loved long walks together, a lively game of one-sided tennis, and chats by the fireplace.

Upon arrival at my parents' home, I was met by the hospice caregiver. "Don't bring that dog in here," he scolded. "This is your father's final hours, and I don't want to be hassled by some mutt."

Devon and I went quickly to Dad's room, ignoring the grumpy man. Not allowed on beds, Devon hopped up nonetheless and settled by Dad's side. Dad was in a coma.

"See, get that thing off!" the aide said.

As I went to reach for Devon, she quietly growled. In the sixteen years of our relationship, this was the only time she had made that aggressive noise.

"Leave her be," Mom said. "Bob has always adored that dog."

Our priest arrived and read Dad his last rites. At that point, I began to weep. Father Joseph also crossed Devon's forehead with holy water and prayed, "Saint Francis, bless your creature who gives such comfort." I shouldn't have glared at the hospice aide, but I did.

My brother and his family arrived. Other relatives stopped in to say goodbye. No one else had an issue with Devon. The hospice man was replaced when his shift ended. I was tempted to say that he had been inappropriate, but I just thanked him. He rolled his eyes as he walked out the door.

Devon rarely moved. Machinery was brought in to keep Dad comfortable. A nurse arrived to take notes and monitor his final hours. The room, at times, was crowded and full of emotion. Devon stayed still. Occasionally, she would lift her head and make eye contact with me. To this day, I can only guess as to her message. I tend to think that this motion was Devon's way of checking that I was alright and to make sure I had not left the room.

The nurse told us that Dad could still comprehend and that we should comfort him with our words. My mother went to sit in the living room as she was in such a state of grief. I wondered if Devon might need to relieve herself after so many hours, but I trusted her instincts.

Eventually, Devon and I were alone with my father. "Dad, I love you so," I whispered. "Everyone is here, and everyone will miss you beyond comprehension. Isn't it wonderful that Devon is by your side? You are the kindest man, and animals pick up on that."

I prattled on and on, recalling stories of our past together. The nurse interrupted from time to time to check Dad's vital signs and make sure he was comfortable. Time went by slowly. And Devon stayed put.

Fourteen hours came and went until my father slipped away. At the exact moment when he took his final breath, Devon sighed. Was this a coincidence? I think not.

We buried my father two days later. He had requested that some of his treasures — a pocket watch that was a precious gift from my mother, and a bottle of his favorite Scotch — were among those items. I added Devon's leather collar.

I read a eulogy that I had written, and Devon stood quietly by my side.

When Devon passed at the age of seventeen I spread most of her ashes on a butterfly garden but saved a small amount for my father's grave.

I went on to raise, show and judge Jack Russell Terriers for many years. But Devon will always be the special one who I hold close to my heart. I do not know how or why she knew all that she knew.

— Kathleen Gemmell —

About a Dog Named Sam

A dog has one purpose in life: to bestow his heart.
~J.B. Ackerley

It was the last year before I retired my Labrador Retriever, Samantha, from her role as a therapy dog. Sam and I had been volunteering in a shelter that offered support for women and children in need. A young mother and her four-year-old son had come to the shelter after leaving an abusive relationship. They had been in the shelter for several weeks, and the little boy, William, hadn't spoken since their arrival.

Every Saturday, Sam and I would visit and play with the children who were staying in the shelter with their mothers. And, every week, William and his mother would come to watch but never participate. We had tried to engage with William when he first arrived at the shelter, but he never left his mother's arms. No one was able to talk to him, come near him, or even touch him.

William and his mother had been watching us from their regular spot in the corner of the yard far away from everyone. His mother would tell me later that, while they were watching, she heard William softly say, "Sam."

Shocked to hear him speak, she repeated back to him, "Yes, honey, that's Sam." A moment later, he began squirming in her arms, and she did something I never thought I'd see: She put him down. He didn't wander far from her reach, but he did take a few steps away from her, standing by himself as he watched Sam play with the other children.

Barely a minute later, Sam, exhausted and needing a break, came to me for a scratch behind the ear, a cookie, and a lot of water. As I bent down on one knee and rubbed her face, I noticed her looking at William, but she knew from experience in the past several weeks that she had been unable to approach him. I finished rubbing her face, leaned in to give her a kiss, and whispered to her, “Go easy with him, doll. This is a big step for him.” She looked in my eyes, and I knew she understood. She returned to finish playing with the other children while William looked on, and that was enough for one day.

Two weeks passed, and each time we came, the same thing happened. William would come out to the yard, stand on his own, and watch Sam with the other children; no words, no playing, just observing.

One rainy day, we were unable to play outside, so we held the play session in the arts-and-crafts room. Moments later, the door opened, and William stood there with his mother. He immediately left his mother's side and went to a small, carpeted area away from all the other children and Sam.

I noticed Sam's attention turn from the other children to William. She slowly got up from her spot and went over to where he sat. She stood there for a moment, and their eyes locked on one another, as if in silent conversation.

He smiled, and she lay down on the farthest part of the carpet from him. He giggled, and she crawled a few steps closer. He giggled again, and she did the same. This continued until Sam had reached his side and rested her head on his legs.

It was the most amazing thing I had ever seen Sam do.

The two of them sat in silence, with Sam's head nestled in William's lap and him slowly stroking her fur, like two old friends who hadn't missed a beat. When the play time came to an end, William kissed Sam on her head, and she licked his face, nuzzling her nose in his neck as he hugged her goodbye.

The very next weekend, we saw a change in William again. He had begun speaking during the week and had left their room several times to eat in the dining room, each time walking and sitting on his own. He allowed staff members and a few children to talk to him.

When Sam and I arrived that Saturday, we joined the swarm of excited children in the yard. As the children headed for the swing sets and jungle gyms, they called for Sam to follow them. William stood all by himself just looking at Sam. She went to him. Embracing her, we heard him say, "I love you." Then he got up from his knees, with Sam beside him, and ran off to join the other children.

The following week, William and his mother left the shelter to start their new life. I ran into William's mother a few months later at a fundraiser we were hosting to raise money for the shelter. Hugging me, she thanked me for bringing my Sam to her son. William was adjusting well to his new school and their new apartment, and he had told his mother he planned to ask Santa for his very own Sam.

As months went by, Sam's body and health aged, and I decided it was time for her to retire from her role as a therapy dog. The following year, a staff member from the shelter called me to let me know that, in Sam's honour, they had decided to create a program of ongoing dog therapy in the shelter—a program that still to this day carries on in her name. Sam's plaque hangs in their memorial hallway as the first therapy dog in the shelter's thirty-year history. It is a testament to the healing that comes from a dog's love.

—Nanette Norgate—

A "Tail" from the Other Side

When I needed a hand, I found your paw.
~Author Unknown

I didn't want to keep my husband awake after bedtime, so I slipped into the guest bedroom to devour a couple of research studies that had grabbed my attention. Before long, I was ready to turn out the light and go to sleep.

Then, around midnight, a noise woke me up. At the same time, I thought I could feel the mattress sinking next to me. My heart started racing. I also felt some weight against my back and a strong sense of a physical presence. With my right hand, I touched something that felt like a dog's paw on my left shoulder. But my fear overshadowed that moment, and whatever I had sensed immediately disappeared.

As someone who prided herself on being a rational, evidence-based person, I dismissed the whole experience as a grief-related hallucination (sometimes referred to as a "bereavement hallucination").

A month earlier, my husband and I had said goodbye to our beloved black English Labrador Retriever. Our loyal friend would never take another walk with us, snuggle with us in bed, or look at us with his knowing eyes. Ranger was forever gone — or so we thought.

A year later, my husband and I decided we were ready for another dog — another black English Labrador Retriever. We found a picture online of an adorable puppy for sale. When I called to ask about the dog, the breeder gave me basic information about him, including his birthdate: March 29, 2013. Then she said, "There is one other thing you should know. The dog is already registered with the AKA as Midnight Lone Ranger." I thought to myself, *That's an interesting coincidence.*

While he had a much different personality than our first dog, Ranger II immediately became part of our lives. As an exceptionally social individual, he also became a member of our community, stopping to greet neighbors whenever he saw them. It didn't take long for the dog to have human and dog friends everywhere he went. Because of this guy, my husband and I became much more connected to our neighbors and community.

My husband developed a sturdy bond with Ranger II; they were nearly inseparable until my husband passed away nine years later. The last thing I remember my husband saying to me before he had a fatal heart attack was, "Make sure you get our boy in to see the vet soon; he's limping a bit." I promised my husband that I would take Ranger in for his scheduled check-up the next day.

Even though I was still numb with shock, I kept that promise. Other than being overweight, the dog was fine.

After my husband passed, Ranger II became my constant companion. One evening, when I felt like my heart was being crushed with grief, Ranger reached out his paw and placed it on my shoulder as he lay next to me on top of my bed. At that moment, everything "that is or ever was" felt interconnected; it was as though the universe was speaking to me — to that rational, evidence-based woman who still had so much to learn.

As I waded into the uncertain waters of widowhood, Ranger was there to comfort me and keep me connected to a different kind of evidence I could not rationally explain. One afternoon while walking with Ranger near a pond that my husband had often visited, I felt one of my widowhood pangs of sadness. My old dog stopped in his tracks and looked at me. I cried out to my husband, "Where are you? Do you even exist in some form?" Just then, a hummingbird zipped past me, literally flying right under my nose. My husband had loved hummingbirds and enjoyed watching them gather each morning at a feeder outside our dining room window.

In some ways, my old dog was a guide for my journey as a widow. With Ranger II's help, I learned to embrace a sense of wholeness that I can't logically explain.

When Ranger II was diagnosed with bladder cancer I knew I would need to say goodbye to my sweet companion, comforter, and guide. I would think of him as part of something bigger that I do not fully understand.

Ranger II passed on June 14, 2023. A couple of months later the image of another black English Labrador Retriever popped up on my computer; that puppy had been born on June 14th. He became Ranger III.

— Paula Marie Usrey —

A Dog Called Delta

A puppy is a bundle of joy with four tiny feet.
~Author Unknown

Our convoy pulled into the staging area after a long night working with our Iraqi Police counterparts. Somehow, we had one more passenger than we had originally taken on the mission. A young puppy had appeared in the debriefing area.

I closed my eyes and took a deep breath. "Where did the dog come from?" I asked as everyone smirked and shrugged their shoulders. Nobody owned up to it.

I knew this was a group effort. I had watched my soldiers feeding and petting the feral puppies. Although they were wild, the young puppies did not have a distrust for humans yet.

There was no way we could keep her. Bringing animals onto our operating base was strictly prohibited. Somebody would find out, and trouble would surely follow.

"Everybody leaves us alone," Lee, one of our civilian contractors, announced. "She can come back to my camp, and y'all can visit her whenever you want."

I thought to myself, *Why not just give her a name and make it official?*

"I reckon we should call her Delta on account of her living here," Lee proposed. The group agreed.

In the days ahead, soldiers were sneaking meat out of the chow hall every evening. One of them capitalized on our working relationship with a K-9 team for dog food. As one of our local interpreters returned from his weekend at home, he took a bag of dog food back with him "just in case anybody needs it."

Our living area was on the other side of the base, and I kept myself too busy to go visit. I had too many meetings to attend and too many operations to plan. I probably put more responsibility on myself than I should have, and I tried to control things that were not entirely in my control. I was desperate to bring everybody home safely. I became more and more detached from people as the stress accumulated. Building emotional walls is a common response to that kind of pressure.

After a patrol, Lee told me he would be waiting outside the operations center when the nightly meeting ended. His group was having a campfire with appetizers and near beer. (Drinks with alcohol were off-limits.) Someone had Budweiser barbecue sauce sent from home and coordinated chicken wings from the chow hall. Another had some fancy cigars shipped over. One of my soldiers got ingredients for homemade guacamole. It sounded like exactly what I needed, but I politely declined because I had too much work to do.

When the meeting got out, I heard, "Let's go, Dean." Lee was waiting for me and said that "no" was not an acceptable answer.

"I have a few minutes, and then I need to get back," I told him.

I got in the truck and went to his camp, where some of my soldiers and his contractors were hanging around. One of them walked over and handed Delta to me.

She was ten, maybe twelve weeks old, a brown dog with white markings and some black streaks around the eyes and snout. Her ribs weren't visible through her body anymore, like when I first saw her. She was soft. They had done a great job feeding her and cleaning her up.

I cradled her and scratched under her neck. She sniffed my face. *Please don't lick my face*, I thought. She licked my face.

"Is Dean smiling?" one of my soldiers asked.

"Someone take a picture!" another proclaimed. "He's showing an emotion!"

Delta fell asleep quickly. I couldn't move without waking her up, so the Budweiser wings were gone before I had a chance to get any food.

I held onto the puppy and let her sleep as a few of us made small talk by the fire. She slept for quite some time, so I just hung out for the night like a real person. It was the first humanizing experience I had felt in months.

They had to drag me there, but I needed it badly. Delta's nap forced me to take some time to relax and recharge. By the end of the evening, I felt much better, and I had a new friend.

— Elton A. Dean —

He Brought Back My Dad's Smile

Before you get a dog, you can't quite imagine what living with one might be like; afterward, you can't imagine living any other way.
~Caroline Knapp

I sprinted into the hospital's emergency entrance. "What room is my father in?" The receptionist, who knew me from high school, pointed down the hall on the right. "Follow that hall to the dead end and turn left. Room 417." Before I started off in that direction, she added, "I think he's stable now."

This was the third time that something horrible had happened to him since Mom died. The first two were little infections that could have easily been treated but were ignored until they got out of hand. It made me secretly worry that Dad was purposefully not taking care of himself, especially since he'd always taken care of himself before he lost his wife of forty-five years.

"Hey, Dad." I greeted him with as much of a smile as I could form. Underneath, I was working to keep the tears from streaming down my cheeks. To say I was worried about whether he'd be around in a year, a month, or even a day, was an understatement.

But he saw through the smile. He knew what I was thinking. "Don't worry, I wasn't ignoring anything this time."

I had to laugh at his directness. "So what was it?"

"Sepsis."

I nodded, although I had no clue what sepsis was at the time.

"The fever hit so fast that I started hallucinating. I called up Ann and started complaining about how she'd sent me one hundred texts in less than an hour. Turns out she never sent a one."

"Good thing she knew something was wrong and came to check on you," I said. Ann was a family friend and I was grateful to her.

"Yeah," he said, pausing in a way that made me feel unsettled. "The doctor said that I was only a few hours from death. If I hadn't gotten to the hospital when I did, I might not have made it."

The news struck too hard for me to react. I sat there, motionless, being rocked by the thought that my father had been that close to dying. The conversation moved to an awkward exchanging of pleasantries as both of us were apparently too shaken to think further about how he'd almost died.

As I sat in the hospital room, I prayed for him to find the will to thrive again. To find a reason to smile again.

A few weeks later, after Dad had been discharged from the hospital and given time to fully recover, he called and invited me up for a visit.

"Hey, Dad," I called out as I opened his front door. "How are…"

My jaw fell open as I looked into the room.

"Who…" I struggled to speak.

"What do you think?" Dad beamed, getting a good laugh at my shock, and gave the large, eighty-pound dog sitting next to him a scratch between the ears. "His name is Tank."

"That's a fitting name," I managed to say.

Tank, indeed. He was enormous, and gorgeous, a Chow mix.

"Can you believe he's still young enough to have some growing left? They think he'll be closer to ninety pounds once he's finished."

"No, I can't believe it."

But, most of all, I couldn't believe how big my dad's smile was. How long had it been since his smile had stretched all the way up to his ears?

"He was part of a training program at the prison. Watch this," Dad said. He motioned with his hand by bending it to bring the fingers down to the thumb, like a mouth closing shut.

Immediately, Tank let out a loud "Woof!"

"Ha!" Dad cheered and praised Tank with more scratches. "I can't wait to show the family that trick at Christmas. What do you think?"

"I love it!" I said, working to keep the tears from forming as happiness and relief poured through me. He was talking about Christmas. That meant he was planning on sticking around! I loved seeing Dad and Tank playing, but, most of all, I loved seeing Dad's smile and hearing his laughter again.

— Katrin Babb —

Special Bonds

A Light in the Darkness

I think the most beautiful thing in the world
is watching the light live on in someone
you love after they're gone.
~Robert M. Drake

Jeffrey's deep, rhythmic breaths fill the silence of the room. His head rests on my chest, his heartbeat a soft thrum against mine, steady yet fragile, as if he's still trying to find his place in this world. I look down at him, his eyes half-closed, and I'm taken back to the day when everything changed for both of us — the day we lost Dan.

The door to Dan's flat had creaked open slowly, revealing a room filled with my best mate's treasures — his guitar leaning against the wall, his mechanic tools scattered on the table, and a stack of old vinyl records by the window. But the room felt different, weighed down by a heavy stillness. I stepped inside and saw him lying there, still and quiet. My heart dropped. And there, beside him, was his greatest treasure — Jeffrey.

Only eight months old, Jeffrey lay pressed against Dan's side, his eyes filled with confusion and grief. He had been there for two days, waiting, guarding his person. I could see his little body trembling, his breath coming in heavy, labored sighs. He had tears on his face. I never knew dogs could cry like that. Jeffrey was more than just a dog to Dan; he was his constant companion, his solace during tough times. And now, Jeffrey had lost his best friend.

Dan wasn't just anyone — he was my best friend, an extraordinary mechanic who could bring any engine back to life, and a musician whose songs carried both joy and sorrow in their melodies. His smile was the kind that could light up a room, and his laugh was contagious. And he adored Jeffrey. That dog was his world, his anchor. Even when life got tough and the darkness closed in, Jeffrey was his guiding light.

On the kitchen counter, I found a note, the ink smudged with what could have been tears. "Take care of Jeffrey," it read. A simple but powerful request. And there, in that quiet, somber room, I made a promise — to Dan and to Jeffrey. I scooped up Jeffrey, his little body still shaking with sobs, and took him home.

When we arrived, he didn't stop trembling for hours. His breathing was erratic, and he seemed lost. I had never seen a dog in such a state of grief before. But my family welcomed him with open arms, and our other dogs seemed to sense his pain, giving him the space he needed. Slowly, Jeffrey began to settle, finding comfort in the warmth of a new family. But his eyes still held that deep sadness, a longing for the friend he had lost.

Jeffrey and I became inseparable in our shared grief. He was my link to Dan, a piece of him that I could still hold onto. We were both navigating a world that suddenly felt emptier, darker. Yet, in those quiet moments, when I'd look into Jeffrey's eyes, I felt a sense of purpose. We were meant to find each other. Two lost souls helping one another through the dark.

As Jeffrey grew into his late adolescence, he started having some negative experiences with other dogs. He became reactive, fearful of the world around him. I was working as a vet nurse then, and despite my love for animals, I didn't feel equipped to support him the way he needed. But I knew I had to learn. I owed it to Dan, to Jeffrey, and to myself to be the best guardian I could be.

That's when I decided to change my path and pursue a career in dog behavior. I reached out to Ian Shivers from Bondi Behaviourist, a man known for his compassionate, science-based approach to training.

I wanted to learn how to communicate with Jeffrey in a way that would help him feel safe and understood, just as Dan would have wanted.

Our first session was a revelation. Ian watched Jeffrey closely, then turned to me and said, "You need to listen to him." Those words hit me like a bolt of lightning. I realized that understanding Jeffrey wasn't about controlling him; it was about connecting with him, honoring his experiences, and building trust.

With Ian's guidance, Jeffrey and I began a journey of healing. Step by step, I learned to see the world from Jeffrey's perspective. I learned to celebrate his small victories and be patient with his fears. Our relationship grew stronger, built on love, empathy, and understanding. The more I learned, the more passionate I became. I continued my studies, diving deeper into behavior science, driven by the desire to help dogs like Jeffrey find peace in a world that often feels overwhelming.

Today, I specialize in reactivity-based behaviors, working alongside incredible dog guardians and their beloved dogs. Jeffrey and I are still learning together every day, growing and evolving. My goal has always been to provide him with a life filled with safety, love, and understanding — a life that Dan would have been proud of.

Jeffrey wasn't just a dog who came into my life during a time of loss; he was a guiding light who helped me find my purpose. Through him, I've found a way to honor Dan's spirit and his unwavering love for his best mate. We may have started as two broken beings, but together we've created something beautiful — a bond that will forever light the path ahead.

— Camille Hartnett —

Echoes of Love

Dogs leave paw prints on our hearts.
~Author Unknown

It's been a couple of decades, but the memory will remain with our family forever. Our daughter Jessica had a Parson Russell Terrier named Bailey. He was beautiful, white with a freckled belly and a larger-than-life personality—everyone he met fell in love with him.

Jessica got him when she was eighteen, and he went everywhere she went. After graduating from community college she decided to move to California with some friends. Of course, Bailey went, too.

In time, Jessica realized that her busy lifestyle wasn't suitable for him, so she made the painful decision to send him back home to live with us. We picked him up at the Albany International Airport with several bags of luggage that contained his wardrobe, toys, and various snacks that he enjoyed.

We loved and cared for Bailey for several years. One day, he fell ill. The vet said that he had a rare muscular cancer that had permeated his insides, and he wouldn't survive surgery. We had to let him go because he was in such terrible pain.

We decided to bury him on our property. We live on the upper Hudson River in upstate New York. Across from our property is a beautiful foothill. There aren't any homes there, just lots and lots of trees. Several years ago, we became aware that when we yelled toward the hillside there would be an echo. Sometimes, for fun, we'd shout out our names or lyrics to a song. We hadn't done it for years though, and we'd never heard an echo from anyone or anything else.

Jessica didn't even know it had happened because it was so sudden. So we had to call her and break the news. That sad day, at dusk, we chose the spot for Bailey's little cardboard coffin, and we called Jessica. Of course, she cried. We all did. And then, as we said our goodbyes to Bailey, we heard something unexpected. In the distance, we heard a dog bark. Then, we heard his echo. It was as if Bailey was saying goodbye to us, too.

We couldn't believe our ears. Jessica heard it too. We had never heard a dog bark there before.

In time, Jessica returned home to live in New York. She moved back with three Pit Bulls this time around. The two males returned to their original family but the female stayed with Jessica. Eventually, she and her partner Chad adopted another Pit Bull as well.

Time passed, and we heard the two males had died. And then the female died, too. Jessica decided to bury her alongside Bailey.

And that's when it happened. As we put the last clump of earth on the new grave, we heard something through our tears. A dog barked, and then an echo followed, just like years ago with Bailey. It was another magical moment. But what we heard next was a shock to us all. We heard at least two or three other dogs bark in the distance. It wasn't the echo this time, though. It was as though the barks were coming from somewhere else, as though the other family dogs, the ones who had already passed, were there.

No one spoke at first, but then Chad broke the silence. He had heard the story about how we had heard Bailey bark back in the day, but he admitted that he hadn't really believed it. I mean, do things like that really happen? But he was here with us this time. He heard it as plain as day. We could only nod and smile at what we had all just experienced.

Since that day four years ago, we haven't heard any dogs barking.

There seems to be such a thin veil between the now and the

hereafter. I feel relief knowing that those threads that connect us, both heart and soul, can withstand time, distance, and space and can never be broken.

— Kim Garback Diaz —

My Temporary Tommy

Since there is nothing so well worth having as friends,
never lose a chance to make them.
~Francesco Guicciardini

A beautiful Golden Retriever bounds up to me by a bench in the park. A breathless man arrives a few strides behind and commands, "Sit." The dog and I both sit. The man and I laugh, and then he sits, too.

"What's his name?" I ask.

"Tommy," the man says, "and I'm Ben." Then he commands, "Tommy, shake."

Tommy lifts his paw, and I lift mine, and we shake. I stroke his shiny coat. Tommy snuggles up like an old pal.

"He really likes you," says Ben.

"Oh, I bet he's like this with all the girls," I say, surprised. It's been a long while since I've felt and reciprocated such sudden approval.

"Not really. He's been kind of a one-man dog his first two years."

We all stroll the park like pals. Ben emails days later, and we three meet near my house for an outdoor supper. Tommy adds spontaneity to every moment. Ben also has a puppy-like appeal.

Ben tells me he is divorced with a daughter living far away. When he was going through a hard time recently, Tommy cheered him up.

I feed Tommy crusts under the table, so he won't feel left out. He devours them with gusto. I admire how Tommy obeys Ben's commands: "High-five, sit, speak, pray, love."

We talk about favorite performers and make a ten-dollar wager about the title of a Willie Nelson film. Ben goads me to the point that I must prove I'm right or lose face.

I lose face and ten dollars, as verified by Google, and he and Tommy walk me home to get the money. After sniffing everything, Tommy makes himself comfortable and offers up his abdomen to me for a scratch.

"Hey, whose house is this?" I feign indignation but like having him there. This is good practice for a dog relationship, if not for a human one. I love Tommy's ingratiating way of sneaking his head under my hand to get attention. We have a chemistry that Ben encourages. I sense Ben is keeping something secret, while Tommy reveals everything.

The next time he visits me with Tommy, Ben brings me a Willie Nelson biography and my own dog bowl.

"This feels so sudden," I say. Then, Ben takes a breath and tells me.

"We've just met, and I feel awkward telling you, but I'm in end-stage renal failure and high on the list for a transplant for an older donor's organ. Rather than waiting seven years for a younger organ, which everybody wants, with so few to go around, I've elected to accept a transplant from someone older. I'll be grateful for a chance after five years on dialysis, although sad that someone has to lose their life to save mine."

"Oh, Ben, I'm so sorry," I say.

He further explains, "And I'm sorry to ask this of you as you're such a new friend, but I have no local family." He laughs and adds, "And most of my other friends are cat people. I've been looking at kennels and finding them pretty unpleasant. Tommy isn't so crazy about other dogs. He prefers human company."

Near tears, he asks if I would care for Tommy should he need to go into surgery in the weeks to come. Without hesitation, I say yes. I feel chosen, not burdened by the idea.

The call comes three days later. Ben's second on the transplant list, but the first person on the list has the flu and can't proceed. Ben will drive three hours to the hospital to which the kidney is being helicoptered on ice. His surgery will begin early the next morning after he's prepped and scrubbed. Late that night, he brings Tommy and his dog bed.

"Don't worry," I say. "I'll take care of him. Call as soon as you can and let us know how it goes."

Ben is deeply grateful, and Tommy whines in empathy. Ben has waited for years on dialysis three days a week and will be glad when that phase is over. My heart aches for him. He asks if I will care for Tommy for as long as it takes him to get out of the hospital, or far more if something goes wrong.

"He has really taken to you. No one else feels as right as you do. Believe me, I've been looking."

"Of course, I'll keep him as long as it takes," I pledge. "We'll cross all our fingers and paws for you."

This all feels fated, somehow, that I be Tommy's temporary caretaker and Ben's friend at this intense time.

Moments are spent orienting me to Tommy's additional supplies, with Tommy getting used to my yard. The two have a calm and resolved farewell. Will I walk Tommy two to three times a day? Will I keep his water bowl full? Will I keep him on his leash except for runs in our neighborhood park?

"Yes to everything. Don't worry, we'll be fine. Now you go get yourself well."

Then off Ben drives into the night. After some whining by the front door, Tommy settles in cozily for his stay.

A nurse calls the next night and reports that the operation was long but successful, and Ben is convalescing. I'm very glad. I tell Tommy the good news and get a lot of wags in answer.

As days pass, every night, Tommy goes to the door and barks, looking for Ben. I take his big head in my hands, and I explain gently that his daddy will be back soon.

Tommy looks from one of my eyes to the other. Perhaps this is another trick that Ben taught him, but I feel he understands. He sighs deeply and sidles up to me for another evening. He sleeps on the bed by my side, and I like feeling close and needed.

Ben phones from his hospital bed four nights later, frustrated.

"Sorry to say that the organ is rejecting me," he says.

"Oh, no!"

"It's a common thing, but I have to go back on dialysis and heavy drugs until it accepts me."

I get a crazy idea. "Put your cell phone on the kidney," I tell him. He does.

"Tommy? Speak," I say to the Golden.

Tommy looks bewildered, cocking his head until he hears Ben's voice command him to "speak" over the speaker. Then, he whines, barks, and then barks again sharply. I tell him to "pray" and tell Ben he does. I truly believe that precocious Tommy gets what's going on. I just hope the kidney gets it, too. I yell, "C'mon, kidney!" for extra support.

Within twenty-four hours, the reluctant organ takes hold and begins to cooperate. Ben calls to tell us he's on the mend, and we all bark and cheer.

Ten days later, a thinner but happier Ben returns. Tommy is ecstatic, leaping and yelping.

We pack up Tommy's things and say so long. Tommy gives my face many kisses, and I give both hugs as they head out my door.

And being Tommy's temporary caretaker got me ready for a creature of my own.

— Melanie Chartoff —

The Wonder Dog

Caregiving often calls us to lean into love
that we didn't know possible.
~Tia Walker

"I'm going to be very honest," the oncologist said as she looked into my eyes with trepidation. "You're looking at three to six months at best."

A lump formed in my throat, and I tried to catch my breath. I almost grabbed her garbage can to throw up. Just months? I covered my face and sobbed in her office. Charlie, a handsome eleven-year-old Jack Russell with a perfectly placed mohawk genetic mutation, still played like a puppy. But he was newly diagnosed as diabetic because he had an insulinoma tumor that created too much insulin in his body. The diabetes put him in a dangerous state. If he could be stabilized, we would need to maintain his insulin at the correct levels for the rest of his life while fighting the tumor.

I'd always wanted a dog, and I found Charlie during my second year of law school when he was eight weeks old. He put a paw print on my heart when, out of all his brothers and sisters, he was the only puppy to sit and wait his turn to meet me. He was the smallest and only fully white puppy, with a brown ear and brown patch around his eye.

When it came to naming him, that was easy. Growing up, I was a fan of the X-Men superheroes, and like the X-Men, Charlie also had a mutation with his mohawk. I will never forget my brother saying, "He's like a member of the X-Men with that mohawk," and he was right. With no question, we agreed he would be Charles Xavier, and like the Charles Xavier in X-Men, he was brilliant and would spend his life protecting me with every piece of his heart and soul.

Charlie started his life with me on Long Island, in a suburb of New York City, filling my days with love and sometimes crying when I had to leave him while I studied. He never left my lap as I submarined for three months for the New York Bar Exam. He seemed to love watching the study videos with me.

When I moved to New York City to start a new life after a failed engagement, he made me laugh through the tears and adjusted to the city flawlessly. Although the apartment was a small space, he found joy in every nook and loved sitting in front of the window so that he could bark at the dogs strolling down his street.

When my father unexpectedly died three months after we moved there, he licked my tears and slept on my chest. When it came to dating, he was steadfast in skepticism and judgment — until he met my now husband, Jarrett, who had him at the first morning walk.

Over the next four years, Charlie survived a tornado in Connecticut with my mother, lived in three different states, and was overjoyed when my husband and I bought him a house in the mountains.

He had already survived so much, and he had supported me through so many ups and downs. Giving up on him was not an option. He never gave up on me.

As I sat in the oncologist's office, I took my hands away from my face and inhaled deeply. "It's not his time yet. Let's try." I met the doctor's eyes, which were now filled with tears of relief. We stared at each other. In the silence, there was mutual respect and understanding.

"I'm glad you made that choice. Let's keep him overnight to see if he'll pull through."

Even though Charlie was dying, he managed to lick me as I handed him off to the hospital. Concern for himself did not exist; only love for me did. If I were to tell you I slept at all that night, I would be lying. It was one of the longest nights of my life.

The next morning, Jarrett and I got a phone call that filled us with what I can only describe as unequivocal hope. The hospital was astonished by Charlie's resilience and strength. When we picked him up, he nearly wriggled out of the nurse's arms. He put his paws on my chest, licking my entire face while he wagged his tail furiously. Our little X-Man was coming home. I remember leaning my head against the window in the car with Charlie on my lap as we drove home, rubbing his soft ears in my hands. I closed my eyes and smiled. It was not his time yet.

It's been a year and a half since we were told that Charlie only had three to six months to live. Not a single moment goes by when I forget the gift of these moments. He spends his days chasing squirrels and tennis balls in the mountains of Connecticut, barking at animals on the TV, cuddling with his favorite stuffed lobster and, most importantly, giving his parents more love than we could imagine.

When people ask us how we handle his care, we tell them that we just do. To say it is difficult to balance it all would be an understatement. When we cancel or turn down plans because we don't want to leave his side, it's because every minute with him counts. I made the choice to be his mother thirteen years ago, and I'm going to see that through to the end. The truth is, unless you've experienced the pure love of a dog, you'll never understand the sacrifices you're willing to make. They devote their lives to giving us every piece of their heart and deserve nothing less than that from us.

One evening, Jarrett and I came home from dinner and looked through the window to see where Charlie was. He was perched on the couch, staring out at the sunset over the ridgeline. We looked at each other, overwhelmed by the beauty of this moment. Charlie was truly living his best life. "The Wonder Dog" is what his vet calls him, and that couldn't be truer. He truly is a Wonder Dog. Maybe that should be his X-Man name.

— Annmarie Sitar —

To Love Again

Dogs come into our lives to teach us about love,
they depart to teach us about loss. A new dog never
replaces an old dog. It merely expands the heart.
~Erica Jong

The story of my Collie, Chivas Regal, began with the death of my pet rabbit, Boof. One cold autumn day, I arrived home to find Boof lying on his side by the patio door where he'd usually wait for me to come home.

He was alive, but barely. I believe he hadn't given in to death only because he wanted to say goodbye. Within twenty minutes of my arrival, Boof passed away.

For the next month, I could barely function. I'd go to work, come home, and fall asleep. Boof's absence left an enormous hole in my world.

A month after losing Boof, I made a stop at the local coffee shop and noticed an ad featuring a Sheltie on the shop's bulletin board. The ad read: "Losing our house. Seeking a good home for Chivas."

The proprietor noticed my interest.

"Sad situation. The guy got laid off, and the house is in foreclosure," he said. "The dog is seven. Seems nobody wants an old dog."

"What are they going to do if no one takes the dog?" I asked.

"He's probably going to have to take it to the shelter," he replied. "They don't have much choice."

I returned to my car feeling sick. I felt sympathy for this family, but there was no room in my heart for another pet.

Over the next few days, I couldn't get Chivas out of my mind. What were the odds of anyone adopting an older dog within the next week? I imagined them taking Chivas to the shelter. I imagined the dog looking hopefully at visitors. I imagined a veterinary technician leading the poor creature to the room where he'd be euthanized.

I made a deal with myself. If the ad was still on the bulletin board in five days, I'd give them a call.

On the morning of day five, I walked into the coffee shop and copied down the phone number. I studied the picture of the dog; his eyes seemed to look right into mine.

"Are you still trying to find a home for your pup?" I asked when they answered the phone.

"We were going to take him to the shelter tomorrow," a man said. "Please come over and see if you like Chivas. If you can take him, we'll love you forever."

As I pulled into their driveway, I saw a thirty-something husband and wife, an infant, and a red-headed boy of about six years of age. The boy's face was blotchy, as if he'd been crying. The husband looked dejected, tired, and guilty.

I studied the wife and knew Chivas was her dog. I saw a pain so deep that it could never be expressed without breaking her. Parting with the dog was the hardest thing she'd ever done, and I sensed it would weigh heavily on her soul.

Then, I noticed the dog and gasped in wonder. What I had thought was a Sheltie was actually a beautiful Rough Collie that looked exactly like Lassie. He appeared dejected—tail drooping, his head cocked at an angle.

I got out of the car and introduced myself apologetically, knowing I would be taking away a precious member of their family.

"His name is Chivas Regal," the man said, sniffing. "We were trying to give him a Scottish name since he's a Scottish breed."

The red-haired boy looked at me with anger and confusion, his arm draped protectively over the dog.

The woman tried to keep a brave face.

"I taught Chivas some neat tricks. Let me show you what he can do," she said.

Suddenly, she began sobbing and ran into the house, apologizing along the way.

I wanted to explain that I, too, was suffering, but that seemed selfish. My pain was different. Boof had died in my arms after a long life. Their dog was in his prime, and they were losing him to a stranger.

I called Chivas to me, and he jumped up and woofed into my face. He seemed to sense my sadness as he laid his head on my shoulder and whined. He was big and fuzzy and sad. I fell instantly in love with this gentle soul.

Watching the family bid farewell to Chivas, I felt a welling of guilt and grief. Though their pet hadn't died like Boof, they'd likely never see him again. The woman had returned to bid farewell to the dog she had loved for years. I watched as she whispered something into his ear and held onto him as if she were drowning.

In my rearview mirror, I watched the family stand in shock. Tears were running down their faces, and I, too, began to cry for their pain.

When Chivas and I arrived home, I felt the last vestiges of Boof's spirit float gently away. Bringing a new pet into his domain seemed like the worst betrayal. I put my head in my hands and wailed, until a cold, wet nose interrupted my pity party.

While wallowing in my own misery, I had forgotten the dog's pain. He had just lost his family and didn't understand why. I saw his confusion. What had happened to his people? Wasn't he a good dog?

I threw my arms around his neck, and we mourned together.

Chivas lived another seven years. He was such a beautiful soul, so gentle, intelligent, and loving. Although I invited his former family to visit, they never did. I understood it would be too painful.

Over the next couple of years, I sent them photos and holiday gifts in gratitude. One day, the gifts were returned, undeliverable. They had moved.

A year later, I married, moved to a farm, and gave birth to my daughter, Justine. Chivas was protective of her. Otherwise, he wouldn't hurt a fly. Our chickens and cat had nothing to fear. Even the wild rabbits stood their ground when Chivas emerged from the house, knowing the big dog was no threat.

Time marched on, and Chivas grew old and arthritic. Then came the day when Chivas could no longer get up to go outside. He'd whine softly, looking into my eyes, communicating his pain. I held my precious dog against me, my arms around his beautiful scruff, hating what I knew had to be done.

We carried Chivas to the car, holding him gently as he tried not to cry out in pain. Chivas loved everyone, even the veterinarian. At that moment, I hated the veterinarian, knowing what he would do to my dog. I prayed for a miracle.

Chivas woofed happily at the veterinarian and licked the hand that held the syringe. I wanted to scream. Instead, I held my dog, looked deep into his eyes, and saw he was ready to go. I squeezed tight and remembered Boof, who was still alive in my heart. I felt Chivas sigh and then relax. His pain was gone. Mine had just begun.

We took our beloved Collie home and buried him next to Boof under the juniper bushes. The sorrow lingered, but I accepted it with grace. Grief is natural after a profound loss.

In the end, Chivas taught me a lesson. I learned that adopting Chivas was never a betrayal to Boof. Love is never limited. It's like a flame that is never diminished by sharing its light. Boof and Chivas share space within my heart. And there's still plenty of room for more.

— Rose Panieri —

The Most Special Visits

The bond between a dog and their human
is unlike any other.
~Charles Schulz

Have you ever been so dog-tired that you can't even muster the energy to fetch a tennis ball? That's how wiped out I am right now, so obviously I don't feel like writing this Chicken Soup for the Soul story for Wood-daddy. But he knows my weakness for dog biscuits, so here I am pawing away at his keyboard.

My name is Murray. I'm a ten-year-old Boxer and I'm named after the late Pulitzer Prize-winning sportswriter Jim Murray. My dad is a sportswriter too.

Why is my long tongue dragging, you ask? Because my two favorite people in the entire universe were just home to visit me, that's why! No offense to Alpha Pops and Mama Lisa, but My Girl and My Boy make my heart race double-time and my tail wag faster than a Ringo Starr drumstick.

This is saying something because I adore Mama so much that I am her constant shadow. Even if I'm snoozing in a warm, sunlit spot, I'll jump up and follow her if she leaves the room — except when My Girl and My Boy are home.

And for the past two weeks, My Girl was home for the first time in ages. I was so surprised to see her that I did my trademark "helicopter" greeting where I spin around and around and around while simultaneously bucking up and down and up like a bronco with a spur under its saddle. U.S. Olympic gymnast Simone Biles would be envious of my gold-medal floor routine.

At my age, I needed a short nap afterward, but first I had to take My Girl for a long walk and show her the neighborhood again.

When I was a puppy, My Girl lived away at college. But two things really bonded us. First, she is the only one who lets me break the "Murray, get off the bed!" house rule. Second, a few years ago, I needed eye surgery, and she took time off work and came home to Southern California from the Bay Area to nurse me while lovebirds Mama and Pops were on an anniversary trip in Ireland. Since then, we've been BFFs.

My Boy, however, has been my bestest best friend from Day One when he picked me out of the litter. I slept in his lap during the long drive home. He was a high-school freshman, and every day after track and cross-country practice I would keep him company when he took an ice bath for his legs. I was so small back then that I had to stand on my hind legs to see over the edge of the bathtub.

Now I'm eighty-nine pounds — "all muscle and mischief" My Boy likes to say — and we still gator-wrestle on the ground like two young pups. My joints are old now, but I'm forever young with him. He even pretends not to notice that my muzzle has grown gray.

My Boy now lives in New York City, so I don't get to see him very often, but we sometimes Skype. I always recognize his voice right away and do a few "helicopter" spins. Some people won't believe this, but I knew with a sixth sense when he was coming home to see me five minutes before he walked through the front door. I was so happy that I almost flew to the ceiling doing my "helicopter" with extra enthusiasm!

For four days — it seemed like twenty-eight — my wagging tail didn't rest because My Boy and My Girl were home at the same time. It was like old times. It was nirvana, I tell you, doggy heaven.

So, you can imagine my hangdog face when I saw them packing their suitcases. I have been napping even more than usual since they left. And my dreams have been a long road of happy memories with My Boy and My Girl.

As I hold loyal sentry at the front window, watching for my two best friends to return once more, I am comforted by a quote attributed to Dr. Seuss: "Don't cry because it's over. Smile because it happened."

I can't wait until it happens again.

— Woody Woodburn —

Imaginary Dogs

My dog is not just a pet; he's family.
~Author Unknown

My husband and I both grew up in wide open spaces where the chickens, pigs, dogs and pretty much all animals roamed free. So now that we lived in the city, we didn't want to get any pets that would have to be confined.

Our two sons, however, loved dogs. The first word my older boy, Caleb, learned to say was not "mom" or "dad." It was "woof." He would be on his bed ready to go to sleep, and when he heard the neighbor's dog barking, he would sit up and say "Woof, woof!" over and over.

Even before he learned to read, all our younger boy, Jared, would pick for me to read to him were books about dogs. At three years old, he knew more about dogs than I did at age thirty.

One day, they were playing in the backyard when suddenly we heard Jared crying very loudly. Most moms can tell when it's a serious cry, and this was the real thing. I rushed outside, thinking maybe he had hurt himself, but I couldn't see anything amiss.

I asked him what was wrong. With tears streaming down his cheeks and between sobs, he said, "Caleb doesn't want to lend them to me."

"What doesn't he want to lend you, Jared?"

"The dogs!"

"What dogs?"

"We were playing we had dogs, and he doesn't want to lend them to me!"

At this point, I almost burst out laughing, but instead I asked him, "How many dogs are there?"

"Twenty!" he exclaimed.

Caleb was just standing there looking somber, and I felt that inside he was stubbornly holding on to his twenty imaginary dogs.

I felt this was serious for them in their little minds, so I tried to settle the dispute just as if Caleb needed to share something real, not imaginary.

And then I went inside and told my husband. We had a good laugh but decided then and there that we needed to get them a dog. So we did. We got them a little Chihuahua they named Fifi.

— Ellie Sanchez —

Cardinal Blessings

Until one has loved an animal, a part of one's soul remains unawakened.
~Anatole France

Our five-pound Yorkie, Burke, was nearing the end of his eighteen years on Earth. He was blind and finding it hard to get around the house. We let him find his own way, which sometimes meant bumping into furniture or walls, but we wanted him to keep his independence as long as possible.

Burke and I had bonded immediately the day we met, and I had been his person ever since. He would follow on my heels wherever I went, and he loved nothing more than to lie in my lap.

It had gotten to the point where Burke was incontinent and wearing doggy diapers. We had to carry him outside to go potty and keep him in a kennel at night. He had always slept in our bed, so this was sad for all of us. He was becoming frail and thin, as he would just nibble at his food. We tried mixing his kibble with his favorite, healthy "people snacks" — blueberries, carrots, potatoes — and his treats, but his interest in eating was dwindling.

One day, he just stopped eating. My husband had to fly up north for work, so I spent Burke's last days with him. He slept in bed with me, and we shared sweet talks about our memories: Burke hiking six miles on his little legs but keeping up with us; Burke riding in a bike basket on our cycling trips; Burke riding shotgun on all our road-trip adventures; and Burke running on the beach, chasing gulls. I wanted to keep him with us until my husband returned, but it became obvious that he was getting weaker. Although he didn't seem to be in pain, it didn't feel right to keep him alive when he was ready to go.

I called the vet and made an appointment. I spent our last day rocking him in "our" rocking chair, singing to him, and sitting out in the warm Arizona sun with him on my lap while I cried buckets of tears. On our ride to the vet, I talked quietly to him, and I think he was comfortable and at peace.

The vet had a side door that we could go through into a softly lit meditative space. We didn't have to go through the lobby, which was a blessing since Burke didn't like going to the vet.

We were given as much time as we needed, so we sat quietly on the comfy sofa while I told him what a good boy he was and how much I loved him. When it was time, the vet gently administered the injection. Within seconds, Burke was gone.

The house felt too quiet without our baby, and I kept expecting to see him come around the corner or hear him crying for attention. On the second day after his passing, I was setting up a little memorial table for him when I heard a tap-tap-tapping somewhere in the house. I went looking for it and found a beautiful red cardinal sitting on our windowsill, tapping on the glass. We had never seen cardinals in our yard before, and I knew in my heart it was Burke's messenger checking on me and letting me know that he was okay.

The following day, I was taking a walk in the neighborhood, imagining that Burke was walking next to me, and a cardinal landed on the sidewalk ten feet in front of me and flitted around. Another message from our little guy that he was with us.

My husband came home, and the house seemed so empty with our little family member absent. We were sitting at the dining room table one morning having coffee and tearfully talking about Burke when a pair of cardinals landed on the tree outside our window. That same day, the pair of cardinals again tapped on our window.

I had heard that cardinals were messengers from our loved ones who had passed, and my friend has had many cardinal visits since her son died. I didn't know that beloved pets could also send messengers, and it fills my heart to overflowing to know that we are only separated by a thin veil.

Recently, I attended a reading by a psychic at Miraval Spa in Arizona. She was beginning a reading for another person, and I asked if I could leave to go to the bathroom. She said, "Yes," and I stood to leave but then she stopped me as I was opening the door. She said, "I see a rainbow around you and a teeny, tiny dog, a Terrier, trying to get your attention. He is so excited to see you and wants you to know he is always with you." I was stunned and started crying.

I love these confirmations that the love continues. Even in my sadness, my heart is full.

— Margie Pasero —

Sunny and Emie

When you feel lousy, puppy therapy is indicated.
~Sara Paretsky

I immediately recognized the song "Für Elise" playing on my phone. It was my daughter April's ringtone. I got nervous at first as my young granddaughter was home recovering from hand surgery.

"Is something wrong? Is Emie okay?" I quickly answered. I heard a tiny voice on the other end.

"Hi, Grandpa. Will you come with us to get my new puppy?"

I was relieved at hearing Emie's voice but also surprised because I didn't think that my daughter would want to bring a puppy home this soon after surgery.

"I sure would," I said. "How are you feeling today?"

"My hands hurt, Grandpa. Want to talk to Mommy?"

April got on the phone and told me how Emie had woken up with painful hands that day. To comfort her, they began reading about dogs. Of course, Emie immediately asked if she could get a puppy. My daughter thought it might be a good idea and suggested to Emie that they might want to consider a rescue dog.

They got on the computer and came across a not-so-small Labrador Retriever named Sunny. What caught their attention about this particular dog was that the summary said he had a deformed paw. Emie told her mom that she should have this dog with a special paw because she had special hands.

That Saturday, we all packed into the van and headed for the kennel. When we arrived, the clerk knew we were there to see Sunny. She explained that Sunny had been there for quite a while with no takers. But that day, a young couple had appeared and they were down at Sunny's kennel. She took us to see him anyway, and on the way, she reminded us that Sunny was a little older than a pup and that his front left paw was deformed.

"The paw appears lifeless, just hangs there. You'll see what I mean when we get there. It's possible he was born that way."

As we approached the kennel, the smile on Emie's face got bigger and bigger, but we couldn't get very close because the young couple was standing in front of us. We then heard the lady tell her husband that this was the dog she wanted. Hearing that, Emie began crying. The lady turned around and saw our little girl crying and her hands all bandaged up.

She looked at April and back at Emie. "What's the matter, honey?" she asked.

"I wanted Sunny. He has a special paw just like my hands."

The young woman looked at April. "May I ask what happened to her hands?"

April explained that Emie was born with a prenatal condition called Amniotic Band Syndrome. Before birth, string-like tissue in the amniotic sac broke loose and wrapped around her hands, which prevented them from growing normally. She told the young woman that the doctors said she would need numerous surgeries up to adulthood to improve function, and they would never be normal. April continued telling the story of how they read dog books and decided to look on the computer for a rescue dog, which is how they came across Sunny.

The young lady listened intently and, for a moment, just stood there very quietly. Slowly, she turned and looked at Sunny in his cage and at his paw. She then turned and whispered something to her husband and turned back to Emie. With tears running down her cheeks, she bent down and told Emie, "Honey, if you want this dog, then he's yours! There's plenty of other dogs that I can choose from. I think you two were meant for each other."

Emie screamed with excitement and gave the young woman a hug.

Before long, we were in the van on our way home with Sunny. Emie was excited, and so was I.

Sunny, however, did not come without baggage. We felt he must have been severely abused and had some sort of anxiety issue. When left alone, he did thousands of dollars of damage to the furniture and walls. He tore holes in the leather couch and chairs and chewed the corners off the dining room table. He walked and ran with a limp due to his "special" paw and wouldn't play fetch or chase anyone. And he never, ever wagged his tail. Even with all these issues, the family was committed to keeping Sunny.

Through the years, Emie and Sunny grew up together. Every night, when the family went to bed, Sunny would make his rounds and sniff each bedroom door. When he was satisfied that everyone was safe, he lay down at the foot of Emie's bed to sleep.

Emie had many more surgeries, and after each one, she would lie on the floor with bandaged hands and try to pet Sunny's paw and whisper secrets in his ear. Sometimes, she would pick up his tail and wag it for him or put her arm around him and take a nap. Sunny was very protective of Emie, and he provided her with immeasurable comfort and unconditional love through the years. Emie, in return, provided Sunny with a special bond and purpose in life. As the young woman said, they were meant for each other.

I often reflect on that moment in the kennel when that young woman made the decision not to take Sunny. I wonder if she has any idea of the impact that one generous decision had on my granddaughter and Sunny.

One summer day, years later, we were all out in the backyard for a picnic. Emie came running up to me and grabbed my arm. "Grampa, come look at Sunny. You won't believe it. You just won't believe it." We walked around the corner of the house, and there stood Sunny watching everyone play, finally wagging his tail. I couldn't believe my eyes. I never did figure out what made this day so special for Sunny that he began to wag his tail, but once he started, he never stopped.

—James B. Zambelli—

Murphy and Jerry

To love a person is to learn the song in their heart and sing it to them when they have forgotten.
~Arne Garborg

On a chilly autumn day, my father's dog and I drove to my parents' home for our "normal" visit. As always, when we exited the highway, Murphy paced in the back seat and barked with his usual excitement.

My father Jerry loved dogs… as a young boy… as a teenager… as an adult. He had Rollo, Dardy, Leo, and Prince, and he always took good care of them. As Jerry got older, so did his dogs, and each one died of old age.

For a while, my dad went without a dog. We all noticed that, for him, something was missing. That's when Jerry met Murphy. As soon as my father walked into the animal shelter, a giant mountain of fur ran over to greet him, sat down, and gave him his paw. Jerry knew they'd become good friends. So, he took Murphy home.

Every day, my dad took Murphy to work with him at his car dealership. Murphy loved sitting in the back of a truck or the front seat of a sports car. They were happy together. Then, something strange happened. My father began to forget things. He couldn't find his keys or his shoes. Occasionally, he even forgot to turn off the kettle after he made a cup of tea. He became very confused.

There were times when my father forgot to feed Murphy. We noticed that Murphy would stand by his bowl and bark until Jerry came into the kitchen. When Murphy started gaining weight, we realized that sometimes my dad fed him twice.

My parents went to different doctors to find out why my father was forgetting so much. After many visits and a lot of tests, we discovered that he had Alzheimer's disease.

Soon afterward, Murphy sensed that his new job was to take care of my father. And that's what he did. At home, Murphy was always beside my dad with his paws on Jerry's feet. We noticed when they went for walks that Murphy stood between the curb and my dad, so Jerry wouldn't trip or fall. And when Jerry walked in the wrong direction, Murphy always guided him home. Eventually it made more sense, though, for Murphy to live with me and visit his human dad.

On the day of my visit, Murphy and I walked through my parents' house. When Murphy saw my father out back, he pulled on the leash. My dad, in his cozy jacket, hat, and gloves, was sitting in his favorite chair on the deck, surrounded by beautiful trees, some still with a few leaves.

I kissed my dad and sat down next to him. Murphy lay at my father's side and put his paw on Jerry's foot to say hi, but my dad didn't notice. I was telling my father about the events of the week when suddenly he looked down toward the dog, petted Murphy's head, and said in a clear voice, "Well, hello, good boy. You're a good boy. What a good boy!"

It was amazing! My father was back. Besides our singing "Red, Red Robin" together, I hadn't felt my dad's sense of presence in a very long time.

Murphy noticed, too. He leaped up and licked my father's face. Then, with all his 110 pounds, he tried to climb onto my dad's lap! When he couldn't, Murphy twirled and raced in circles, each time coming back to Jerry, licking his face and hands.

Then, my father looked directly at me, and I knew he was "there." With tears in his eyes, he said, "I love you. I'm so sorry. So very sorry."

I took his hand, and we hugged. Murphy kept licking him. We sat together until our beautiful moment was over.

The next day, my father died.

Hundreds of people came to pay respects in the week following my father's funeral. It was too much for me, and at one point, I needed a respite. I walked with Murphy to a cove at a nearby lake, where he and my father had often gone together. As we approached the cove, Murphy howled and he wouldn't stop.

At the edge of the cove, there was a canoe nestled on the shore. Murphy ran full speed ahead and barked at it. The boat was not tied up, and it started floating into the center of the lake. The dog sprinted back and forth along the shore, yipping and howling. I am certain my dad's spirit was in that canoe and Murphy was saying goodbye.

—Dr. Dale Atkins—

Learning to Love the Dog

Don't Pick Me, I'll Pick You

When you have a dog, you never truly walk alone.
~Author Unknown

I wasn't looking for a dog. I had nothing against the canine set; I was just more of a cat person.

But my husband pestered me for a dog, thinking it would be good for us. It would get us out. We'd get exercise. And given that we're both autistic, he reasoned that a dog would be an ideal emotional support animal.

I ignored his pleas. And when that didn't work, I tried logically explaining that we could ill afford to bring another hungry mouth into the household. He was undeterred. He was, pardon the pun, like a dog with a bone.

He became obsessed with the idea of getting a dog. That's one of the ways his autism manifests itself. He becomes completely fixated. He also has a complete lack of practicality.

My husband's mind is a wondrous place of paint and music. And he lives in a world of barely organized chaos that almost causes me to hyperventilate because I am a creature of habit, holding fast to facts, figures and order. I guess opposites really do attract.

I love him. And my one weakness is that I can't say no to him, at least not for long. He wore me down. If a dog was what he wanted, a dog he would have.

I found one on a local buy-and-sell site. Two Border Collie/Australian Shepherd/Great Pyrenees mix males were left from a litter of five, and one caught my eye. He was fluffy with an adorable mix of black, white and brindle. And he had the cutest blue eyes.

I looked at his picture over and over again for a day or two and then made the call. Soon, we were off on a forty-minute drive to a farm in the middle of nowhere to pick up our boy.

Only, we didn't.

Oh, we drove to the farm alright. And as we entered the yard, the object of my affection, along with his mother, father, grandmother and three or four other dogs, came bounding up to me. I crouched down and gave them all some love.

My boy was so adorable, so sweet and happy. He licked my face and eagerly pounced all over me while his brother, handsome in his own right, with more black in his fur and soulful brown eyes, watched timidly from the step.

With our choice made, the couple selling the pups, Stepfanie and Burton, invited us in to complete the transaction. We followed them toward the house.

And that's when our lives changed forever. My husband slipped on the ice and hit the end of the driveway with a thunderous thud. He went down like a ton of bricks. Well, 250 pounds of bricks, to be exact.

And the little pup from the step came running. He made a beeline for Carl and gently licked and pawed him. His sweet, chocolate-coloured eyes were full of so much compassion.

When he saw that Carl was okay, he began to jump on him playfully.

Carl got up, and we proceeded toward the house. This little guy kept jumping on his leg and making cute, little puppy noises.

He was relentless. He had made his decision. We were his humans. He picked us. And, in that moment, we picked him back.

He took over our home and hearts. He's added so much joy to our lives, and I can't even imagine an existence without him.

It turns out my husband was right. We do get out more, and we do get more exercise. He's lost about twenty pounds just from our daily walks. And my social anxiety is much less severe when Rudy's out and about with me. Suddenly, I can engage in everyday chitchat with others without being crippled by fear.

Not bad for a pup. And, just think, it was him who picked us! How lucky are we?

— Misty Rae —

DadsRules4TheDog.doc

Most owners are at length able to teach themselves to obey their dog.
~Robert Morley

My computer crashed, and suddenly I remembered I had forgotten to back up my life. Not even the "genius" at the Apple Store could coax the "tech-antique" to cooperate. Thus began the nightmare of digging through a bag of jump drives in a feeble effort to reconstruct a few of the files.

That's how I discovered a long-forgotten file: DadsRules4TheDog.doc. Curious, I opened it—having zero recollection of what it was.

The file dated back to the year our family was considering a move from Washington to Ohio. Our daughters, ages five and ten, bawled and howled their aversion to leaving the only life they'd ever known—that is, until I made the ultimate bribe.

"Tell you what, kids. Daddy will let you get a puppy if we move." (Up until this point in their lives, Daddy was always Mr. Bah-Humbug when it came to a pet.)

Deal done.

"But girls," I warned, "this will be your dog. Daddy will have nothing to do with it. It's a big responsibility, and it's all on you. You will have to pay for everything pet-related with your allowances. You'll have to exercise, feed, clean up after the dog, bathe..." I may as well have been talking to cardboard cutouts. They weren't listening.

I suppose that's why I felt the need to put everything in writing. Thus, "Dad's Rules for the Dog."

In this manifesto, I spelled out every conceivable scenario where I might be inconvenienced by a mutt. "Dad will never exercise the dog. Dad will never feed the dog. Dad will never pet the dog. Dad will never look at the dog. And, of course, Dad will NEVER clean up after the dog. All fiduciary responsibilities will rest solely upon Lindsey and Claire. These costs will include — but are not limited to — vet bills, grooming fees, food costs, dog toys, dog bags, pet therapy, etc. Dad will never spend one penny on the pet. Moreover, the dog will never be allowed in the house. Should the owners of this pet be in violation of any part of this agreement, thereupon on that day, the dog shall surely die...." You get the idea.

One weekend when I was out of the country, Mom and the girls found an eight-week-old Maltese/Poodle and named him Skipper. (I wanted to name him "Repent," so I could go through the neighborhood calling "Come Repent, come Repent!" As a minister, I figured the dog could be a tax deduction.)

Don't ask me how, but Skipper soon became "Dad's dog." Yep, I walked him every morning. Bathed him. Picked up after him. Happily paid for everything. You get the idea.

I even turned into one of those obnoxious pet owners, constantly posting about their pets. Videos. Blogs. Pictures. And I forgot all about my magnum opus, "DadsRules4TheDog."

When Skipper was seven, he fell ill and wouldn't eat or drink. He lost nearly half his body weight. His eyes sparkless. His breathing shallow. He lay in sad silence as if swallowed by a fog of fatigue.

That weekend, while I was officiating a wedding, Mom and the girls took Skipper to the pet ER. She texted updates: "Doesn't look good... They're not sure what's wrong... They may have to do surgery... The X-ray shows he got into some cat litter."

During the lighting of the unity candle, I replied, "I don't care what it costs, just PLEASE keep Skip alive."

I still wonder: How does a guy go from "I won't spend a penny on that pet" to "I don't care what it costs"?

Good news: Skipper survived the cat-litter scare. And lived another nine beautiful years. Recently, our family once again took him to the pet ER. Only this time, there was no hope for healing.

Saying goodbye felt like heartbreak in slow motion. The grief hit hard. And still hurts. But his sad eyes let us know he was ready to rest.

So, being that "obnoxious" pet owner, I took to social media with this final post:

Sweet sixteen. Skipper made it to within 4 months of the "sixteen." But he had the "Sweet" in spades. This is not to suggest he was flawless; he could be ornery. And mischievous. But his heart was as pure as a pearl.

This morning, I missed my 5:30 alarm—the "little man" resting his paws on my pillow and whimpering softly to let me know it's time for our three-plus-mile walk. But, after fifteen years of this routine, I was wide awake without the whimper.

Goodbye, sweet Skip. You taught me the stuff that matters most:

- Forgive fast.
- Be curious.
- Stay active.
- Be available.
- Show loyalty.
- And, above all, love hard—fiercely, unconditionally, and always.

Thank you, Skipper, for enriching my life so profoundly. I miss you beyond measure.

—Karl Haffner—

The Gentle Giant

It's just the most amazing thing to love a dog,
isn't it? It makes our relationships with people
seem as boring as a bowl of oatmeal.
~John Grogan

I had been divorced for quite a while and had moved from the northern tundra of North Dakota to the desert heat of Arizona. After staying mostly indoors during the summer's intolerable heat, I was eager to get out when autumn finally came. I also craved companionship, so I went on one of those dating apps. After more than a dozen misses, I finally found someone who intrigued me. After more than a dozen emails so we could get acquainted, we decided we would meet for a pizza. It went pretty well, and on the fourth or fifth date, after we had been to a movie, she invited me in for a nightcap.

While we were having beer on the couch, sitting side by side, I heard something that I thought was a door. I looked questioningly at my new girlfriend. Did she have a roommate? She answered, "That's just Dude." A male roommate? This was not turning out well. That's when I saw a king-sized German Shepherd come around the corner.

"This is Dude," my new girlfriend said. "He's my baby."

I am a dog lover myself, but after six Dachshunds, I couldn't believe the size of this "baby." I estimated that he was close to 110 pounds. (I wasn't too far off. I found out later that Dude weighed in at 106.) But I learned that he was well-trained and well-behaved. He lay down at his owner's feet and went to sleep.

After we had enjoyed our beers, I didn't want to overstay my welcome, but I wanted a goodnight kiss. As I "moved in position" to "make my move" and put my arm around her shoulders, that giant German Shepherd jumped up on the couch right beside me. With me sitting and him standing up, he was clearly a head above me, and I imagined him saying, "Not with my mommy, you don't." Also, I didn't want my obituary to read that I was mauled by a jealous German Shepherd in my girlfriend's home.

But Dude settled in beside me and didn't growl or snarl, so I thought I was okay — for now. But color me concerned! And who wouldn't be, sitting beside a German Shepherd (in his territory), who could inflict a bite of my whole head? But I wanted that kiss, and I wasn't going to give up that easily. So, I pulled her to me, but before our lips met, I could feel Dude closing in on me. My thought at this time was, *Oh, no! At best, I am going to lose an ear!* I tensed up, waiting for him to attack. And then, he licked my bald head!

Myriad thoughts went through my mind, but leading the pack was thankfulness. My adrenaline was still flowing, bringing relief, comfort, deliverance, and reduced danger. My girlfriend was laughing uncontrollably and said, "I think Dude likes you." And that was the time, I think, when I fell in love with both of them. With that dog kiss, he welcomed me into the family.

My girlfriend became my "significant other," and we have been together for ten years. Sadly, Dude left us when he became too lame and was in much pain. And both of us miss him. Dude was a gentle giant.

— Doug Sletten —

Never Judge a Pug by His Breed

The pug is living proof that God has a sense of humor.
~Margo Kaufman

"We've got a foster dog for you," said the rescue's tireless leader, Sylvia, the minute I arrived. I dropped my coat and bag in the office and followed her to the vet's building, running to keep up with her.

"A foster?" I repeated, surprised since I was still new and there were plenty of more experienced staff.

"Yes, he has to go to a house with no other animals or children."

My stomach flipped as an image of an antisocial monster flashed into my mind. But Linda was still talking, and that image quickly dissolved as she described a puppy abandoned by a breeder for having megaesophagus, a condition that meant it was dangerous for him to eat solid foods. I nodded as it became clear why she had picked me. I was the only staff member with no dogs of my own (or kids), and they couldn't risk him getting into other animals' food or eating scraps dropped by children.

"That's his main issue anyway," she added, somewhat ominously. Then, she opened a crate containing a tiny, six-week-old Pug, the sorriest-looking puppy I had ever seen.

With their squashed noses and bulbous eyes, Pugs can be

funny-looking at the best of times, but this little guy was something else. In addition to his digestive issues, which had left him painfully thin, he had a growth protruding from the centre of one orb-like eye, giving him a decidedly alien appearance.

Good lord! I thought as I stroked his minuscule ears and listened as Linda listed the care he needed. Eye drops, medications, liquid food, regular checks for fluid in his lungs… The list went on and on, and I started to wonder if I was up to the task.

When I started working at Many Tears Animal Rescue, I knew I would be fostering dogs. It was one of the reasons I had taken the job. My nomadic lifestyle prevented me from having my own dogs, so working with them and offering them a temporary home was the next best thing. I'd always loved big dogs, so when I imagined myself with a foster, it was an old Labrador, a regal Alsatian, or one of our wolf-like crossbreeds, never a Pug! There was no way I'd ever have chosen such a small breed, with their ridiculous faces and lack of athleticism.

But this was the lot I had been given. Whether I felt ready or not, this neglected Pug puppy, with his myriad issues and endless care requirements, was mine to look after until he was happy, healthy and ready for his forever home.

It soon became apparent, however, that he had no idea he was supposed to be an invalid, or that he was a lapdog breed. In his mind, he was King of the World and didn't care who knew it. From the second he came home with me, he made himself comfortable, peeing all over the place, chewing anything I left on the floor, scratching paint off the walls, and howling when I put him in his crate at night. He was, in short, your average naughty, entertaining, adorable puppy.

I started calling him Piglet because of the way he ran around my flat, squeaking with his curly tail in the air. This soon evolved to Puglet, and Puglet he was for the next four months as he became my little sidekick.

He came to work with me and spent his days terrorising the other staff members' dogs, who didn't know what to make of this tiny troublemaker. He took to his dietary regime like a champ, slurping up meat smoothies and liquid treats as fast as I could make them. He raced along on walks, his little legs working overtime in his urge to explore the world. He attracted attention everywhere we went, and people constantly stopped to ask about the little Pug with the strange eye and the big-dog attitude.

But though he was happy and popular, he didn't yet have a clean bill of health. He was eating well and gaining weight, but my efforts with drops and medications weren't fixing his eye. Instead, it was getting worse because his impaired sight meant he often bumped into things, knocking the growth on his eye and whimpering in pain. Eventually, the vet decided there was nothing else for it; that eye had to come out.

As soon as he was fit enough, he was knocked out, enucleated, and neutered at the same time. He woke up wearing a plastic cone, several stitches, and a one-eyed glare that said he thoroughly disapproved of being treated this way.

But there was no denying that it helped him. Once that painful, swollen eye was gone, he went from strength to strength, running even more riot now that he had no fear of bashing into things. He reached a healthy weight and was a chubby Puglet with a rotund belly replacing the visible rib cage he'd arrived with. But this health and happiness came with a downside; it meant his time with me was ending.

Of course, by then, I had fallen madly in love with him. But, as much as I wanted to, I couldn't keep him. I was going travelling in a few months and would be gone for over a year. So, if I couldn't adopt him myself, I would do the next best thing and make sure he went to the best home possible.

I updated the rescue's website regularly with adorable pictures, stories of his improved health, and videos of his mad antics. I didn't want anyone reading his medical history and thinking they were getting a retiring little invalid. Whoever took on this ball of energy and mischief needed to know what they were in for!

All too soon, it worked, and a woman emailed saying she thought she could offer him the perfect home. She had three other dogs for him to play with, and one of them also had megaesophagus, so she was well-versed in the care he needed. It sounded too good to be true, but she passed all the rescue's checks (and mine), met him, and fell for him instantly. In a matter of days, he was gone.

A few weeks later, we received an email telling us how well he was settling in. So far, he had established himself as King of the Pack, damaged an antique Chesterfield sofa, and humped his new owner's leg in front of a whole church congregation. He was having a whale of a time, and she couldn't be happier with the new addition to her family.

The successful adoption was bittersweet, but the Puglet-shaped hole in my life didn't last long. Within a few days of his leaving, I had volunteered for a new foster dog: April, another abandoned puppy with another lengthy list of health issues. And, against all odds, another Pug. Because who was I kidding? From the first moment I'd met that skinny, wonky-eyed, mischievous, little Puglet puppy, I had officially become a Pug person.

— Anita Gait —

Strength Through Weakness

Opening up your life to a dog who needs a home is one of the most fulfilling things you can do.
~Emma Kenney

His name was Mr. Chips, though he never knew it. Born deaf, he navigated the world with quiet grace, never burdened by what others might call a handicap.

Mr. Chips was a striking, double-blue Merle Sheltie, the result of breeding two blue Merles, a process often discouraged due to the genetic risks involved. While the Merle coat is sought after for its unique beauty — no two dogs share the same patterns — there's a 25-percent chance that puppies from two Merle parents will inherit serious genetic defects like blindness or deafness. Mr. Chips could have been considered one of the unlucky ones. But despite his hearing loss, he possessed an undeterred spirit and an intelligence that surpassed even my expectations.

I adopted him when he was just a year old. The breeder, no longer wanting the responsibility of a deaf dog, was happy to let him go. But to me, Mr. Chips was perfect. His brilliant blue eyes, gleaming with curiosity, and his thick, snowy fur peppered with gray spots made him nothing short of breathtaking. I fell in love instantly.

However, it didn't take long for me to realize that he wasn't house-broken. How does one housebreak a dog who can't hear commands or praise? I couldn't yell "No" when he squatted to urinate in the house or give him effusive verbal affirmation when he did his business outside.

Luckily, I was finishing my first year of veterinary school and had brought Mr. Chips home to my parents' house for the summer. What I couldn't teach with words, he learned by observing. He followed my parents' dogs out to the fenced-in backyard and watched them. Soon enough, he figured out what to do. It was remarkable how quickly he adapted, almost as if he intuitively knew what was expected of him.

At the time, I lived in a townhouse. Mr. Chips chose my upstairs bedroom closet, just above the entryway, as his favorite sleeping spot. Every day when I came home, I'd tap on the ceiling with an umbrella that I kept just inside the door for that purpose, and the gentle vibrations would wake him. He'd come racing down the stairs in seconds, his eyes sparkling with excitement, eager to greet me.

He learned hand signals for "come" and "stop" with ease, but getting his attention was a different story. I often found myself jumping around or wildly waving my arms, earning puzzled looks from passersby. But to Mr. Chips, this was just normal communication. His calm, laidback nature allowed him to take everything in stride. Nothing rattled him, not even the five times we moved to new homes. Each time, he settled into a routine within a day or two, as if he'd lived there his whole life.

Even though Mr. Chips couldn't hear my voice, I talked to him constantly. Maybe it was wishful thinking, but I was convinced he understood me by reading my lips or simply sensing my intentions. A few years after I got him, I adopted a stray I named Orphan Annie, who quickly became his helper dog. Whenever I couldn't find Mr. Chips, I'd tell Annie, "Go find Chippies," and she'd take off, locate him, give him a nudge, and guide him back to me.

The house alarm went off one day while I wasn't home, and the police were dispatched to investigate. When I pulled up to my house, I found officers in my backyard, standing by the glassed-in Florida room. One officer approached me solemnly and said, "I'm sorry, ma'am, but your dog is dead." My heart stopped momentarily as I glanced through the glass, only to see Mr. Chips curled up, fast asleep, oblivious to the chaos. I burst out laughing and explained that he was deaf. I knocked firmly on the window, and Mr. Chips sprang to his feet, much to the visible relief of the officer.

For nearly seventeen years, Mr. Chips was my constant companion. Despite his deafness, he was the most intelligent dog I ever had. Somehow, he always knew when a plate of leftovers had been placed on the floor, no matter how quietly I set it down. To this day, I have no idea how he did it. In Mr. Chips's world, deafness wasn't a limitation. I doubt it ever occurred to him that he had a handicap. Deafness was simply his reality, and he embraced life with a spirit full of joy and resilience.

I was humbled by the obstacles he overcame. He taught me that we don't have to be defined by what others may perceive as weaknesses. True contentment comes from accepting who we are and living fully in that truth. Mr. Chips never let his deafness stop him from enjoying life, and in doing so, he left an indelible mark on mine.

— Ellen L. Fannon —

Whiskers and Tears

There is no psychiatrist in the world like
a puppy licking your face.
~Ben Williams

"Now, don't be mad," my friend Sam began when I answered the phone. But her tone was light and teasing, so I smiled as I waited for her to finish. "I found a dog, a puppy actually, that I think would be perfect for you."

My heart skipped a beat. We had lost our three beloved furry children — two dogs and a cat — all within six months of each other. We hadn't discussed getting another pet yet, but Sam had not only found another little Shih Tzu (like the other two), but she wanted to gift him to us.

I waited anxiously for my husband to get home from work, and when he finally pulled up in the driveway, I was on the steps waiting for him with a strained smile on my face, which he noticed.

"What's the matter?" he asked.

"Now, don't be mad," I said, laughing at my use of the same phrase Sam had used on me. Sam had sent me a picture, which I showed to him, and we both were smitten. Who wouldn't be by a fluffy little guy with the sweetest button nose and big brown eyes that seemed to beg us to come and get him? Which, after quite a bit of discussion, preparation, and anticipation, we did. And when my husband held him in his arms, and he nibbled on my nose when I nuzzled him, we were happy with our decision. We named him Floki.

It wasn't easy. We hadn't had a puppy for over twenty years. Puppies can be extremely challenging, and we were not as young as we were the first time. But we'd made a commitment and were going to stick to it.

The challenges continued to grow when he proved stubborn to train. (Shih Tzus tend to be that way.) Then the vet discovered he had myriad health conditions, some that would be lifelong. We also realized we were still grieving our previous losses.

We wondered if we had been too hasty in getting another dog when we hadn't even been sure we wanted one.

Since I was at home all day it was up to me to train him, walk him, and play with him. My husband helped me when he was around, of course, but I did a lot of the heavy lifting, so to speak. I wrestled with my feelings a lot. One of the Shih Tzus we'd lost had been like a therapy dog to me, and I was still devastated. I wasn't even sure I wanted to fill his place, and since this one was so young and undisciplined, it was hard to imagine the dog he would become.

But he grew, became well-trained, and developed a personality—one that made us laugh and brought some joy back into the house. He began to grow on us. But, for some odd reason, I was still cautious, and I spent a lot of time trying to figure out why.

Eventually, I realized something: I wasn't letting this dog into my heart because I was afraid of him breaking it. Not because he was a bad dog or anything like that. I knew that if I fell in love with him, one day he too would die and take part of my heart with him.

Then I had my epiphany. He was happily trotting ahead of us during a walk at the park, and I was talking animatedly to my husband. I let out a "fake sob" in my story. Floki stopped sniffing, turned around, and came running over to me. He jumped up and pawed at me to lift him up. When I did, he began to lick my "tears." And as he continued to gently lick away, his whiskers tickling my face, I realized it was already too late.

Then, the real tears started. Sensing my distress, Floki started licking even more, which made me cry harder. Pretty soon, I was laughing instead of crying. I knew that it would all end in tears one day when he would no longer be there to comfort me, but every moment until then would be worth it.

— Kristi Cocchiarella FitzGerald —

Matchmaker, Matchmaker

Love — that which biologists, nervous about being misunderstood, call "attachment" — fuels the bond between dog and master or mistress.
~John Bradshaw

My older sister Lisa had many rules growing up, such as always controlling the remote, staying away from her Lite-Brite, and not taking her clothes. Being the obedient little sister, I abided by most of her rules. Ten years after we'd last lived together in our childhood home, I moved in with her in Chicago, and she still had rules — more rules than living with our parents, it seemed. One of them was "no dogs allowed" in the condo.

I wiggled my way in with her friends in true little-sister form. During our first week living together, we hosted her friends for dinner. Lisa had previously introduced me to her friend, Aaron, a nice Jewish boy, and I had had my eye on him ever since. Aaron and I got to know each other at this dinner. He was cute, kind, and intelligent, and we instantly connected. We began dating immediately, and four years later, we moved in together. First order of business… get a dog! We got a Goldendoodle and named her Ivy after the famous foliage at Wrigley Field just down the street.

Aaron and I were a match, and we are forever thankful to Lisa, our matchmaker. In *Fiddler on the Roof*, Yente is the town's Jewish matchmaker. In Yiddish, yenta means gossip or busybody, but because of the movie and its famous lyrics ("Matchmaker, matchmaker, make me a match…"), it has become synonymous with matchmaker.

Since Lisa helped me find my bashert (Hebrew for "meant to be"), it was only fair to put my yenta-ness to use as her matchmaker if the right person came along. I had been begging her to let me choose someone or scan the dating sites for her for years since she hadn't picked well thus far.

Lisa's wish list: funny, Jewish, attractive, and family-oriented.

Aaron's wish list for a future brother-in-law: sports fan!

My wish list: someone different than she'd ever dated before!

In my mind, I filed all this away in what I call my matchmaking Rolodex. Little did I know that I'd have two furry assistants to help.

As a teacher, I had summers off, so I enjoyed taking Ivy on long walks around our bustling Chicago neighborhood. I loved to meander past the school where I taught, catch up with past students, and stop in the shops to browse and talk — dogs allowed! In good pet etiquette, we said hello and did a quick sniff with the neighborhood regulars. I didn't always remember the humans' names, but I knew the dogs' names: Mia the Husky next door with one green eye and one blue eye; Simba the Golden Retriever from dog daycare; and Charlie the big, furry Bernese pup always lounging in his front yard.

One day, I noticed a new dog and owner strutting down the street. It was hard to miss a massive Rottweiler and a sleeveless owner with an almost-as-massive Jewish star necklace. He looked as if he had just come from a night of clubbing. I cordially said, "Hello," and the dogs sniffed. The next day, I gossiped with the shop ladies about this new guy in the neighborhood. Who was he? Where did he come from? What did he do? We speculated, but no one really knew.

The next time I passed him, I stopped to introduce myself and Ivy. I learned they were Jake (the Rottweiler) and Dan (the owner), who had just moved to the neighborhood that winter. Ivy, quickly smitten, rolled over to show her belly, a universal dog sign of trust. I declared Jake her new Jewish dog boyfriend. This was my first match, but not the last.

Almost every day that summer, we stopped for chitchat and the dogs for belly rubs. Jake and Ivy would take turns rolling, sniffing, romping, and barricading the sidewalk, blocking commuters' paths. I was honored when Dan told me I was among the few people not scared by Jake's size and breed. Only a few people or dogs stopped to socialize, apparently. Jake was the biggest sweetie, a teddy bear, a 150-pound leaner, and he loved just as hard. I always looked forward to seeing Jake's massive doggy smile and nubby tail wag when we approached.

September was back-to-school time for me, and long walks had to wait until the weekends. I didn't see Jake and Dan as often anymore. Then, one Saturday, Aaron, Ivy, and I were strolling down the street and ran into them. I introduced Aaron and asked Dan about his upcoming plans for Rosh Hashanah, the Jewish New Year. Aaron will say I interrogated him that morning, but honestly this man talks more and louder than anyone I know. He told me his life story: He's a chef, hates shirts with sleeves because they are restrictive, is a Packers fan, his sister lives in Seattle, and his parents would be out of the country for the holiday!

Previously, I was skeptical of this seeming meathead character until this conversation. I didn't judge Dan's dog by breed, but here I was judging him—shame on me! The more he talked, the more he checked off the lists. Funny: check. Jewish: check. Attractive: check. Sports fan: check. Family-oriented: check. Very different from anyone she's dated previously: check!

My yenta vibes were tingling! "I want you to meet my sister," I blurted out. He agreed, and we exchanged numbers. I set up the date. Lisa, Dan, Aaron, and I all went on that first date to the bar that Lisa and I used to live above. Unfortunately, no dogs were allowed there either, but there was puppy love. Lisa and Dan clicked as fast as Jake and Ivy—without the butt-sniffing.

Speaking of love, Lisa hadn't loved a dog since our childhood Westie. Lisa was less than impressed by Ivy, mostly because of the sneezing. But after a few months of dating, Lisa went from "no dogs allowed" in her condo to walking a dog bigger than herself and letting him move in! There were still a few sneezes, but it was worth it to her.

Jake became the highlight of Lisa's new Instagram account @ Jake_the_Rottie, reaching over 20,000 followers. He became a local celebrity, attending movie premieres such as *The Secret Life of Pets*, being the life of the party at Yappy Hours, getting invitations to stay at fancy dog-friendly hotels, and being featured in the *Chicago Tribune*!

There's truth in the saying, "Love me, love my dog." Lisa and Dan got married two years after that first date. And now that Ivy and Jake are doggy cousins, Ivy is allowed in Lisa's condo for doggy play dates.

Matchmaker mission accomplished!

— Melissa R. Friedman —

Delighted to Meet You

A dog is the only thing on earth that loves
you more than he loves himself.
~Josh Billings

His name is Wilson, but when we first met him, it was Lukas. To be perfectly honest, it was really my father-in-law Stan's fault — plus the fact that it was too hot to go outdoors and feed the geese and ducks after our weekly lunch. The Humane Society offered respite from the heat, as well as an opportunity to interact with animals. So that's where I took Stan after our Monday lunches during that hot summer.

We would walk into the pound, choose a dog who looked like it could use a bit of attention, request the use of a "playroom," and gain a new friend for an hour or so. I watched while Stan poured love into a new dog each week, exclaiming the same thing every time: "I've never held a dog before! What do I do?"

As much as I adore dogs, my joy came from watching Stan with the animals. He let them lick his hands and face — something he likely would not have allowed before Alzheimer's became his "new normal." He held them on his lap and rubbed the undersides of their chins, while they wagged their tails in gratitude.

There was a particular dog, one Monday, who was barking incessantly, as if to say, *Please don't overlook me! I know that my ears are too big for my head, and I'm far from the cutest dog you've played with here, but what have you got to lose for an hour of your time?*

I can answer that question in two words: my heart.

I lost my heart that day because it was stolen by the scenario that played out in front of me. Once again, Stan said, "I've never held a dog before! What do I do?"

Luckily for Stan, Lukas took care of the rest.

I couldn't look away. Stan didn't have to remember a name, a prior conversation, whether or not he was still in grade school or the fact that he had been a prominent architect in St. Louis for his entire adult life. All he had to do was love this pup who had been found roaming the streets of Riverview Gardens.

Lukas was unencumbered by the fact that Stan no longer made memories but lived every moment as if it were a brand-new experience. Lukas was unaffected by Stan's repeating the same questions or statements to him. The sound of his gentle voice was enough to bring comfort to a dog who just wanted to be loved.

Returning Lukas to his cold metal "cell" wasn't easy. As I looked back at him, his eyes pleaded, *Really! I'm sorry about the ears! Can't we overlook them?*

Later that afternoon, I brought my daughter back to meet Lukas.

Back at home, a brief conversation ensued in which she asked her dad, "Don't you think you'd learn to love him?"

He responded, "I'm sure I'd learn to love him."

We interpreted that as the "go-ahead" we sought and returned to the pound.

You're back! You reconsidered the little issue with my ears!

Paperwork completed, we legally adopted Lukas, got to know him for a few days, and renamed him Wilson.

Stan had no recollection that Wilson was the dog with whom he had become so enamored on that hot August day at the pound. Yet, Wilson remembered Stan and greeted him with exuberance at every visit.

When Stan left us, there was a hole in our hearts too big to fill. Wilson is a reminder of the happiness that a rescued mutt brought to a man who had lost his memories, but not his ability to love. Not only that, it also demonstrated that even in the midst of unrelenting cognitive loss, Stan brought delight to a dog who had been abused and needed to learn how to trust again. Wilson had, indeed, chosen the right person in whom to place his faith.

— Sheri Block Glantz —

A Change of Heart

We never really own a dog as much as he owns us.
~Gene Hill

"Ginger's in the basement?" I asked. I had stopped by my dad's house. To the average observer, this would not be considered odd at all, but this was my dad we were talking about. If either my sister or I had been living in a place that allowed dogs, one of us would have taken my brother's dog when Jon deployed to Afghanistan. However, my sister was living in an apartment that didn't allow dogs, and I was living with my elderly and asthmatic grandmother who was highly allergic.

I thought back to when we were kids. My dad had said that we would never, ever have a dog, or any pet for that matter, except maybe fish since they weren't messy. Maybe.

Then, he had discovered a stray kitten in the wheel well of his work truck. After bringing him home to us and adopting him, as well as a couple of hamsters, gerbils, rabbits, birds, a frog, and an iguana, he had finally relented on the "no dogs" rule.

First, we had one dog, then two, living in the house with us. This lasted until we went away for a week. Our neighbors came over several times a day to take them outside and play with them, but the dogs got bored without their humans around and pulled up several strips of linoleum flooring in our kitchen. Upon discovering the damage, my father built an elaborate kennel and declared that henceforth and forevermore they would be strictly outdoor dogs. I believe his exact words were, "I don't care if it's forty below zero outside. I will heat that kennel before they ever set one paw in this house again."

And he did. Granted, it was a huge building with a door, windows, foundation, and even electricity. In many ways, it was more of a house than a kennel, but from that point on, they were not allowed inside. Our older dog had passed away several years prior, leaving Ginger, who was Jon's dog. When my brother deployed, my father had stepped up to take care of her, but never in a million years did I anticipate that he would allow her inside the house.

"Well, she's been so depressed ever since Jon left," Dad explained. "Since she's used to being outside and has her winter coat, I was concerned that having her upstairs would get too hot for her, but the basement is a little cooler. Plus, I spend so much time down there, so I think that's good for her." I nodded, wondering who this man was and what he had done with my father.

"Okay," I responded. "I just need to grab a few things before I head back to Grandmom's."

"Sure," he replied. "Hey, if you need to go down in the basement, don't turn the light off. I leave the light on down there whenever I'm not able to be with her. I don't think it's good for her to be alone in the dark. She's depressed enough as it is."

The next time I went home, Ginger had been promoted to the kitchen and there was a steak cooking on the stove.

"Hey! What's going on?" Dad asked me.

"Not much. Are you making lunch?" I asked.

"Well, Ginger hasn't had much of an appetite lately," he replied. "She's refusing to eat her regular dog food, so I've been trying to get her to eat something. She misses Jon so much. I've tried salmon and tuna fish since they have strong smells. You know, dogs like those foods with strong smells. I've tried making eggs and other food for her, but she just isn't very interested, so I thought I'd try this steak. I've just got to get her to eat. Maybe if I chew it up a little before I give it to her... That might help her eat."

As I left the house that day, I realized that this went far beyond an old Golden Retriever and a man who hated having dogs in the house. This was about the young man serving on the other side of the world. This was about helping each other cope with his absence.

My dad couldn't be with my brother to protect him as he served his country, but he could take care of my brother's beloved dog. Because of this, he had thrown everything he had into caring for her, including cooking her steak and offering to chew her food for her. Ginger gave Dad a way to help my brother while he was on the other side of the world, and, the truth was, he needed her just as much as she needed him.

— Elizabeth S. —

Stepping Up

The average dog has one request
to all humankind. Love me.
~Helen Exley

When I joined social media, I never envisioned grieving the death of someone I had never met, let alone adopting her dog. But that's exactly what happened.

I made my first online friendships before Facebook was a household word. It started in an eBay forum I had joined when trying to sell my original art online. The group consisted of a few dozen fellow artists who had come together to show off their latest work while sharing sales tips.

That's where I met Wendy.

Wendy had recently retired due to chronic health problems. Now living on her sister's pecan farm in Northern California, she spent her days creating whimsical animal portraits. She painted cats in military uniform, bunnies wearing Elizabethan ruff collars, and hamsters wearing party hats. But her favorite subject was her prized Toy Manchester Terriers. She doted on her three dogs, dressing them in eccentric costumes and creating fanciful illustrations that ended up on greeting cards and calendars.

Over time, our group's cordial discussions turned into witty banter and random silliness. We talked less about art and more about our shared experiences as pet owners. I formed a close bond with the group and looked forward to checking in with them every day.

When Facebook came along, eBay closed their forums, and many of us migrated to the popular new site. It was there that I also connected with Wendy's sister, Peg.

Over the next nine years, we all celebrated new pet adoptions while simultaneously grieving the ones that had passed. During that time, I lost one dog and rescued two more. I also saved two feral kittens, which brought my feline population to five. Wendy lost two of her Terriers, leaving her with only one, her ten-year-old male, Popgun.

Wendy became ill, and all of us stayed in close touch with her. As her health declined, she became too exhausted to continue her art projects, and she devoted her time to photographing her beloved dog. Popgun developed a Facebook following of his own, always looking dapper in a bow tie and top hat. Wendy didn't want to worry friends with posts about her failing kidneys. Instead, she filled her page with fun posts.

The private messages between Wendy and me told a different story. She sent me texts from the hospital during her many trips to the emergency room. She was often sedated and her messages incoherent, but I did my best to comfort her. For reasons I may never know, she had chosen me to reach out to, and our bond grew even stronger.

One morning, I was awakened by the sound of a phone alert from Facebook Messenger. It was a message from Peg. "We lost Wendy last night. She came home from dialysis and never made it to the front door."

Peg broke the news on Facebook that morning. Her page was immediately filled with posts from friends and family offering condolences. While everyone who knew Wendy was heartbroken, we could at least take comfort in knowing that Popgun would remain on the farm with Peg. However, that would change in a matter of days.

Things weren't working out for Peg. She was busy trying to run the farm, and Popgun kept escaping. At night, Popgun angered her husband when he tried to sneak onto the bed. She felt her only choice was to rehome the dog.

She posted an adoption notice on Facebook. The many people who had flocked to Wendy's page to post their condolences were suddenly silent. When no one came forward, Popgun's breeder took over and posted a public adoption notice. This resulted in numerous inquiries from strangers. It seemed that everyone wanted to fly Popgun to the East Coast. He'd be thrown into the cargo hold of a plane and then have to learn to adjust to a cold climate. It was too much trauma for a senior dog, especially because he was already confused by the sudden absence of his caregiver.

My heart broke as people competed for this treasured pet, as if he was some kind of toy.

That's when I did something about it. And it was all too easy to do, from the comfort of my home, seated in front of my keyboard. I hit the reply button and wrote: "I'll take him."

A few days later, I drove north from my home in Los Angeles and met Peg at a rest stop in Central California. We hugged and shared memories of Wendy, and then Peg handed me Popgun and drove away.

The minute Popgun walked into my house, he began lifting his leg and urinating wherever he pleased. He proceeded to tear apart all the plants in my garden. If I left him alone in a room, he let out a piercing scream. Did I mention he ate poop? Not only his own, but any he could find in the yard. When one of my cats puked up a hairball, he snatched it up—and gobbled it down. I tried to stop him, but he bit me.

My response to all of this? I curled up in a ball, too overwhelmed and exhausted to do anything but cry. I had intended to do the right thing for someone else but ended up doing the wrong thing for me. I logged into Facebook to contact the breeder. I saw no other recourse but to ask her to place the dog elsewhere. But when I logged into my account, my page was flooded with messages telling me that I was a hero. I certainly didn't think of myself as a hero, but maybe Popgun did.

I revisited the photos Wendy had posted. They reminded me that I wasn't the only one whose life had been dramatically altered. Popgun had lost the only home he had ever known and the only person who had ever cared for him. Maybe we both needed time to adjust.

Maybe he deserved a second chance.

Popgun settled in. He stopped peeing on the furniture. He learned that destroying my garden angered me. As he felt more secure in his new home, he stopped the unbearable screaming.

As for me, I settled in, too. I agreed to disagree on the matter of eating poop and vomit. Sometimes, you just have to compromise.

It's now been four years since Popgun arrived, and while he continues to test my patience, I can't imagine my home without him in it. I love it when he sleeps on the bed at night and snores like an old man because I imagine Wendy going to bed each night comforted by that sound. I also imagine her going to bed each night comforted by the knowledge that her dog would be in a loving home after she passed.

Sometimes, I lie awake and think about my own mortality and the likelihood that that I, too, will leave pets behind when I'm gone. When that day comes, I hope someone out there will hit that button and be a hero to the animals I love.

— Kathy Valentino —

What a Clever Dog

Going with the Flow

What do dogs do on their day off? Can't lie around — that's their job!
~George Carlin

Right from the day she pranced into our house as a puppy, our Border Collie mix, Sneeks, proved to be a character. Quirky, smart, and rebellious, she constantly dreamt up ways to surprise us.

One summer day, I noticed Sneeks standing on the deck that bordered our in-ground pool. Sneeks was dipping a front paw into the pool and pulling the water toward her. The reason for her action became clear when I noticed a tennis ball bobbing in the waves a short distance out from where she stood.

I assumed the tennis ball must have fallen into the pool, and Sneeks was trying to get it out. Sure enough, once the ball drew closer, Sneeks leaned forward and plucked it out of the water.

But it was her next action that really got my attention.

Sneeks carried the ball partway around the pool until she came to the spot where one of the underwater jets pushed water out to keep the pool's contents circulating. Sneeks dropped the ball into the water right at the jet's location.

The ball drifted away from the side of the pool and then caught the current. It floated parallel to the side of the pool, with Sneeks keeping pace beside it, barking occasionally to encourage it to keep moving.

Sneeks raced ahead and then stopped and waited for the ball

to catch up. Once she deemed it had come close enough, she leaned forward, dipped a paw into the pool, and started pulling the water toward her. The ball drew closer, and finally she was able to reach out and seize it in her jaws. She trotted to the next jet to continue her game.

I just shook my head. I'd heard a saying that if you don't keep Border Collies busy, they'll find their own entertainment. Despite my initial skepticism, Sneeks had just provided all the proof I needed. Tired of waiting for me to play fetch with her, she'd figured out a way to play fetch with herself. Now if I could just get her to take herself for walks, I'd be all set.

—Lisa Timpf—

My Little Tap Dancer

Everyone thinks they have the best dog.
And none of them are wrong.
~W.R. Purche

Our little dog Max, part Maltese, part Shih Tzu, had developed cataracts. At twelve, he was still up for chasing his toys and performing a trick now and then. We'd recently purchased a multicolored kitchen rug, bold and cheerful. There was a big problem, however. Poor Max couldn't find his treats anymore when I tossed them onto the rug. The poor dog would search and search, unable to locate the tasty morsels.

I came up with the best solution I could think of. After I'd toss a treat or two, I'd tap near the treat with my foot, letting him know where to find it. This worked pretty well, and we both seemed happy with the solution.

I, too, am growing older, often unable to locate the contact lens I'm attempting to place in my eye. Days later, I'll find the dried-up piece of plastic sticking to the place in the bathroom where I dropped it.

One morning, I was moving slower than usual. Max was anxious to be fed. I tried consoling him with gentle words as I slipped a contact on my index finger, lifting it slowly toward my eye. Max suddenly jumped against my leg, and the contact dropped off my finger, heading to parts unknown.

"Oh, no, Max, not another lost contact!"

Carefully, I searched the entire sink. No lens anywhere in sight.

That's when I heard a tap-tapping on the tiled floor. Looking down, I witnessed the most amazing feat ever. There was Max, tapping his claws against the floor, directing me to a minuscule item sparkling in the sunlight.

"My contact!"

I smiled down at Max, clapping my hands before retrieving the lost treasure.

Max gazed up at me with pleading eyes as if to ask, "Now, can I please have my breakfast?"

Hurriedly, we two seniors made our way to the kitchen for breakfast.

— Mary Z. Whitney —

This Dog Kept Her Hair Appointment

Every dog must have his day.
~Jonathan Swift

My friend, Jackie Sturzenegger, always loved the Fourth of July. It's usually a warm summer evening filled with picnics and fireworks. Jackie invited my husband, me, and other friends to watch the fireworks on one particular Fourth. She hosted a barbecue dinner, and then we all gathered in her backyard to wait for the celebration to start.

The Sturzeneggers opened their back gate so everyone could see all the fireworks. Their wonderful Australian Shepherd, Frankie, sat beside Jackie at the show's beginning. Frankie was a fluffy dog about the size of a collie. She had beautiful blue eyes and was very intelligent.

When the fireworks show ended, Jackie was surprised that Frankie wasn't sitting beside her anymore. "I'll go look in her doghouse," Jackie said. But Frankie wasn't there. "I'm worried," said Jackie. "She probably got scared and ran off."

We began to look everywhere for the dog. Jackie and her husband drove around their subdivision to no avail.

Jackie left the gate open that night, hoping Frankie would come back. Her husband drove around the neighborhood again the following day, down the familiar streets and beyond. Again, there was no Frankie.

Jackie called Carol Smith, who was Frankie's groomer. She

apologized, saying she was sorry she couldn't bring Frankie in to be groomed because she had run away during the fireworks. The groomer's receptionist offered to cancel Frankie's appointment.

About forty minutes later, Jackie's phone rang. It was Carol. "Does your dog have a purple collar?"

Jackie confirmed that Frankie's collar was purple. "Frankie arrived on time for her appointment," the groomer said. "She came into our parking lot like she knew where she was. She walked right up to our door and came inside. I remembered her purple collar and her blue eyes."

Feeling a sea of emotions, Jackie asked if Frankie was all right. "She seemed fine, so I groomed her," said Carol."

Jackie still can't imagine how Frankie walked so far to her appointment. The groomer is five or six miles from Jackie's house. Frankie had to cross busy streets to get there. "It's beyond my imagination other than that aliens carried her," Jackie told me.

But Jackie's husband had another explanation. "Frankie's a woman. She wouldn't miss her hair appointment," he said.

Today, we all feel like Frankie's adventure was a miraculous coincidence. If Jackie and I think about it too long, all the ramifications of Frankie's long walk make us crazy. We're both just glad she finally made it home safe.

— Carolyn Campbell —

What My Dog Taught Me About Trust

When the world is at its dismal, dullest
or darkest, your dog will insist on his walk
— and cheer you back to sanity.
~Peter Gray

After we lost my stepson Ryan, the grief felt insurmountable. But it wasn't just his death that weighed on me — it was how his accident shattered everything I thought I could trust. Life had suddenly shown me that everything I held dear could be ripped away in a heartbeat. In an instant, my belief in security, in the safety of ordinary moments, crumbled.

How could I trust anything anymore?

The world felt fragile, like it could break apart at any moment. Simple things, like driving to the grocery store, suddenly felt loaded with uncertainty. I imagined horrible scenarios in my mind, like having a blowout that would send my car across lanes of traffic. If one of our other children didn't return a call or text, I thought the worst every time.

Our Great Pyrenees, Scarlett O'Hara — a fluffy, white angel with paws — came into our lives at just the right time, bringing the kind of comfort only a beloved pet could. But despite her presence, trust wasn't something I could find again. It was like a piece of me had been fractured, and no amount of love or comfort could put it back together. When Michael and I walked with Scarlett at Quail Hollow, I followed behind her almost out of habit, but the familiar paths we had walked for years now felt different. Even though we'd been hiking there long before Scarlett joined our family, the trails held a new uncertainty. But Scarlett… She was never uncertain.

In those woods, she was in her element—sniffing, trotting, taking charge like she had an inner knowledge that we lacked. She always seemed to know when to veer off to avoid mud or when to slow down because something ahead needed our attention. She had a confidence that I envied, a trust in herself and in the world that I had lost. When one of us fell behind, Scarlett would pause at the trailhead, her head turning back to make sure no one was left behind. She wouldn't let anyone get lost—not on her watch.

One day, after a long hike on the Brandywine Gorge Loop trail, we stepped into a parking lot overflowing with black SUVs, all blending together. We wandered from row to row, Michael pressing the panic button again and again, but we heard no response. I was frustrated. How could we possibly find our car in this mess? It felt like one more thing I couldn't control, one more way the world seemed unsteady.

But Scarlett wasn't fazed. She kept walking with purpose, tail held high, and led us straight to our car, stopping in front of it with a calm certainty that I envied. In that moment, I realized that Scarlett was teaching me something I hadn't yet understood. Rebuilding my trust in the day-to-day wouldn't come by having all the answers, or even feeling certain all the time. It would come with taking one step at a time, even when I felt lost, and trusting that eventually I would find my way.

A few years after Ryan's death, on a quiet Mother's Day morning, Scarlett offered us a gift that spoke volumes. We were walking in the park. It was early, and we had the place to ourselves, so we let her go ahead of us as we sometimes did. I was trying to embrace the day, but something was missing. Since Ryan's death, Mother's Day had been bittersweet.

Without warning, Scarlett bounded over to the steps of the still-closed gift shop. She positioned herself in front of them, and then, with surprising grace for a dog her size (over 100 pounds), she began to jump and twirl. Her agility and grace were remarkable.

And, somehow, I knew she was doing more than just playing—she was performing a dance just for me. As I laughed and clapped, tears welled up in my eyes. Somehow, she had a way of sensing exactly what I needed without me saying a word. That day, she reminded me of something I had forgotten: Joy is found in the moment, and it seeps in if you are willing to let down your guard.

Through this small act of spontaneity, she reminded me that trust, like joy, could still exist, even after heartbreak. It was a reminder that life continues to offer unexpected gifts, even when the darkness feels overwhelming.

Trust became our bond.

When we stayed at an Airbnb, a sudden storm on the first night knocked out the power, enveloping the old Victorian in eerie darkness. I was asleep in the master bedroom upstairs, right next to a steep staircase, and the house was plunged into pitch blackness, with even the streetlights out. Scarlett and Michael had gone downstairs before the blackout, and I was left alone in the dark.

I fumbled with my phone, trying to find its flashlight, but the battery had died. Panic began to rise in my chest as the storm outside roared, and with no service and no light, I felt scared and stranded.

Then, I heard Scarlett barking up the stairs, her voice cutting through the darkness. She was determined to alert me, and her persistent barking eventually woke Michael. Using his phone's flashlight, Michael guided me safely down the stairs, where our little family was reunited. We lit candles and we settled on the couch to wait out the storm together.

As I lay there listening to the wind howl, I realized that Scarlett didn't need words or instructions; she knew what to do. Whether we were facing darkness or uncertainty, she always reminded me to trust her and trust life. In many ways, Scarlett danced me back into life, showing me that joy and trust could coexist even in the most difficult times. For that, I will always be grateful.

—Amy Catlin Wozniak—

The Day I Learned to See Dogs Differently

There is nothing truer in this world
than the love of a good dog.
~Mira Grant

My father had so many dental issues that it made me want to brush my teeth all the time. It seemed he was always getting a cavity filled, and he'd had many of his teeth pulled. Most recently, he had really bad toothaches and had to get several root canals over the span of a few weeks. I couldn't even imagine having one root canal let alone several.

Finally, his toothaches were gone, and the dentist declared that he did not need any more root canals. It was a sunny Thursday in late June, and the weather was perfect, around 72 degrees. I assumed that my father would go fishing at his fishing club. No, he said when asked. He was just going to stay home and spend time with his dog Oscar as he had not been home a lot lately.

Oscar was his six-year-old, caramel-colored Dachshund. He looked like a cuddly teddy bear but he didn't act like one. He followed my father around the house, snout held high, as if he was a courtier to a king. If anyone got close to my father, he would glare at them, growl, and bare his teeth. He didn't want to be petted by anyone other than my father either, except on rare occasions.

Then, there was his behavior in the car. When he went for a car ride with my father, he would whine until he was allowed to sit in the front seat. It really sounded pitiful, as if he was a small child alone in the big world, separated from his parent. My father could not stand to see the dog suffer, and whoever was sitting in the front seat was then demoted to the back seat. One time, my friend said she saw Oscar look back at her after she was demoted and smirk at her.

I tolerated Oscar, but to be honest, I never quite understood why my father was so crazy about dogs — especially this unfriendly Dachshund. Then again, I did not understand dog lovers in general. I worked with a woman who talked about her dogs as if they were people. She went on trips with them and couldn't even have a conversation without talking about them. I thought she was certifiably crazy.

That Thursday, I had the day off from work and was going to get my hair done and go shopping. I finished talking to my father and turned to walk into the bathroom when something hit me on my lower calf. It felt like someone had hit me with a very large football, and the force of it almost knocked me over.

I turned around, and that little dog was looking at me. He then ran over to my father and started barking loudly. He kept looking at me and then looking at my father while barking. It was clear that he was trying to tell us something.

Finally, I suggested to my father that maybe something went wrong with his root canal. Perhaps he had an infection. I had read that dogs could sense things like that. It seemed like a long shot, but as we had lost our mother a few years earlier, I thought it might be a good idea for my father to see a doctor. My younger brother happened to call at that time, and after much persuasion, we convinced my father to go to the doctor just to be on the safe side. He made a few comments about how he did not raise kids to be bosses, but then he did agree to go.

After much difficulty from the dog, I finally made it out of the house and commenced my day of pampering and shopping. My brother went with my father to the doctor. At the time, I thought my brother and I were both overreacting, and the doctor would say there was no infection. Maybe the dog just wanted treats.

At about 4:00 PM, I received a call from my brother. Our father had been admitted to the hospital. He didn't have much more information except that my father was there already. I was shocked, and it all felt surreal. What could be wrong?

I was two hours from the hospital and did not get there until 6:00 PM. Both my brothers were there, and my father was in excruciating pain that even painkillers did not stop.

It turns out that my father's "toothaches" were actually small heart attacks. His condition was getting worse and worse and he was starting to have a major heart attack. If he had been at home when the heart attack started and called an ambulance, it probably would not have gotten to him fast enough. As he was already in the hospital when the heart attack started, they were able to save him.

If not for Oscar, my father would not have lived. Oscar, his cranky, little Dachshund, had saved his life. It is one thing to read about something like that, but it's another to experience it.

At that moment, my eyes were opened to the fact that dogs are so much more than little animals. They love us, care for us, and have more abilities than I was even aware of. I suddenly felt a new respect and appreciation for Oscar and all dogs. For the first time, I even felt a kinship with the millions of people who love dogs. I had become one of them.

A few days later, after an angioplasty, my father was ready to return home. We brought Oscar with us, and on the way home, my father insisted on driving. Oscar was super happy to see my father, and my father had to hold him for a few minutes before he was even able to drive. Of course, Oscar sat in the passenger seat next to my father, and this time he was sitting in a new, very expensive car seat that I had bought him. I didn't care if he growled at me again or smirked. As my father drove home, I felt nothing but gratitude for that little dog who taught me that miracles do happen.

— Angela Kennedy —

Charlie Hero

Where there is great love, there are always miracles.
~Willa Cather

Tucker is my 110-pound German Shepherd, whose hobbies include, most recently, eating my couch, chewing my shoes to pieces, sleeping on my deck with all eight hundred of his toys instead of in his bed in my room, and playing tug of war. He's a gentle giant, and I'm very nearly terrified he'll be a puppy forever. He's two and a half, and he shows no hint that he'll soon take up the great sport of adulting it, canine-style. Tucker did teach my three-and-a-half-year-old, Charlie, how to play, though, and that has made us a healthier and happier family.

Charlie, the aforementioned older but much smaller Chihuahua, has learned two forms of play: He has recently learned to fly from one piece of furniture in my house to the next and is king of the game "Don't Fall in the Lava on the Floor," a game most humans with children and grandchildren know well. And he is quite proficient at figuring out how to get things he wants. This second skill, less purely designed than the flying, recently saved Tucker's life.

I woke up in early April 2023 and, feeling sick, headed for the bathroom. I fell, hard, and I couldn't get up. I had to use my emergency necklace to summon help. I spoke calmly with the dispatch at 911 and started plans for my rescue. I explained that I was weak but probably not in need of a doctor, so they called the police. The paramedics working at Waldens Ridge Emergency Service were on their way to my house. I discussed the dogs, too, because Tucker is so huge that he often looks ferocious when he's really just a big ball of fur, begging for belly rubs when he isn't eating furniture.

The dispatcher relayed this information to the relevant parties and was told that a county sheriff's deputy had already arrived and said Tucker was unduly aggressive.

Now I panicked. I worried about how the officer would treat my dog. I told him to have the deputy wait for the Waldens Ridge paramedics outside. I said that if the officer would just call Tucker by name and hold his hand out slightly with his palm down, Tuck would lick his hand. The guy was too antsy, though. He didn't want the volunteers to witness his fear or something.

By the time the paramedics arrived, there was no sound from Tucker, and Charlie had raced faster than I'd ever witnessed (we're talking lazy Chihuahua here) into my bedroom to be with me. The deputy ignored my questions about Tucker. I was begging to know where he was and if he was okay. I had more than a sneaking suspicion that my dog had been tasered. I can't say for sure, but I knew he was hurt because he didn't come back to my room after the deputy came in.

The deputy stood inside my bedroom and waited for the paramedics, ignoring my panic over the dog. He moved to the door as the paramedics arrived, and then I saw the deputy and the ambulance driver drag something toward the back door.

The paramedics got me up and to my bed. I couldn't walk. But I refused to go to the hospital unless they brought Tucker into my room. They did not.

I'll admit I was paranoid. A person who is septic tends to be paranoid and have hallucinations, too. We found out later that I went into septic shock.

So, back in bed, basin by my side, I refused to go to the hospital, and I was unreasonable. I called Tucker repeatedly, but it wasn't until 4:00 AM when I heard him crying from outside the dog door two rooms away.

"It's okay, Tuck," I called out to him. "I'm coming."

But I wasn't. I couldn't.

I called Tucker inside, but he didn't come. I offered him treats, and I knew he heard me because he cried every time I called him. But he couldn't get in.

Finally, I talked to my little guy. "Do you think you can get Tucker, Charlie? Will you go find Tucker?"

Charlie headed out of the room like a flash. He came rushing back. He had not exited the dog door that leads to my fenced-in backyard, but he acted like he had seen Tuck.

I held up a chewy chicken treat. "Charlie? If you help Tucker, I'll give you a treat!" I held up the treat for the little guy to see.

"Charlie, go get Tucker." I patted him on the rump and… it was a thing to behold. Mind you, it was not a Lassie moment. Charlie didn't tell me that Timmy fell down the well or anything like that, but it was beautiful nonetheless. The little guy was rooting around in the laundry room, where the dog door goes into the yard. I heard bumps and more bumps. Dragging ensued and then a tumble of… books? I was certain of it. After the books fell down, I knew Charlie could get to Tucker. Charlie ran back into my bedroom with a look that said, "I hope you can hear how hard I'm working, Mom!"

"Good Charlie!" I encouraged.

In about a minute, horse hooves were beating down the dog door. Not really, though. It was just Charlie leading his bigger, younger brother back inside.

"Tuck!" I yelled, overjoyed. "And Charlie Hero!" I officially changed Charlie's name that day after he rescued his brother. Then, the dopey dog took his untouched treat to Tucker and laid it down. He was better than a hero.

A laundry basket with books in it had been shoved up against the dog door so Tucker couldn't get in until somebody rescued him. Somebody did. Charlie.

Tucker licked his gift and started to eat it. This is a treat neither dog ever refuses. Tucker changed his mind. He stood up and grabbed the treat and said, with his eyes, "Nah. You keep it."

I'd never seen two dogs refuse their favorite treat, but I saw it then.

Charlie finally ate the treat, and we all slept. I didn't realize I was growing sicker by the minute and that my blood had infected my brain. I ended up in the hospital shortly after Tucker's rescue where I was rescued too. I survived and came home to my babies.

And that's the takeaway: I have canine family, my babies. And now they love each other too.

—Marla H. Thurman—

I'll Hide, You Seek!

The dog lives for the day, the hour, even the moment.
~Robert Falcon Scott

My dog loves to play hide-and-seek. Although Charlie is a Goldendoodle, I suspect she inherited way more Golden Retriever genes than Poodle. Not only does she look and shed like a full-bred Golden, but she maintains both the dopey sweet temperament and clinginess of the beloved breed.

Linked to her intense clinginess is a need to constantly know my location. She follows me everywhere. If I get up from the couch, she gets up from the couch. Heating up leftovers in the kitchen? Charlie is heating up leftovers in the kitchen. Occupied in the restroom and don't fully close the door? In no time, Charlie is also occupied in the restroom, gazing at me from only inches away. She despises closed doors, which impede her ability to properly trace my whereabouts. And unless doors are latched shut, she will shove them open with her cream-colored snout.

One can sense her panic as she arises from a nap or re-enters the house after playing in the backyard to realize she can't see me. She runs from room to room until she finds me.

We made a game of it. I began to deliberately hide from her, first in easy spots like an open closet or behind a door. As soon as she found me, she would jump with joy, lick my face, and sprint around the house.

In no time, Charlie learned where the easy hiding spots were, so I had to up my game. Once I shimmied underneath my king-sized bed, only inches to spare between my face and the solid wood frame. As I heard the pitter-patter of Charlie's paws trotting through each room, searching for me, it appeared I had finally stumped her. She even retraced her steps, searching each room again, her unease rapidly escalating.

My own anxiety began to mount as I became claustrophobic under the bed, so I released a couple of playful sounds to alert her to my location. Finally pinpointing me underneath the bed, her enthusiasm was so great that she slithered her own body halfway under and began aggressively licking me in delight. Attempting to lurch free of her wet tongue, I smacked my face on the bed's wooden under-frame, earning a delightful wound on the bridge of my nose. Co-workers found it quite amusing in the weeks to come when I explained that the source of my battle wound was a vigorous game of hide-and-seek with my pup.

Playing fetch with Charlie one evening more recently, she decided to take our hide-and-seek game to the next level. With a stuffed toy hotdog in her mouth, she chased her neon-orange ball down the hallway, quickly leaving my line of sight. When she didn't immediately return, I assumed the ball must have bounced into a dark corner or gotten stuck under the nightstand.

I went to investigate. I peeked down the hallway and into my bedroom: no Charlie. I swiftly glanced into our bathroom to find it similarly empty. I scanned the guest bedroom where she enjoyed looking out the window at wildlife in our backyard: no Charlie. The workout room was likewise empty.

Following a moment of confusion, I began connecting the dots. After all our rounds of hide-and-seek, was Charlie reversing the roles and hiding from me?

"Oh, Charlie. Where are you?" I called out, suspecting she might emerge from her hiding spot at the sound of my voice. Not a peep. I rechecked each room and finally found the corner of her stuffed hotdog just barely sticking out from underneath the king bed. Crouching onto all fours, I peered under the bed to see Charlie's sweet face staring back at me.

"Charlie girl! Were you hiding from me?"

She was beyond ecstatic to have been found and emerged from the darkness to cover my face in wet slobbers. I'm not sure if Charlie or I was more excited. I lavished her with praise for not only successfully hiding, but for selecting such a tricky spot and staying quiet as I searched.

I still chuckle at the thought of her patiently watching me from underneath the bed as I searched room after room looking for her, refusing to stir even as I called her name. After always doing the seeking, she clearly wanted a turn hiding. Hopefully, next time Charlie wants to reverse the roles, her hotdog won't give away her position.

— Emily C. Marszalek —

A Winner After All

Be the person your dog thinks you are.
~C.J. Frick

It requires fortitude, or a persistent Lakeland Terrier, to draw you out for a walk on a damp spring morning in New England. Fortunately, I had the latter to keep me moving one day. We finished our three-mile trek with a stop at our mailbox. Teddy joyfully sniffed the golden daffodils budding beneath as I reached my mittened hand inside.

After thirty years of making music, I thought my ambition had dried up. But as I scanned *International Musician*, a monthly job publication for professional musicians, my pulse quickened at the words, "Principal Harp Audition."

As a professional harpist, I had read those words a dozen times, and they were always for orchestra positions in distant states or distant countries. Full-time jobs didn't turn up very often.

As we made our way up the driveway, I read that this audition was for a local orchestra. But it was on the same day as my twins' awards assembly at school. It was also the day of my husband's mandatory off-site work meeting.

How could I slip away to take an audition? How could I find the time to prepare for an audition? Did I even have the courage to do it?

Inside the house, Teddy barked impatiently as I continued to stare at the newspaper. He was ready for his post-walk towel rub and cookie.

"One minute, Teddy," I told him. "I'll just email to find out the repertoire, to satisfy my curiosity, nothing more."

But it was a slippery slope. "The Nutcracker," "Symphonie Fantastique," "Tzigane," Verdi, Britten — I had played all the required repertoire. In fact, I had performed all of it.

I'd practiced those parts at the Conservatory until hot, red blisters formed on my fingers. I had performed them with community orchestras in New England and as substitute harpist with many professional groups, too. I knew those excerpts inside and out.

I looked down at Teddy. Well, I knew the parts before barking replaced harp arpeggios in our house. I had known them sixteen years ago, before I had my son, before my twins, before my laundry, cooking, cleaning, driving, parenting gig.

The next morning, after my husband left for work and the kids for school, Teddy and I headed to the file cabinet. The parts were frayed at the corners, yet I could still hear my teacher's voice as I scanned a tricky, technical section.

I placed the music on my stand.

An hour later, I pushed the harp from my shoulder. My back felt tight, and my fingertips tingled. The sound wasn't the rich, warm tone I remembered, but the notes were fantastic. Passages came back to me like old friends.

But Teddy, where was Teddy? I tore through the house calling him. He wasn't in the kitchen or the bedrooms, not the TV room or the attic. Back downstairs, I panicked as I wondered if he had pushed open a door or fallen out a window. Finally, I saw his tail protruding from my closet. His head was inside a brown paper bag, and chocolate wrappers littered the floor. He had found my stash.

"Teddy!"

Fortunately, four ounces of milk chocolate is not poisonous for a fourteen-pound dog.

The following day, I placed Teddy's bed next to the harp and four Milk-Bones on the music stand. He stayed on his bed quietly while I practiced for two hours.

The next day, six Milk-Bones and three hours of practicing.

A few weeks later, we had worked up to four hours of practice in the morning, a quick lunch break, and two hours in the afternoon. We traded our walks in the park for five minutes of running laps in the backyard each hour. It was quicker than walking, and we both felt better.

Soon, I lost count of how many Milk-Bones and how many practice hours. But I knew exactly how many days until the audition and how many notches on the metronome until I would be playing at tempo.

Then, I agonized over my solo. Handel was the traditional choice. "Whirlwind" was a contemporary showpiece. The risk was that everyone else auditioning would play Handel, but on the other hand, the judges might not like the contemporary choice, "Whirlwind."

I played both pieces for Teddy.

The first time I played "Whirlwind," he sat up straight on his bed and perked his ears. The second time I played it, he threw back his head and sang. I say "sang" because he rounded his lips and matched the pitch ringing from the harp. He moved his head and rocked on his haunches until the final four pianissimo notes.

"Wow!" I exclaimed. There was no denying it. My playing had elicited a physical response.

Teddy sang every day after that. In fact, if he was in the kitchen eating his dinner, he would race through the house to sing with "Whirlwind."

It made my husband and children laugh, but it stirred something inside me. "Whirlwind" would be my solo.

The day before the audition, the metronome was having trouble keeping up with me. My fingers felt strong, my tone sounded warm, and the parts were all memorized. I was ready.

Professional orchestra auditions take place behind a screen. It removes the element of bias, but you have no idea who is listening to you. They don't give you any feedback except "You have lost" or "You have won."

I lost.

The next day was my twins' graduation. I had missed Awards Day, but I was at school for the final ceremony and festivities. Teddy was home in his crate.

That night, my husband returned from his off-site with lots of stories. Teddy and I sat in the kitchen and listened.

Summer started. There was cooking, laughing and late nights with my teenagers. I didn't play the harp.

A few weeks later, I found myself home alone. The house was quiet, too quiet. I put my book down on the couch. Where was Teddy?

"Teddy?" I called. "Teddy? Teddy?"

I moved through the rooms. I found him next to the harp, sitting on his bed.

Our eyes met.

"Are you waiting for me to practice?" I asked.

He wagged his tail.

I pulled the harp back and played "Whirlwind."

He flung his head back and sang.

For an hour, we were lost in the musical space we both loved.

Teddy reminded me that we make music for the sheer joy of it, to release that which lies silent within. Continuing to do what you love takes courage. When mine faltered, my Terrier drew me back.

After the music, we both felt so elated that we took a few laps around the yard.

— Sarah Stuart —

My Dog Can Talk

Dogs do speak, but only to those
who know how to listen.
~Orhan Pamuk

Our six-month-old Pug, Oski, with his toasted-marshmallow coloring and soft, curvy wrinkles, happily zipped across the grass in our yard, his new forever home. We called them "zoots," a combination of zoomies and scoots because Oski ran with his backside dangerously low to the ground until his hind legs buckled and he tumbled over. My husband and I thought the zoots were the cutest.

"This is not cute," our veterinarian said at Oski's check-up. Oski's zoots, as well as his signature waddle walk, were signs of a potentially painful, genetic spinal abnormality. An X-ray confirmed hemivertebrae, an abnormal wedge-shaped bone in the thoracic region that pinched Oski's spinal cord and restricted nerve function to his hindside.

"It looks like a twisted roller-coaster track!" I said, gasping at the disturbing image of Oski's warped spine.

"Considering quality-of-life options for a dog his age," our veterinarian continued, "I'd advise surgery to stabilize the spine, or Oski could quickly become fecal incontinent and lose all rear mobility." The rest of the appointment was a blur.

"I feel so guilty," I said to my husband on the way home from the vet. "How did we miss the signs?" My mind raced with questions. *Did it hurt? How bad was the pain? Can I afford a wheelchair? Where do*

I buy doggy diapers?

I wished I had done better by Oski.

"If only Oski could talk," I said as I showered him with several squeaky kisses through my tears. "Then, he could just tell us if he's in pain." Little did I know that my wish was about to reveal itself in a little, plastic word button made for animals.

At the same time that Oski was successfully recovering from spinal surgery, I stumbled upon a news article about a pediatric speech and language pathologist who taught her dog to communicate using recordable word buttons. With these assistive language tools called Augmentative and Alternative Communication (AAC), Christina Hunger recorded a word into a button, and her dog Stella pushed it with her paw to hear the word. Then, Hunger verbally and physically modeled the word to help Stella understand the meaning.

Eventually, Stella learned to associate the word with the action and pressed the buttons independently to express her needs and wants. I wondered, if I had these buttons, would Oski learn to talk to me, too? Could he tell me when he was in pain?

"AAC means we're not replacing communication," I explained to my husband as I excitedly unpacked the box with my new buttons, "but adding to it."

Using tips from the Christina Hunger article, I started teaching with words that were already familiar to Oski. I recorded the word OUTSIDE into the first button. Oski pressed down with his paw to hear my recorded word, and I repeated it before taking Oski to the backyard for reinforcement. I did this multiple times until it appeared that Oski understood that pressing this particular button got me to open the door and let him out.

Over the next several months, I continued to add and model words, including PLAY, UP, and TREAT. Most were associated with basic needs like meals (EAT, FOOD, HUNGRY), going potty (PEEPEE, POOP, OUTSIDE) and family members (MOM, FRIEND, GRANDMA). Gradually, I added more advanced concepts like time (NOW, LATER, SOON), emotions (FRUSTRATED, HAPPY, SAD), and self-care (OUCH, VETERINARIAN, HELP, MEDICINE). Suddenly, Oski had more than eighty buttons!

I set out on a journey to teach Oski how to tell me when he hurt. Two years later, I found myself inside a whole new world of communicating with my dog. Oski appeared to use his word buttons to share observations, ask questions, argue, advocate for himself and others, express feelings, and demand treats.

He pressed these buttons one at a time, in combination and in context. Oski appeared to tell me when it was time to nap (BLANKET) and argued for his treats in a timely manner (NO, NOW). I think we had a lengthy conversation about CHEESE and why there was none in the refrigerator (WHERE, HMM?). He informed me when the cat was out of water (ALL DONE), when he wanted company to leave (BYE), and when he was hungry (EAT).

As Oski learns, his presses aren't always clear. The average adult has 15,000–35,000 words in their vocabulary. Oski has 80. We don't use full sentences with syntax so our conversations sound more like toddler talk. Because of the limited vocabulary, Oski learned to choose his words creatively to get his point across.

"He's making the words do double-duty!" I said to my husband after months of modeling the buttons. I was amazed to realize that Oski could use one button to mean multiple things in context. He was using DRINK after taking a sip from his water bowl to narrate his current situation, or to inform me that his water bowl was empty, and also when he observed me drinking my morning coffee. The more I connected with Oski, the better I got at interpreting.

Recently, Oski started showing weakness in his rear legs again. His waddle became a wobble. His back left foot dragged. Zoots were a memory. I wasn't surprised when Oski lumbered to his soundboard one day, tilted his head, and pressed OUCH, VETERINARIAN.

"Are you feeling okay, Oski?" I whispered, snuggling up to him. But I knew. A trip to the vet confirmed intervertebral disc disease. Unrelated to his spinal abnormality, IVDD is a condition causing weakness, nerve damage, and pain. This time, I was ready. I was able to address Oski's medical needs without any uncertainty. He told me so.

Oski continues to thrive despite his diagnosis and still presses his buttons, albeit a little haphazardly. I'm grateful that teaching AAC gave Oski a voice, and I'm fascinated by its impact on the study of animal cognition. Maybe someday it will be possible to discern how our pets can talk and to what extent.

Now bonded to each other like best friends, we sit near the buttons with Oski on my lap enjoying delicious, leg-thumping scratches behind his ears. One day, when I stopped, Oski slid toward the board and pressed I LOVE YOU… MORE. My heart melted. I leaned over and pressed the same button. "I love you, too, Oski," I said. "I love you, too."

—Alli Straus—

Who Rescued Whom?

Along Came a Spider

The unconditional love you get from a pet
is something you carry with you
for the rest of your life.
~Kyra Sedgwick

It was a rainy night when my mom jumped out of the car. She had seen a small, shadowy figure in the driveway. What she thought was a stray cat or maybe even a drowned rat turned out to be a shivering, black Teacup Poodle weighing under three pounds. Of course, my mother swooped him up, got him inside, cleaned him up, and got him warm. He had ear mites, rotten teeth, and a mess of black hair.

My mother had been saying "no more animals" for months after losing feral cats and adopted dogs. But this little dog had left her no choice. It was almost like he knew which house to pick.

The next day, we contacted our city hall and put his information on Facebook. Given his condition, an owner probably wouldn't step up, but we wanted to put his picture out there just in case. After a few days, it was clear that the little man was here to stay.

Naming him was a whole other issue. He was balding in spots and was so little, with huge, buggy eyes and a strange little waddle due to a bum leg. From a distance, he looked almost like a strange rodent or large bug. So, we decided upon the name Spider.

It wasn't long before we adult children had been replaced by the little interloper, as Mom always had to get home to take care of him (even though the dog slept probably twenty hours a day). But he became the new project and love of my mother's life (and even my father's—who came along under duress but couldn't help himself).

My mother and father, even though they are in their seventies, are very busy people. In addition to the two of them and my family of four in a large house, there are always comings and goings. It should be noted that, even though there are six of us in the house, there was only one person that Spider acknowledged—my mother. Any of us could walk past his bedding area without a single peep, but the moment she stepped into the house, he would whimper. If she didn't immediately go to him, the whimper transitioned into barking until she picked him up.

My mother is one of the bravest women I know and as a general rule is not moved by much of anything. Having survived a heart attack and more than her share of emergency surgeries, her feathers very rarely get ruffled.

But it was different when the pandemic hit. Her nerves were often shot, and her anxiety was pretty high about the choices that she needed to make about work, family, and all the other uncertainties that a national emergency brings. But two things calmed her: her faith in God and the by now almost hairless, little old man that would squirm his way into the crook of her knee when she would lie down on the couch.

Spider took advantage of her new availability. He figured out that if he barked at 3:00 AM, she would come get him and return with him to their usual spot on the couch—him hidden under the covers, snuggled next to the woman who brought him peace, and her sleeping soundly with the hairless wonder that brought her peace during a scary time.

I'm sure he didn't understand what was happening in the world. But he was content knowing that, in a world of chaos, this was where he was safe. And, in a weird way, I think my mom felt the same way. Sometimes, when we are afraid and feel alone, love is all it takes to make us feel safe—even if that love comes from a bald, toothless three-pound dog.

Spider passed away in my mother's arms after a series of seizures.

The vet said he was in his late teens, a real wonder. My father and son dug a hole in the pouring rain to bury him. His little headstone reads: "If love could have kept you here, you would have lived forever." Truer word were never spoken.

— Corrie Lopez —

Sunny Delight

He is your friend, your partner, your defender, your dog. You are his life, his love, his leader. He will be yours, faithful and true, to the last beat of his heart.
~Author Unknown

The blast from a gun echoed through the valley between my neighbor's house and my office. I pressed my watch for the time — 2:10 in the afternoon. What was that?

I rose from my desk and looked out the window facing the valley. That's when I saw her for the first time, running for her life. With her tail tucked between her legs, the small, yellow dog ran as fast as her short legs could carry her, stopping only after she made her way to the top of the hill in front of my office, a good hundred feet in front of me.

Soon, she settled down into a small heap, panting, head resting on her front paws as she scanned the horizon. Another stray was not a surprise. The gravel road behind my office had no houses for miles. It was the perfect spot for dropping unwanted animals in a county where no animal shelter existed. My neighbor or I were the recipients of these strays, who foraged for food, water, and kindness in an unkind world.

My neighbor, however, wasn't as understanding as I was. He'd taken in his share of strays, nursed them back to health if the expense wasn't too great, and found homes for them, but only if it required little effort. I wondered why he'd fired the shot to scare this one off. I found out soon enough.

I opened the door and made eye contact with the frightened creature on the hillside. From where I stood, I couldn't see the severity of her problems. I called to her, and her tail wagged. I coaxed her to come toward me, anxious to know if she was friendly. She picked herself up from her prone position and looked at me, tail still wagging, probably wondering if it was safe to approach.

I went out to the porch and opened the plastic bin where I kept dog food for these emergencies. I poured out a generous helping of tasty morsels and proceeded toward her, encouraging her to trust me. We met halfway. Only then did I understand my neighbor's reluctance to let her stay.

Her swollen face made her eyes look like slits. Her neck was puffy and raw, with the fur gone from her legs, face, and neck.

Mange!

I'd never had dealings with mange, and I was hesitant to touch her because I had other dogs to protect. However, she didn't know she had mange, and her tongue drooled at the smell of the food I had placed before her in the plastic bowl. She consumed it in five bites and then licked the bowl, her small face looking up at me for more.

I would not let her suffer if something could help her. I made a frantic call to my vet.

"I have a stray dog here, and she's covered with mange. What should I do?"

"Any signs of anything else?"

"No. She appears normal in every other way, has a good appetite, and is friendly with a wagging tail."

"Will she let you touch her?"

"I haven't tried."

"Bring her in. It's not the end of the world for her. Mange is treatable."

"What about my other dogs? Is she contagious?"

"It depends on the type of mange. Let me look at her before you let the other dogs around her."

"I'll be there soon."

That's all I needed to hear. I gave water to the dog, which she lapped appreciatively.

I grabbed a clean towel to wrap around her, opened the back door of my van, placed the towel around her, and picked her up. She offered no resistance as I put her in the back and closed the door.

The vet met me outside. "Looks like red mange to me. Let me scrape her skin, and I can tell you in a few minutes."

I waited outside while he took in the skin cells to examine. The verdict came back as he had said: red mange.

"Can it be treated?" I asked.

"Yes, but red mange is the hardest to work with. We can get rid of the infection with a high dose of antibiotics, but it'll take about a year for her hair to return."

"Is she contagious?"

"No, red mange is hereditary. It's in her blood. It passes to dogs from their mothers. We can keep it under control, but she should never have pups. We'll need to spay her as soon as we clear the infection."

"Okay, let's get started."

"Do you have a name picked out for her?"

A name? I wasn't expecting such a bundle of neediness to knock on my door. As I looked at her, her tail wagged in tune with my thoughts, and I saw her smiling with those puffy eyes. She was the color of sunshine.

"Sunny Delight."

"Okay, let's get Sunny Delight inside to begin her treatment." He picked her up and carried her through the door to his examination room.

Her thin, bony body trembled as I reached and touched her head for the first time.

The next few months brought significant changes to Sunny D's appearance. With daily antibiotics, the infection went away. Her eyes soon looked normal and bright as the puffiness subsided, and fur grew over the once-raw skin. She developed a healthy appetite but no longer wolfed down her food as if it were her last meal. The scar from her spaying healed over. Happiness exuded from her as she made friends with the other animals that called my rescue farm their home.

A year later, Sunny D shows almost no signs of red mange. She's a fat, healthy bundle of joy who lives up to her name. She greets me enthusiastically whenever she sees me and rides beside me in the golf cart every day as we check the fences. Nothing goes unnoticed by her now-clear eyes. She chases butterflies through the meadows and barks at bluejays when they fly down at her. Her love for the farm pond goes without saying as she stands knee-deep in the water, barking at the fish as they nibble at her.

My neighbor who'd shot up in the air to scare her away saw her for the first time the other day as we rode through the pasture on the golf cart.

"Where'd you get the cute dog?" he asked, unaware of his shortcomings. "My kids would love her."

"Oh, she was a stray who adopted me," I told him. My heart swelled with pride as I looked over at her, facing forward, ready to take on whatever came next. She's my hero.

— Carol W. Huff —

Anxious Alice

Every puppy should have a boy.
~Erma Bombeck

We'd been in the Northwest Territories for two years and had already adopted a lovable Husky named Roxy. We were now seeking a companion for her at Yellowknife's SPCA animal shelter. As we stepped in from the cold, we learned they had a new litter of puppies. They were almost ready to be weaned.

The mother was a tall, extremely slender, grey-haired dog. Her puppies were blond. "The mother is a Whippet, and we believe the father was probably a golden Lab," said the young lady who was showing us around.

I studied the thin mother. Whippets just didn't make sense in our Arctic climate. How could these dogs possibly survive in -40°C conditions? They had no body fat and lacked the proper insulating fur.

Still, we'd been hoping for a young companion for our Husky, so we eagerly adopted one of the golden-haired puppies and named her Alice after the Northern Lights (Aurora Borealis).

Unfortunately, Alice grew from a goofy pup into a neurotic adolescent. A Whippet has a unique physique that closely resembles the Greyhound. However, it's their absurd personalities that distinguish them from nearly every other breed. They are extremely vocal with grunts and groans that sound almost human. They have a high prey drive, which in Alice manifests as her flinging her kibble all over the house and chasing it down with single-minded fervour.

But it's the anxiety that is the big problem. Alice cannot stand to be separated from her human pack. She has chewed up doors, carpets, and garbage cans when left alone. Kennels couldn't keep her contained, muzzles seemed uniquely cruel, and anxiety meds didn't work. She has cost us thousands of dollars in damages. It was exasperating to come home to destruction time after time, and perhaps we would have found her too much to deal with if not for one invaluable trait: She had the innate ability to calm my autistic son.

Preston would have meltdowns when he was younger. It wasn't unusual to hear him throwing the Nintendo Switch controller against the hardwood floor and screaming in rage and frustration. Meltdowns in autistic individuals occur due to emotional regulation issues. In other words, their brains haven't made the connections needed to control (behaviour inhibition) the knee-jerk reactions we all have when emotionally overwhelmed.

But Alice knew what to do. She would crawl into his lap and soon he would be giggling. "Alice. You're silly!" And just like that, the meltdown would be over.

It wasn't until she began to make a habit of interrupting his meltdowns that I realised what an enormous service she was providing all of us. As soon as Preston began a meltdown, she'd leave my side, often hearing his frustration before I did. It seemed instinctive for her.

I began to spy on them, sneaking behind her so I could watch how she helped him. Sometimes, she nosed him. Sometimes, she licked his face until he was drowning in saliva. And, sometimes, I'd find her lying across him, using her body weight to pin him as she demanded his undivided attention. It was the latter approach that had me purchasing weighted blankets because he obviously liked the pressure.

She had a variety of techniques that she cycled through and she seemed to know what he needed in the moment. Over the years, his meltdowns tapered off from daily to weekly to so few and far between that I almost forgot that he ever had them. And I know a lot of that was due to Alice. It was practice for Preston's brain. It helped build the connections that were needed to soothe the raging storm of the meltdown until eventually he could manage them himself.

Alice is an absurd, exasperating and anxiety-ridden dog who became a miracle worker for our family. I can't help but think that her own struggles with overwhelming emotions developed within her a sense of empathy that drove her to ease those same emotions within my son. She knew how he felt, and she was determined to make it better. To this day, the two are inseparable. And no matter how many doors, carpets, or garbage cans she chews up, our loyalty for her will never waver. She could cost me a million dollars, and she'd still be worth every penny.

— Carina Middleton —

Running Partners

The one absolutely unselfish friend that man can have
in this selfish world, the one that never deserts him,
the one that never proves ungrateful
or treacherous, is his dog.
~George Graham

After our Poodle, Cookie, died from seizures, I had no desire to adopt another dog. The trauma of Cookie's painful death made me hesitant to connect with another animal, fearing they would endure similar suffering. Unfortunately, my desire to remain dog-free ended abruptly five months after Cookie died. My younger sister, Elena, wanted to adopt a Standard Poodle named Lady. I was upset by this news. Even if I wanted another pet, five months after Cookie's death seemed too soon.

But Elena explained why our family needed to adopt Lady. "The house feels empty without Cookie. Plus, Lady needs us as much as we need her. Her last owner was evicted and had to surrender Lady to a shelter. The shelter said the owner wanted to come back for Lady in a month but never returned."

Elena showed me a picture of Lady. Her white fur was so overgrown and matted that we could barely see her eyes. Lady was eight years old, with several benign tumors and an eye infection. The shelter was so eager to get rid of her that they told Elena they'd give her two free tickets to SeaWorld if she adopted her. I guess if I had to find a silver lining, at least this new dog would get us a free ride on the Manta roller coaster.

Even so, I couldn't shake the fact that Lady was eight years old. Cookie was twelve when she died. Why would I bond with an animal who could die in a few years?

Despite my concerns, my parents also wanted to adopt Lady. A couple of days later, I came home from my part-time job to find Lady sitting on our couch. The shelter had shaved most of her fur, exposing her big, brown eyes and ribs. It looked like she hadn't eaten in weeks.

She hopped off the couch and sniffed me like I was the intruder. Then, she stood on her hind legs and tapped my thighs, as if she was trying to say, "Pet me!" I petted her head for a moment before heading to my room. I feared that if I petted her for too long, I might start liking her.

For the next couple of months, I continued to avoid Lady as much as possible, but her clinginess made her difficult to ignore. Most mornings, I'd wake up to her big eyes staring up at me.

"Leave, Lady!" I'd say and point toward the door, only for her to wag her tail and jump on my bed. Then, when I kicked her out, she'd cry and claw at my door until I reopened it.

Lady's clinginess wasn't exclusive to me; she simply hated being alone. The first time we left her home alone, she panicked and jumped through my window screen. Luckily, we lived on the first floor, and she landed on the grass. My family calmed her anxiety by feeding her treats or pieces of chicken.

Eventually, that skittish, skinny Poodle I found on the couch became a peaceful, plump dog. Our vet shamed us for overfeeding her and recommended that Lady lose some weight.

Around this time, my doctor suggested that I also lose weight. I was a junior in college who had gained thirty pounds since freshman year. Between the stress of school, work, and the growing balance on my student loans, I used food to calm my nerves. Although I wanted to lead a healthier life, I had no clue where to begin. I didn't have enough money to join a gym. Neither did I have the self-motivation to work out alone at home. If I was going to exercise, I needed a workout partner.

I asked friends to run with me, but no one had the time or desire.

Then, one day, I woke up to Lady clawing at my door at 7:00 AM. Unlike my friends, Lady had the energy to wake up early. She also needed to lose weight. This got me to thinking. What if Lady became my running partner?

On a cloudy spring morning, Lady and I went out for our first run. The moment we stepped outside, I immediately wanted to walk back in. I couldn't run without my sides aching or feet cramping. I'm sure my neighbors could hear my heavy breathing. Ashamed of how out of shape I'd become, I hid under a baseball cap, keeping my eyes on the ground.

Lady also kept stopping. She'd hit a stride, only to stop abruptly to smell another dog's pee. Afterward, she'd zoom past three or four houses, only to stop again so she could poop. This was a bad idea. No way were we going to run around the block without me falling flat on my face. Also, running around with a big bag of poop made it even harder to breathe.

Fortunately, my neighborhood sat on a steep hill with a paved walking trail. After finding a trash can, I took Lady down this hill to see how she'd behave. Upon reaching the bottom, I realized this was a great spot for her. Few dogs came along this path, so she had nothing to sniff.

As we walked up the hill, I stopped several times to catch my breath. Every time I stopped, I looked over at Lady, who stood beside me, wagging her tail like an approving trainer. During some rest periods, I'd bend down to pet her, and she'd lick my cheek. Her support re-energized me.

When we got home, Lady waited by the bathroom door as I showered. At night, she hopped onto my bed and fell asleep beside me with her head on my pillow. I nudged her. She scooted even closer to me and made her body heavier, like she was gluing herself to my bed. Lady made it clear that she was here to stay.

At that moment, I decided I was tired of pushing her away. Lady was a sweet dog, and if she wanted to sleep next to me, I'd make room for her.

From then on, Lady and I hiked down and up the hill every other day. Eventually, our walks became runs. I never thought I'd enjoy running, but running with Lady was like meditating. When I ran with her, I didn't worry about school, work, or money. All I focused on were her paws pitter-pattering against the pavement and our goal to make it to the top of the hill.

After several months of running and eating healthy, Lady and I reached healthier weights. I couldn't believe that a dog had helped me live a more active lifestyle, just as much as I couldn't believe how much I'd grown to love Lady. She was the companion I didn't know I needed. While her age still worried me, running away from her was a waste of time. I'd rather make the most of our short time together by running beside her.

— Bianca Sanchez —

I've Been Waiting for You

Our pets are our family.
~Ana Monnar

I'm a sucker for most hard-luck stories, human or animal, which is how I ended up with some of my most precious, fuzzy friends. Thankfully, any dogs that had abusive pasts were eventually able to put it behind them with a lot of love, patience and kindness. Once they realized there was nothing to fear, they adapted and quickly become the rulers of house and hearth, whether or not I approved of the change in the chain of command.

Fur-covered little bullies.

I have always adopted, never paying anything more than adoption fees for my furry friends. I don't believe that there is anything wrong with purchasing a purebred, but (1) I can't afford to, and (2) the rescues I've adopted seemed to know that they'd dodged a figurative bullet and were doubly grateful for their rescue.

It was never a planned encounter; we simply found each other. That's how it was with Trixie. Her first home had been with a woman in her eighties who had traveled from Ohio to Michigan to purchase her but had passed away within months of bringing her home. The woman had no children of her own but had left a stipend in her will for someone to take the dog. Despite this, Trixie was dropped off at the shelter and then failed to find a forever family as prospective adopters kept returning her. After her last surrender, the sixth, she was dangerously close to her final go-round.

My mother had lived with me since developing dementia and had recently lost her beloved Bichon, Charlie, to cancer. Although I explained his absence to her multiple times a day, Mom continued searching for him, eyeing me suspiciously as she did. She couldn't remember specifically who I was, but she sure missed her Charlie, and I was suspect number one. It was time to get her a dog who needed her as much as she needed him or her.

We began to visit local shelters, but her response was always negative. I think that she was still searching for her Charlie, whom she had adopted after he had been abandoned in a downtown postal office. She delighted in telling his story and of her rescue of him. He appeared to be a full-blooded Bichon, with the biggest feet I have ever seen on such a small fellow, and he was so cockeyed that he could see around corners without turning his head.

That dog had a heart of gold and was just waiting for the love of his life. Mom's jaw dropped when she saw him. She had wanted a lapdog, but this guy was an over-lap dog. But there he was, freshly bathed and fluffed, because the shelter had prettied him up for his potential adopter. He wore a plastic cone around his neck because he was also now minus, well, certain masculine attributes.

Mom had brought him home, and the two were devoted friends for over ten years. And now, despite dementia's cruel grip, she remembered her Good Time Charlie and searched for him still in the faces of the unwanted, abandoned and abused.

At an out-of-town shelter, Mom continued to waffle back and forth. Working her way down the line, searching the pens with hope in her heart, she was looking for the white dog that she had loved so much. I didn't want to rush her or try to push her into just any dog. I was hoping that she would fall in love with a dog on her own.

As she peered into pen after pen, I drifted to a high-sided, concrete structure to sit and wait. And there was Trixie, a little pup with the ears of a mule. She looked up at me, her tail swinging frantically and irresistibly. I lifted her into my arms while keeping an eye on Mom and saw she had a beautiful little face. But, boy, those ears resembled canine satellite dishes. It took only a moment for me to realize that if Mom didn't choose her, then I'd be going home with two dogs, hers and mine.

The puppy had been placed in a concrete structure, much like a watering trough, as though she were no longer a viable candidate for adoption. I wondered if she had been culled. There had been a seizure of puppy-mill dogs that morning, and the employees were having to make some hard decisions.

Mom joined us, prepared to announce that she still hadn't found her Charlie—until she saw the puppy I was holding. She held out her hands and smiled when I placed the puppy in her arms. She began murmuring softly to the wriggling, ecstatic dog, who was busily washing her face with licks and kisses.

When all the paperwork and fees were completed, I pulled Trixie into my arms. Encircling my neck with her front legs, she clung there, holding tightly as I too received a face wash. She buried her head against my neck as though saying, "I've been waiting for you."

Holding her for a moment, I then placed her back into Mom's eager hands and caressed one of those precious, ridiculous ears. I thought to myself, *And we've been waiting for you...*

— Laurel L. Shannon —

A Golden Gift

Not everything needs to be figured out.
Some things are best left to unfold naturally.
~Author Unknown

When my husband and I finally purchased a home of our own, we put getting a dog high on our list of priorities. Visits to local humane societies offered a few possibilities but no "I'm your dog!" moments — until the day I spotted a little, golden ball of fluff huddled in the back of a run. Sad, dark eyes blinked at me above a pink nose. *Cute face,* I thought.

The information card on the front of the run identified her as Gretchen. Under "Reason for surrender," the message read, "Jealous of new baby." She was three years old, already housebroken, leash-trained, and knew basic obedience commands. The previous owners labeled her a Golden Retriever mix, although she looked like a lap dog as she watched me from her refuge. Perfect.

When I greeted her by name, she lifted her head and wagged her tail. Did a spark of life come into her eyes? My husband agreed she was interesting, but when we asked a staff member about seeing her outside of the run to get acquainted, the response was horrifying.

"She's quite aggressive," the woman told us. "Our staff members are afraid of her. She snaps and snarls at everyone. We can't get a leash on her. We're just awaiting a veterinary consultation to order her put down. We can't let her out of the run. Too big a risk."

"I must have given you the wrong kennel number. The dog I saw was very calm," I said. "Let me go back and double-check."

This time, I approached the run with caution. If that vicious dog was near the sweetie pie I had found, I didn't want to be startled by it nor have her upset by it. I crouched by the gate and made eye contact with the Golden inside. This time, she crept up to the gate. She thrust her nose through the wiring, nostrils twitching. Obeying the guidelines for meeting a strange dog, I put my hand close enough for her to smell, but not close enough to bite.

I watched her tail start a slow sweep back and forth. Her ears lifted to attention. What looked like a smile lifted the corner of her mouth. I could almost swear I heard her say, "I was right. You're the one."

The staff member joined me in the kennel corridor, leash in hand. "Found the right number?" she asked.

"This one," I said, pointing to my Golden find. Gretchen sat down, pulling her nose clear of the gate. She lifted her head as if to offer easy access to her collar.

"But… how did… what did you…? She hasn't behaved like that since she came in. This is the vicious dog I warned you about. Why isn't she snarling and carrying on?"

"Maybe she likes me," I said. "Could we try her on the leash, please?"

Did I note a slight tremble in the woman's hand as she reached for the gate? Once she opened it and stepped inside, I saw a look of confusion cross her face. Gretchen didn't make a sound. The woman clipped the leash to Gretchen's collar and led her outside the kennel.

In two steps, Gretchen was beside me, tail sending semaphore messages of joy.

"Gretchen, sit," I said. She sat.

The bemused worker handed me the leash. "Be careful she doesn't turn on you."

"Gretchen, come." She walked between my husband and me as we headed for the visiting area. Once we arrived, I ran through the litany of basic obedience commands. She knew sit, lay, come, and even shake hands. I was in love with this Golden beauty.

"What do you think?" I asked my husband.

"I think we don't have any equipment for her at home."

"Do you suppose they'll hold her for us overnight?" I was worried we might have found her only to lose her to someone more prepared, or worse, to an unfortunate vet visit.

He laughed. "If you go by what they think of her, I'm pretty sure they'll be glad to see us take her."

When we headed back to the reception area, a volunteer came to lead us back to Gretchen's kennel. She maintained a careful distance as we walked along the cages.

"Be careful when you put her in the cage," she warned. "She might revert."

I knelt beside Gretchen and looked into her eyes. "Here's the deal. We want you to have a nice bed and good food when we take you home. Maybe even some toys. We have to go shopping. So, be good until we come back tomorrow morning, okay?" Did her wagging tale indicate agreement or just happiness to receive attention?

She stepped into the kennel and lifted her head. I unclipped the leash. She headed back to the blanket in the corner where I had first spotted her. No noise, no trouble.

We completed the paperwork to apply for adoption and paid the adoption fee. I wanted to be sure that no one else could spirit her away. We headed to a pet-supply store and spent a ridiculous amount on the things we thought she needed or might enjoy. We set everything up for her: dog bed, food and water dishes, toys, leash, collar and so forth. That night, I dreamed of curling up with my newfound friend.

The next morning, we drove to the humane society with the new leash and collar. My excitement was tempered with concern. After all, I'd never adopted a grown dog before, only puppies. Would she have adjustment issues? How would we measure up to her previous owners?

"I don't know what you did, but she's been a perfect angel since you left." The volunteer at the front desk didn't attempt to mask her surprise. "Your paperwork is all done. Let's get your dog."

When we arrived at her kennel, Gretchen was sitting quietly at the gate. The volunteer shook her head in disbelief. Once we had swapped out the old collar for her new one and attached her new leash, she was ready to go.

The three of us marched past the ranks of the other potential adoptees, through the waiting area and its group of pet seekers, and out to our car. We were homeward bound with our Golden girl. Gretchen shared our lives for ten years and left us richer for her Golden presence. What a gift she was!

— Mary Beth Magee —

Amazing Gracie

When our heart is open, everything
we do becomes love.
~Mimi Novic

In 2011, my husband David left a long and storied career, a move I never saw coming but was delighted to see. He was offered a lucrative new position, and the timing seemed appropriate. I had recently retired, and it all felt right.

The plan was to take a week's vacation before David started his new job. We went to Arkansas' scenic Boxley Valley, a 260-mile drive from our Kansas City home. We rented a farmhouse at the end of a long road shared with a small church at the entrance to the drive. It was a bucolic setting, complete with a pasture full of cows and their "guard donkey," a friendly fellow who enjoyed the apple slices I fed him when he meandered to the fence. It was just the sort of place to unwind and enjoy early fall in the Midwest.

It was early evening, and we had finished a lovely, barbecued steak dinner with grilled hamburgers prepared for the next day's lunch. David wanted to enjoy the evening breeze and the view from the porch, but I set out for a walk down the gravel road that led to the church. Evening services had just been released, and the members of the congregation were chatting in the parking lot.

My presence was scarcely acknowledged, nor was the small, scraggly dog desperately seeking anyone's attention. She was thin, dusty, and tremendously thirsty, a medium-sized, tail-less mutt. She waffled between excitement and exhaustion, and I wondered if she could remain upright much longer. I bent to pet her and asked if she belonged to anyone, but I was rebuffed with "She's a stray," "Probably dumped," and "I wouldn't touch her if I were you" as several individuals tried to shoo her away.

"Maybe she could have some water…" I tried to interject, but the consensus was that I should go away and take my little dog with me. So much for charity and "do unto others."

More than a little indignant, I mumbled something about it being "mighty Christian of them" and headed back to the farmhouse with my new four-legged friend in tow. I found myself talking to the dog I elected to call "Gracie" as I hummed "Amazing Grace." I didn't know if she could make it as far as the rental house, where I could get her a bowl of water.

When we got to the farmhouse Gracie struggled to climb the stairs. She desperately tried to get to David, who questioned what in Heaven's name I was doing with a stray dog. I informed him that she might have been on the side of the angels, but seeking help from our church neighbors down the road clearly didn't pan out, and I wanted to feed her. And feed her I did, with two of the burgers designated for lunch the next day!

We couldn't let her in the house because it was "no pets," but I found an old rug in the laundry room and brought it out for our guest, who flopped down, exhausted from the start of her new adventure. We decided that if she was there the next day, we'd try and find a shelter that would take her in.

In the morning she was still there but the nearby town had no shelter. David called Alane, a good friend and animal rescuer extraordinaire, for advice. We never expected her to plead that we bring the dog back with us. But Alane's mother had just lost a pet and would give Gracie a home.

Had she lost her mind? Did she expect us to make a five-hour drive with a strange dog? Suckers that we were, we drove into town and found a collar and leash at a local variety store, along with a flea collar, dog food, and a package of plastic sheeting to line the back of our SUV.

On our last morning in Arkansas, we packed the car, loaded our newfound friend, and headed home. With only one bout of car sickness, Gracie rode proudly in the back of the car for the trip home. She consumed a plain McDonald's burger and an ice-cream cone without digestive issues. Life was good!

Alane met us at the house and took Gracie to her mom's, where the dog found her own baby mattress bed and all the accoutrements a spoiled dog could ever want. Gracie stayed by Anita's side for a decade, loyally remaining there until Anita died. It was a tremendous loss for Gracie, but she remained a steadfast family member when Anita's granddaughter, Reghan, who'd recently lost her dog, chose to adopt her.

Gracie's next adventure began with a road trip to Boulder, Colorado. It took a few days to acclimate to her new surroundings, some crying nights, and difficulty warming up to her foster brother, Tucker, now a permanent member of Gracie's family.

A social media sensation, the little stray is now part of @GracieandTucker_ on Instagram. While Gracie is at least thirteen years old, and arthritis has set in, she still gets around thanks to acupuncture, stroller rides, and love. What a life this little stray has lived! As the hymn goes, "I once was lost, but now I'm found." It sums up God's plan for Amazing Gracie, living happily ever after.

— Marla Anne Bernard —

Magical Maggie

My little dog — a heartbeat at my feet.
~Edith Wharton

I walked into the Austin Humane Society just to look. I had recently lost my cat and was ready to add a dog to the family. I met two-year-old Savannah, a Terrier mix, who was heartworm-positive, an owner surrender, and underweight. She was shy, scraggly, and a little scared, but she jumped up on the bench and immediately lay down next to me. It was clear we were meant for each other! I immediately changed her name to Maggie.

I remember stopping for gas when we left. I watched her nervously follow me with her eyes as if to ask, "Where are you going? Are you leaving me, too?" I reassured her as I got back in the car that I would never leave her, and we headed to the pet store to stock up.

I noticed her calmness and sweet demeanor immediately. There was no barking at the shelter, even while a cacophony of barks was going on all around us. In the pet store, she sat quietly in the cart while I showed her toys, beds, and blankets that I hoped she'd like. When we made it home, she went in a pen that I set up for her and fell asleep.

As the months passed, she became my shadow. We went everywhere! She helped me deal with my grief, and I helped her come out of her shell. I have always been quite introverted, and she forced me to go outside. I met my neighbors and new friends at dog-friendly restaurants, and I even created an Instagram page for her so the world could enjoy her magic!

One day, while talking to my boss about her, he said, "You should bring Maggie into the office to see how she does." She was so calm and quiet that I was allowed to bring her with me every day. I had a blanket for her on a chair, and she was content to be with her human at work. We would take walks around the block, and workers from nearby offices got to know her, too.

Everyone loved having her in the office. "I'm having a bad day. Can I pet Maggie?" I heard that a lot. She was happy to get all the petting and give all her love. While I watched as one of my co-workers petted her, I had an idea. She could become a therapy dog, and we could spread her love to more people!

I immediately started researching therapy-dog organizations, and I came across one that I thought would be perfect: Divine Canines. I called and was asked questions about her, myself, and places I would like to visit, and then I was told about all the requirements to become a Certified Therapy Dog Team.

I immediately started working with Maggie so she could pass her Canine Good Citizen test, as that was the first step. I decided to talk to a trainer and ask what level he thought Maggie was at and what I needed to work on. We met at a training facility, and we went through everything necessary to pass a Canine Good Citizen test.

When we finished, the trainer said, "Congratulations, you passed!"

My mouth fell open, and I happily screeched, "What?"

The trainer said to me, "If I had told you I was testing you, you would have been nervous, and that would have traveled from you, through that leash, to her. Humans get nervous; dogs don't. She didn't need to feel your nervous energy."

I thanked him and was very excited because it meant that we could go through the training to become certified!

We finished training, and Maggie passed her test with flying colors. After graduation, we began our visits. We started with assisted-living facilities, where she was a total hit. We visited hospitals and elementary schools, but our absolute favorite visit was to the local jail. There, we got to visit with men and women who worked hard toward qualifying for therapy-dog visits. Maggie loved it because she got to run around, say hi to everyone, and show off her tricks. She got so much love and attention.

There was nothing better than seeing grown men reduced to tears when they saw this now twelve-pound dog because they missed their own dog. Maggie had so much fun there that she always slept the whole way home. We had business cards provided by Divine Canines, and one of the inmates made a lovely pencil drawing of Maggie derived from her photo on her card. I framed that drawing and will treasure it always.

Maggie and I were road-trip warriors. We traveled about 6,000 miles together and had the best time! One of our road trips was to Utah. We visited lots of beautiful places, including the Coral Pink Sand Dunes in Kanab where, on our way back to the car, Maggie was bitten by a rattlesnake! It was the absolute worst day of my life, but I was determined to get her help. I had never driven so fast in my life, but I had also never been so focused.

We made it to the vet, where they immediately started working on her, while I immediately lost focus and broke down. Maggie survived the bite, and at her follow-up visit the next day, everyone was amazed at how well she was doing. Aside from her snout being swollen, you would have never known she almost died the day before. Kanab is a small town, and when I stopped at a local restaurant, I was asked, "Wait, is this the dog that just got bit by a rattler? Oh, we're so happy she's okay. And look at how well she's doing!" That was Magical Maggie, causing smiles everywhere!

Maggie spent eleven years of her life with me — the best years of my life. She had survived abandonment by her original owners, heartworm treatment twice, and a rattlesnake bite. After an X-ray for something unrelated, I learned she had three pellets by her spine. Someone had shot my baby girl before she came to me.

Even after all that, Maggie had nothing but love for everyone she met. She left this world much too early for my liking, but I am proud to have been her mom and to have shared her with so many people. She was magical!

— Veronica Saldate —

Meet Our Contributors

Becky Alexander is a tour director, leading groups in Charleston, New York, Toronto, and other destinations. When not on the road, she writes magazine articles, devotions, and inspirational stories. She loves volunteering year-round with Operation Christmas Child. Learn more at www.happychairbooks.com.

Dr. Dale Atkins is a licensed psychologist with 45+ years of experience as a relationship expert focusing on families, wellness, aging, caregiving, life transitions, and balanced living. She has authored seven books, including *The Kindness Advantage*. Dr. Atkins lectures worldwide and is a recurring media expert, having appeared on NBC's *TODAY* and CNN.

Katrin Babb lives with her family on a small farm. When not writing, she can usually be found in her flowerbeds or training for her next triathlon/duathlon. Learn more at KatrinBabb.com.

Dave Bachmann is a retired teacher who taught writing and reading to special needs students in Arizona for thirty-nine years. He now resides in California with his wife Jay, a retired kindergarten teacher, writing poems and short stories for children and grown-ups.

Marla Bernard holds a Master's degree with distinction from Baker University and has served as adjunct faculty for a local university. This is her third story published in the *Chicken Soup for the Soul* series. She resides in the Midwest with her family and is writing a short story collection.

Jane M. Biehl has been a librarian, counselor, teacher and writer over a span of fifty years. She has written many books and articles on her hearing ear dogs, her cancer journey and her hearing loss.

Cheri Bunch was born on a small farm in Elma, WA. She received her Associate degree from Chemeketa Community College in Salem, OR.

Louise Butler is the author of four books and numerous articles and short stories. She has advanced degrees in education, administration and economics. She is a regular lecturer at national and international events. Butler uses her love of writing to indulge the storytelling inheritance of her Sámi ancestors.

Anne Calvert is the author of the three titles in the Evie series: *Banderidge*, *Gidesha City*, and *Broken Shell Beach*. In addition, she has three short stories in the anthology, *59 Seconds*, and an article in the July/Aug/Sept 2021 edition of *ZGP Magazine*. Her current work in progress is book four of the series. She lives in West Tennessee with husband, Wesley, and dog, Bear.

Carolyn Campbell majored in print journalism at Brigham Young University. She is the award-winning author of three books and 900 magazine articles. Carolyn is the mother of four and grandmother of three. She enjoys reading, cooking, writing, and swimming.

Melanie Chartoff's an actor (Broadway, *Seinfeld*, *Newhart*, *Ally McBeal*, *Weird Science*, *Parker Lewis*, *Rugrats*, *Jumanji*), and author of *Odd Woman Out*. She's published in *The New York Times*, *Funny Times*, *The Jewish Journal*, *McSweeney*, *Avalon Literary Review* etc. and has now become a wife and stepmom.

Elton A. Dean has written two children's books. *A Yeti Like Freddie: Talking to Kids About Autism* is an introduction to autism. *Brandon Sets Sail: A Story About Sharing Success* is a collaboration with his (then) seven-year-old son. Elton is retired from the U.S. Army and currently works in higher education.

Laurie Dell'Accio has a Bachelor's in Elementary Education and Spanish and a Master's in TESOL from Southern Connecticut State University. She is a middle-school teacher and lives in a small shoreline town in Connecticut with her husband, her teenage son and daughter, and her dog, Lilly.

Lindsay Detwiler is a bestselling romance author of over thirteen novels, including *The Trail to You* featuring her Mastiff, Henry. She is also the USA Today Bestselling author of *The Widow Next Door*. Lindsay is a high school teacher in Pennsylvania, where she lives with her husband, Chad, and her Great Dane, Edmund.

Kim Garback Diaz has her Master's and SAS in education, and a Bachelor's in marketing. She is the owner of Educational Solutions, a consulting business for parents, families, students, schools, and departments of social services. She lives in the Adirondacks in upstate New York with her husband Ray.

Kim Engelmann is a freelance writer and works as a chaplain in addictions and mental health. She is the author of multiple books and articles and received her Master of Divinity from Princeton Seminary and her Doctor of Ministry from Boston University. She lives in the Bay Area of California with her husband Tim and two dogs.

Kristin Evans grew up along the coast of Southern California. She received her Bachelor of Arts in Literature from UCLA before embarking on travels and a career that has taken her around the globe. She resides in Ann Arbor, MI with her family and is hard at work on an action-adventure book for middle graders.

Genesis F. is a college student currently pursuing her Bachelor of Science in Information Technology. In her spare time, she enjoys exploring films and TV shows, expressing her creativity through art, and spending time with animals.

Ellen L. Fannon is an award-winning author, a retired veterinarian, a former missionary, and a church pianist/organist. She and her retired Air Force pilot-turned-pastor husband have fostered more than forty children and have two adopted sons. Ellen has published eight novels and numerous stories and devotions.

Jill L. Ferguson is the author or co-author of dozens of books, including co-authoring the *Whiskey Dog Mystery Series* that she writes with her brother under the pseudonym Faith Walker.

Kristi Cocchiarella FitzGerald has had several stories published in the *Chicken Soup for the Soul* series and *Fine Lines* journal where she's also an editor. She has degrees in English and Theater and is a Willamette Writers member. She lives in Montana with her husband, Shih Tzu Floki and new kitten Freyja.

Alex Flowers is a sophomore in high school. When not working on his charity he spends time with his friends, his two black Labs and boxing. He hopes to study international relations in college.

Melissa R. Friedman received her Bachelor of Science in Early Childhood Education from Indiana University and a Master of Science in Child Development from the Erikson Institute. She is a preschool teacher, mahjong instructor, and the best job of all — mom (one human, one canine). She is an aspiring children's book author.

Anita Gait is a freelance travel writer and author. She is currently based in the UK and loves travelling for work and for fun. Although her lifestyle means she still doesn't have any dogs of her own, she makes up for it by endlessly offering to pet sit for friends, family, and occasionally strangers.

Kathleen Gemmell currently pens for a variety of publications. She is also an animal welfare proponent. Kathleen loves the written word and also a fine pizza. E-mail her at kathleenagemmell@gmail.com.

Robyn Gerland is the author of four novels and a book of short stories. Her work has been featured by The British Columbia Federation of Writers. She is a past instructor of creative writing for Vancouver Island University.

Sheri Block Glantz holds an M.Ed., is a special educator who served five terms on her local school board, has taught pre-school through college, and is a lifelong writer. She finds gratitude in her world daily, and enjoys time with her family, traveling, gardening, pickleball, mahjong, and canasta. She is always up for a new adventure!

Amanda Ann Gregory is a trauma psychotherapist renowned for her work in trauma recovery, notably as the author of *You Don't Need to Forgive: Trauma Recovery on Your Own Terms*. Her writing has been featured in *The New York Times*, *Psychology Today*, and *Psychotherapy Networker*. Learn more at www.AmandaAnnGregory.com.

Karl Haffner is V.P. at Loma Linda University. He has two B.A. degrees, two Master's degrees and a Ph.D. Karl has written thirteen books and 1,000+ articles published in a variety of journals and books. Karl and his wife Cherie have two daughters — and for nearly sixteen years they cherished their favorite furry family member, Skipper.

Ali Hall is an ex-police detective turned writer from Scotland. Her happy place is running along trails with her dogs. Her work has been featured in *Kinship*, *Your Tango*, *Samsung Food* and *Tracking Happiness*. You can also find her on Medium and Substack. She's currently being trained by Lenny, the blue-eyed wonder dog.

Camille Hartnett is a certified dog behaviourist specialising in reactivity-based behaviours. Her dog Jeffrey, a beautiful soul with big feelings, inspired her journey into the industry as she sought to support his unique needs. She is dedicated to helping guardians navigate their dogs' challenges with compassion and understanding.

Kathryn Haueisen began publishing essays while studying journalism at Bowling Green in Ohio. Now retired, she writes historical fiction and stories about good people doing great things for their communities. She enjoys visiting her family scattered across five states.

Nancy K. S. Hochman is a mostly retired English teacher and tutor, leaving her more time to write and publish essays and articles. Her essays have appeared in four other *Chicken Soup for the Soul* books. She is currently working on an anthology on heroism and miracles. E-mail her at nkshochman@gmail.com.

Some of **Carol W. Huff's** happiest memories are wrapped around her deep love for animals. She is lucky enough to own an animal rescue and sanctuary in Georgia, where she cares for over forty amazing critters who all call their farm "home." Writing about their quirky personalities and heartwarming stories is a true joy.

Jeffree Wyn Itrich is the author of three novels, a children's book, and a cookbook. Her stories have been published in over a dozen titles in the *Chicken Soup for the Soul* series. When she's not writing, she's usually making a quilt. Jeffree is married and a mom to a Snorkie dog and two cats.

Maiya Katherine is a published author, transformational speaker, life coach, and podcast host. Since publishing her first book in September 2021, she continues to develop programs, workshops, speeches, books, and courses to help others heal their hearts, follow their life purpose, and live abundant and fulfilling lives.

Judy Kellersberger has written several hundred stories, songs, and poems. Pete Seeger featured her poem/song "Tribute to the Hudson River" for the Quadricentennial. "Tribute to a Firefighter" hit #1 on Cash Box. Judy is completing a book of her collected short stories and adventures.

Judy Kelly lived most of her life in a small community, where she has filled a variety of roles, from wife and mother to insurance agent, choir member, and active participant in many community service projects. She enjoys spending time with her family and friends and taking daily walks.

Angela Kennedy received her Bachelor of Science in Biology from Loyola University Chicago, and has a career in banking. She enjoys yoga, traveling and painting.

Catherine Kenwell is a Barrie, ON author and mediator. She is an avid gardener and world traveler and enjoys adventuring with her husband. Catherine lost her dog Sunny in 2023, and a few months later she rescued a Whippet/Terrier puppy "Potcake" from the streets of Barbados.

Chip Kirkpatrick has published three books—all about animals. He also writes for several metal detecting magazines. This is his third story published in the *Chicken Soup for the Soul* series. Chip is also a popular storyteller, telling humorous stories from his life.

Debbie LaChusa earned a B.A. in Journalism from San Diego State University in 1985 and embarked on a thirty-year career in marketing. After retiring in 2018, she moved to Western North Carolina and began writing creative nonfiction. She has published four books, multiple essays, and is working on a memoir. She also enjoys hiking.

A voice actor by day, **Jody Lebel** writes romantic suspense novels and short stories, which have sold to *Woman's World*, the *Chicken Soup for the Soul* series, and dozens of others. She was raised in charming New England and now lives with her two cats in South Florida.

Robin Stearns Lee is a wife, mother, and grandmother, and she and her husband lead a small group at their church in the South Carolina low country. Her inspirational stories appear in several anthologies, on Inspiration Ministries online at www.inspiration.org, and on Amazon's self-publishing platform.

Corrie Lopez has been a teacher for over thirty years in the heart of America. She has two amazing children, a loving family, an incredible staff, a group of cool students, and a wonderful extended church family.

Mary Beth Magee's faith leads her to explore God's world and write about it in many genres. She is the 2025 Mississippi Poetry Society Poet of the Year, a Storyteller and a speaker on a variety of topics. Magee serves as narrator for The Everyman Puppet Theatre. Learn more at www.LOL4.net.

Irene Maran is a retired high school administrator living at the Jersey Shore with her four cats and six box turtles. She runs a weekly prompt writing group and has a bi-weekly column in *The Coaster of Asbury Park*. Her humorous stories about family, animals and everyday topics keep her readers smiling.

Emily C. Marszalek enjoys the simple pleasures in life with her husband Nick and their two Goldendoodles, Charlie and Lucy, in the Pacific Northwest. She loves Jesus, jigsaw puzzles, rock music, Nintendo 64, and every flavor of birthday cake.

Sandra Martin loves to write about universal life experiences. She has produced a documentary collection, *View from the Inside*, and is publishing her first book of poetry, *Reflections*. Sandra also loves traveling and writing about her many adventures. E-mail her at sandimartin516@gmail.com.

Amy McHugh is a freelance writer living on Cape Cod. Her work has appeared in *The New York Times*, *The Washington Post*, *Oprah Daily*, and *Newsweek* among others. The mother of two college-aged daughters, she loves the salt water and hawks screeching overhead. She's currently working on a memoir, *Permission to Be Human*.

Laura McKenzie is a retired kindergarten teacher living in Abilene, TX with her husband Doug. She enjoys traveling and spending time with her children and grandchildren. Laura loves to read, write and volunteer at her church's food pantry. This is Laura's seventh and eighth story published in the *Chicken Soup for the Soul* series.

Sally Meadows is an award-winning author of children's books and short stories; a four-time national award nominated singer/songwriter;

a speaker; and a contributor to various magazines and anthologies. She is also a fashion color consultant, and she explores her love of color through her photography, art, and paper crafting.

Carina Middleton married her husband in 2010 and has three children. She has lived all over Canada thanks to her husband's job as an RCMP officer. Her son's diagnosis of autism had her moving from a career in Early Childhood Education to a full-time, stay-at-home mother. She plans on writing whenever she has time.

Linda Mihatov was a licensed wildlife rehabilitator for over twenty years. During that time her family shared their lives with a variety of orphaned or injured wildlife species. Retired and relocated to Tennessee, she and her husband enjoy their two dogs, feeding the birds, and seeing the wildlife that frequents their property.

Nanette Norgate is an award-winning Canadian author. Her recent works include her newest children's series, *The Adventures of Lanny Llama*. The first book of the series, *Moving to The New Farm*, was launched July 19, 2024, with the second book of the series in production scheduled for release in Fall 2025. Learn more at nanettenorgate.com.

Dawn O'Herron recently retired as a Registered Nurse. She worked as a school nurse for about thirty years. Dawn raised three children and now has three wonderful grandchildren. She has always had a passion for animals, and animals have always been an important part of her life.

Marie T. Palecek finds wisdom and joy in simple, everyday things. She shares these nuggets in a delightful storytelling style whether speaking or writing. Marie lives in Minnesota, where she enjoys all four seasons with her family and friends. Learn more about her speaking, devotionals, and Bible studies at www.marietpalecek.com.

Rose Panieri is a published author who has worked in journalism for more than twenty years. She loves to write, and she loves dogs (and all other creatures). Rose feels the only downside of having an animal companion is when they leave this earth.

Deidra Parham received her Bachelor of Arts, with honors, and Master of Arts from the University of Memphis. Since 2007, she has taught English to speakers of other languages in the public school system. She plans to continue writing with hopes of publishing more writing for children, young adult, and adult readers.

Margie Pasero is a seventy-four-year-old woman who looks for the beauty and magic in life. She is a snowbird from Washington State to Tucson, AZ and loves the adventures that come with living in these two unique locations. In addition to being a writer, Margie plays alto sax in two jazz bands and a concert band. She enjoys hiking with her husband.

Ree Pashley has degrees in criminal justice and social work and worked for twelve years in Canada before settling down in Tanzania, East Africa. Now she is a mom to eight awesome kids and spends her days writing and chauffeuring her children to and from school and hiking.

Miranda Phelps is a psychologist/writer living in Maine. Previously a freelance writer, she has an MFA in playwriting from Brandeis University and is now writing stories, picture books and a novel. She is devoted to her family—which has always included dogs—and to Buddhist practice.

Winter D. Prosapio is an award-winning novelist and humor columnist. She has two novels, two kids' books, and so much more. She's also a big fan of caves, small dogs, waterparks, wooden roller coasters, and funnel cake, not necessarily in that order. Learn more at WinterProsapio.com.

Misty Rae is a Canadian author based in Saskatchewan. She received her B.A. (honours) and her LLB from the University of New Brunswick. She enjoys writing, photography, reading and spending time with her husband and two dogs, Rudy and Fawn. Misty's novel, *I Ran So You Could Fly* (The Paris O'Ree Story), debuted in 2024.

Marianne Reese lives in Nevada with her husband Gene and the enduring spirit of their beloved Golden Retriever, Gixxer. She's the author of the teen fantasy novel *Skylar Moon*, and has numerous short stories published in various anthologies.

Mark Rickerby owns Temple Gate Films. He has written over thirty stories for the *Chicken Soup for the Soul* series. His narrated and illustrated stories can be found on YouTube at "Mark Rickerby's Tales of Mystery and Adventure." He says, "No matter what I accomplish in this world, my daughters, Marli and Emma, will always be my greatest sources of pride."

Lorraine Rose writes and publishes poems, short stories, and essays. Her favorite subjects include the interconnection between humans, animals and nature. Lorraine has also worked as a reporter for a local newspaper. In her spare time, she teaches English as a Second Language and cares for her four rescued kitties.

In the summer, you might see **Constance Rutherford** on her lounge beneath an apple tree, pad and pen ready at hand to bring to life a short segment of her life. Mackie was a rescue Doberman, one in a long series of adopted dogs who came to live with her, one after the other, about ten years apart.

Elizabeth S. graduated from Pensacola Christian College in 2007 with a Bachelor's in Family and Consumer Sciences. When she isn't writing inspirational and devotional children's books, she enjoys spending time with her family outdoors.

Veronica Saldate has been an animal lover and advocate since childhood. She currently has one dog and one cat. Veronica enjoys spending time outdoors with her dog, traveling, and working with the senior members of her community.

Bianca Sanchez has a B.A. in English from San Diego State University and currently works in communications. Her work has appeared in *50-word Stories*, *Every Day Fiction*, and *San Diego Poetry Annual*. Bianca enjoys writing, reading, taking Zumba classes, and spending time with her two dogs, Lady and Bee.

Ellie Sanchez is a minister's wife and mom of three. She enjoys reading, writing and baking. She also enjoys nature and traveling. She has one published book of poems in Spanish and another one on the basics of being a minister's wife, also in Spanish. E-mail her at elyfraisen@gmail.com.

Joyce Newman Scott worked as a flight attendant while pursuing an acting career. She started college in her mid-fifties and studied screenwriting at the University of Miami and creative writing at Florida International University. She is thrilled to be a frequent contributor to the *Chicken Soup for the Soul* series.

Laurel L. Shannon lives in NW Ohio with Trixie, the little Australian Terrier who inspired this tale.

Annmarie Sitar is a practicing lawyer in New York City and has a passion for writing and savoring life's simple moments. She lives in the mountains of Connecticut with her husband and their dog, Charlie. Annmarie loves hiking, chasing sunsets and helping others. She plans to write a children's book about the beauty of nature.

Billie Holladay Skelley received her Bachelor's and Master's degrees from the University of Wisconsin. A retired clinical nurse specialist, she is the mother of four and grandmother of three. Billie enjoys writing, and her work crosses several genres. She spends her non-writing time reading, gardening, and traveling.

Doug Sletten grew up in the cold of the Dakotas. He is currently retired and living in Mesa, AZ. Doug received his Bachelor's degree from Concordia College in Moorhead, MN in 1968. He has a son, Mitch, and a daughter, Sara. Doug enjoys reading, taking car trips, skiing, and writing. E-mail him at douglas4146@gmail.com.

Anna I. Smith is honored to once again be part of the *Chicken Soup for the Soul* series. Her previous work has been featured in *The Tishman Review* and the anthology *Crows Feet*, among others. When not writing she can be found pursuing her other passions: hosting short-term rental guests and baking. Learn more at annaismith.com.

Amy Soscia earned her MFA in Writing from Albertus Magnus College. She was nominated for a Pushcart Award for winning the Tulip Tree Review's 2023 Wild Women Story Contest. She has been published in literary journals, anthologies, and *Chicken Soup for the Soul: Recovering from Traumatic Brain Injuries*. www.amysoscia.com.

Alli Straus is a picture book author and content creator for her influencer dog, Oski the Pug. She has been sharing their communication journey with AIC on Instagram since 2021. Together, Alli and Oski volunteer their time at local libraries as a literacy therapy dog team helping children improve their reading skills.

Sarah Stuart is a professional harpist and writer on the East Coast. Her home is filled with music, books, and her favorite people.

She is the lucky mother of three children and one tenacious Terrier. Sarah is grateful to Oberlin College and Conservatory where she fell in love with music, writing and her husband.

Sue Sussman writes fiction and nonfiction for all ages. Her adult novel, *The Dieter*, was selected as Pocketbook's first hardcover. She's won awards for her children's science books, and she won an Emmy for the film adaptation of her children's book, *There's No Such Thing as a Chanukah Bush Sandy Goldstein*.

Anne Taylor is a writer living in Seattle, WA. She enjoys writing novels and walking her dog.

Marla H. Thurman was a past contributor to the *Chicken Soup for the Soul* series. Sadly, she passed away in April 2024. She will be greatly missed.

Lisa Timpf received a Bachelor of Physical Education from McMaster University. A long-time dog lover, she currently shares her home in Simcoe, Ontario with a lively Cocker Spaniel/Jack Russell mix named Chet. In her spare time, Lisa enjoys penning poetry, fiction, book reviews, and creative nonfiction.

Aimee C. Trafton is a multi-genre author and eLearning Specialist from Fredericton, New Brunswick, Canada. Her published books include *Amber Tambourine and the Land of Laugh-a-Lot*, *The Misfit Crew*, *Grief Journeys: A Prose and Poetry Chapbook*, and her newest book, *Purple Popsicles: And Other Preposterous Poems*.

Lois Tuffin started writing short stories as a child but found real life eclipsed anything her imagination could conjure up. So, she became an award-winning journalist and Editor in Chief of *Peterborough This Week*. She continues to write nonfiction books, blogs and articles as a freelancer.

Paula Marie Usrey is a writer, researcher, and a retired Associate Professor of Speech Communication. She is the author of *Refusing to Be Invisible: Life Planning Empowerment Strategies for Women 50+*. She is a grandmother, widow, and "mama" to a black Labrador Retriever fittingly named Ranger III (born the same day Ranger II passed).

Kathy Valentino is a former graphic artist and advertising copywriter. She holds an Associate degree in Animal Sciences, a Bachelor's in Business Management, and a certificate from the UCLA Extension Writers' Program. Kathy lives in Los Angeles, CA with her husband and numerous pet rescues.

Jillian Van Hefty is a humor writer from Northwest Arkansas. She won the 2022 "A Hotel Room of One's Own: The Erma Bombeck| Anna Lefler Humorist-in-Residence Program." She enjoys exploring waterfalls, practicing calligraphy, and zipping past slow people on her e-bike. She is a dual US/UK citizen.

Laura Vertin holds Master's in Social Work from East Carolina University. She lives with her family in Dublin, GA. This is Laura's third publication in the *Chicken Soup for the Soul* series. She enjoys reading, writing, gardening and spending time outdoors. Her next goal is to write an inspirational book.

Jessi Waugh's short stories, essays, and poems appear in publications ranging from *The Pregnant Chicken* to *Kakalak Anthology of Poetry and Art*. At her hometown on the southern Outer Banks, Jessi enjoys teaching yoga, volunteering, and spending time with her husband and two young children. Learn more at jessiwaughwriter.com.

When his wife died, **David Weiskircher** was thrown into a torrential storm. Luckily, he had a unique group of friends by his side — herding dogs — which led him to peace. His books, *The Healing Way* and *A Thin Place* are available through Amazon.

Debra White lost her social work career in 1994 due to brain trauma from a pedestrian car accident. At the end of a long recovery, she found a new life in creative writing and volunteer work.

Mary Z. Whitney has written for the *Chicken Soup for the Soul* series for many years. She also contributes to *Guideposts* and *Angels on Earth* magazines. Mary has published a children's book entitled, *Max's Morning Watch* featuring her little dog Max. She has also written an adult inspirational fiction book entitled *Life's a Symphony*.

Marilyn J. Wolf is from Indiana and writes poetry, prose and essays on Medium.com. She is published in anthologies, Indiana's Poetry Archive, displayed in online and physical galleries, and more. *In Celebration of the Death of Faeries* is her first book. She is a past 1st VP, Poetry Society of Indiana, and Director, Indiana Writers Center.

Nemma Wollenfang is a prize-winning, short story writer who lives in Northern England. Her stories have appeared in several venues, including *Northern Gravy*, *Flame Tree Publishing* and the *Chicken Soup for the Soul* series. She loves animals, has volunteered in several animal rescues, and can be found on Facebook.

Woody Woodburn is a longtime national award-winning newspaper columnist—Sports originally and General Interest for the past decade. He is also the author of three books, including the award-winning novel *The Butterfly Tree: An Extraordinary Journey of Seven Generations*. Learn more at woodywoodburn.com.

Amy Catlin Wozniak loves sharing hope through storytelling. A frequent contributor to the *Chicken Soup for the Soul* series, she writes about the stories God weaves in her life. Raised in Nebraska (Go Huskers!), Amy now lives in Northeast Ohio with her soulmate, four kids, three grandsons, and a Great Pyrenees named Scarlett O'Hara.

James B. Zambelli graduated from Slippery Rock College with an undergraduate (1972) and Master's (1977) degree in Elementary and Special Education. He retired as an elementary school principal in 2009. He and his wife, Linda, have three children and seven grandchildren. He enjoys writing, traveling, boating, golf and fixing things.

Meet Amy Newmark

Amy Newmark is the bestselling author, editor-in-chief, and publisher of the *Chicken Soup for the Soul* book series. Since 2008, she has published more than 200 new books, most of them national bestsellers in the U.S. and Canada, more than doubling the number of *Chicken Soup for the Soul* titles in print today. She is also the author of *Simply Happy*, a crash course in Chicken Soup for the Soul advice and wisdom that is filled with easy-to-implement, practical tips for enjoying a better life.

Amy is credited with revitalizing the Chicken Soup for the Soul brand, which has been a publishing industry phenomenon since the first book came out in 1993. By compiling inspirational and aspirational true stories curated from ordinary people who have had extraordinary experiences, Amy has kept the thirty-two-year-old Chicken Soup for the Soul brand fresh and relevant.

Amy graduated *magna cum laude* from Harvard University where she majored in Portuguese and minored in French. She then embarked on a three-decade career as a Wall Street analyst, a hedge fund manager, and a corporate executive in the technology field.

Her return to literary pursuits was inevitable, as her honors thesis in college involved traveling throughout Brazil's impoverished northeast region, collecting stories from regular people. She is delighted to have come full circle in her writing career — from collecting stories "from the people" in Brazil as a twenty-year-old to, three decades later, collecting stories "from the people" for Chicken Soup for the Soul.

When Amy and her husband Bill, the CEO of Chicken Soup for the Soul, are not working, they are visiting their four grown children and their spouses, and their six grandchildren.

Follow Amy on X and Instagram @amynewmark. Listen to her free podcast — Chicken Soup for the Soul with Amy Newmark — on Apple, Google, or by using your favorite podcast app on your phone. You can also find a selection of her stories on Medium.

Thank You

We owe huge thanks to all our contributors and fans. We received thousands of submissions for this popular topic, and we spent months reading all of them. Daniel Zaccari, Crescent LoMonaco, Laura Dean, Kristiana Pastir, and D'ette Corona read all of them and narrowed down the selection for Publisher and Editor-in-Chief, Amy Newmark. Susan Heim did the first round of editing, and then D'ette chose the perfect quotations to put at the beginning of each story, and Amy edited the stories and shaped the final manuscript.

As we finished our work, D'ette continued to be Amy's right-hand woman in working with all our wonderful writers. Barbara LoMonaco, Kristiana Pastir, and Elaine Kimbler jumped in to proof, proof, proof. And, yes, there will always be typos anyway, so please feel free to let us know about them at webmaster@chickensoupforthesoul.com, and we will correct them in future printings.

The whole publishing team deserves a hand, including our Vice President of Production & COO, Victor Cataldo, and our graphic designer, Daniel Zaccari, who turned our manuscript into this beautiful, inspirational book.

Chicken Soup
for the Soul